World Food in the 1990s:
Production, Trade, and Aid

World Food in the 1990s; Production, Trade, and Aid.

EDITED BY
Lehman B. Fletcher

Westview Press
BOULDER • SAN FRANCISCO • OXFORD

Copyright © 1992 by Westview Press, Inc.

Published in 1992 in the United States of America by Westview Press, Inc., 5500 Central Avenue, Boulder, Colorado 80301-2847, and in the United Kingdom by Westview Press, 36 Lonsdale Road, Summertown, Oxford OX2 7EW

Library of Congress Cataloging-in-Publication Data
World food in the 1990s: Production, trade, and aid / Lehman B.
   Fletcher.
      p. cm.
   ISBN 0-8133-8049-9
   1. Food supply—Developing countries.   2. Food industry and trade—
Developing countries.   3. Food relief—Developing countries.
I. Fletcher, Lehman B.
HD9018.D44W67   1992
363.8'09'049—dc20   90-44542

Printed and bound in the United States of America

   The paper used in this publication meets the requirements of the American National Standard for Permanence of Paper for Printed Library Materials Z39.48-1984.

10   9   8   7   6   5   4   3   2   1

Contents

Tables

Statistical Appendix Tables

Figures

Preface

This book, based on materials prepared for a four-session workshop held September 20-22, 1989, in Washington, D.C., explores the following themes:

1. the international economic and policy environments anticipated for the 1990s and the likely organization and operation of world food markets in relation to food security of developing countries;
2. the impacts that multilateral liberalization of agricultural trade and domestic policy reforms in both industrial and developing countries may have on world food production, trade, and food security; and
3. how the United States's foreign economic assistance, including food aid, should be adapted to changes in the world food system and the economic and policy environments of the 1990s.

Chapter 1 offers an overview of the themes of the book and a context to help readers integrate the ideas in the four parts that follow. Part I contains materials drawn from the opening session, which assessed the global setting within which the world food system is likely to operate in the 1990s. Chapter 2 considers prospects for economic growth and trade of developing countries, Eastern Europe, and the former USSR in light of expected growth and policies of the United States, Western Europe, and other high-income industrial countries. Chapter 3 appraises the expected state of world markets for major food and feed commodities in the 1990s. It includes a critical evaluation of the potential contributions and limitations of international trade in food grains to national, regional, and global food security.

Part II continues the theme of changing international and domestic agricultural markets. Chapter 4 examines more closely the prospects for, and implications of, international agricultural trade liberalization and domestic agricultural policy reforms on less-developed country (LDC) growth and food security. Chapter 5 reviews the record on efforts to improve agricultural output and food security in developing countries through policy reforms to open domestic markets, to place more emphasis on exports and incentive prices for farmers, to limit government involvement in production and trade, and to provide more modest and targeted food subsidies to consumers.

Part III draws implications of the previous themes for foreign agricultural assistance and food aid programs. Chapter 6 evaluates past U.S. foreign assistance efforts to boost food output and provide food security and questions whether these efforts will continue to serve useful purposes in the 1990s or should be modified. Chapter 7 reviews the use of food aid as a development resource, based on a realistic appraisal of what donor and recipient countries can do to make more effective developmental use of food aid within the evolving trade patterns and food security concerns of LDCs. Chapter 8 assesses the U.S. legislative and international and domestic political environment and suggests realistic possibilities for policy changes in the context of the 1990 Farm Bill, the General Agreement on Tariffs and Trade (GATT), the Food Aid Convention, foreign assistance, and other national and international accords.

The book contains edited and revised versions of the papers and comments of discussants presented at the workshop. Two working groups reported their strategy and policy recommendations on each of three workshop objectives at the fourth and final session. A panel reacted to these recommendations and then general discussion took place. These recommendations, reactions of panelists, and the ensuing discussion, which were transcribed, have been used as the basis for the concluding Part IV of the book. While an attempt has been made to accurately state the recommendations and fairly interpret reactions and discussion, no specific attribution of views to the organizations of individual participants is intended.

The workshop and the publication of this book were funded

by the U.S. Agency for International Development (USAID) through its Bureau for Food for Peace and Voluntary Assistance. In the workshop's opening address, Phillip L. Christenson, assistant administrator in charge of the bureau, pointed to the timeliness of the workshop in relation to the GATT negotiations on agricultural trade reform and efforts to revise U.S. farm legislation in 1990. He reminded participants of the dramatic changes taking place in the world food production and trade system and asked how these changes and agricultural policy reforms in industrial and developing countries are affecting world agricultural trade and food security. He noted the effects of rising debt service, high interest rates, and large net capital outflows from the developing countries on agricultural trade. He reviewed past foreign assistance programs for agricultural development and wondered how future assistance can best help developing countries improve the productivity of their agriculture and alleviate their hunger and poverty. He expressed particular interest in ideas about the reform of food aid to make it more relevant for the 1990s. He challenged workshop participants to carefully and objectively interpret past trends but boldly propose new policy options needed for the 1990s.

The Center for Agricultural and Rural Development (CARD) of Iowa State University organized the workshop and the publication of this book. CARD and the workshop staff thank USAID for financial support and for the interest and assistance of its personnel. Also, of course, thanks must go to the workshop participants for their contributions.

Lehman B. Fletcher

1

Rethinking World Food, Trade, Aid, and Food Security Issues for the 1990s: An Introductory Essay

Lehman B. Fletcher

Two Conflicting Perspectives on World Food and Agriculture

Concerns about world food and agricultural prospects for the 1990s have coalesced around two conflicting perspectives. One forecasts substantial food shortages occurring during the decade, causing higher world food prices and more hunger in poorer countries. The other foresees a continuation of surplus food production, low or declining food prices, and subsidized exports by industrialized western countries in the absence of a multilateral agreement to reform their agricultural support policies and liberalize international agricultural trade.

Food Pessimism

Proponents of the food shortage perspective support their position by pointing to evidence that food production growth has slackened in recent years. Optimism abounded on the food front in the early 1980s, after world grain production more than doubled between 1950 and 1984. In the mid-1980s, grain stocks in exporting countries reached all-time highs and world (real) prices fell to historical lows, continuing their slow long-term downward trend that dates to the beginning of this century.

International agricultural trade grew rapidly during the 1970s until a world recession in the early 1980s caused export sales to slump. As costs of domestic farm support programs rose to politically painful levels, the United States and the European Community (EC) escalated their use of export subsidies to bolster sales in a world market shrunken by the inability of poorer, indebted, and low-growth developing countries to import enough food to meet their growing consumption needs.

U.S. agricultural legislation in 1985 initiated a trend to lower government support levels for corn, wheat, soybeans, and other major traded commodities. Using export subsidies, both the United States and the EC boosted overseas sales, but at declining world prices and to a degree at the expense of other exporters. By 1989 the volume of U.S. grain and oilseed exports equaled 1983 levels although export value was lower by some $5 billion. Entering the 1990s, world prices for wheat and corn were above U.S. producer floor prices and stocks had fallen.

Drought in the United States and other important producing countries in 1987 and 1988 reduced world grain stocks to their lowest level, relative to world consumption, in two decades. In response, world prices for food and feed grains rose sharply, although by less than in 1972-73 when international prices doubled. A continued shortfall of production below consumption in 1989 further diminished stocks and kept world prices above their trend levels.

Production increases consonant with consumption responses to population and income growth are necessary for replenished stocks and stabilized food prices in line with their long-term trends. The "food pessimists" cite reasons to believe that pushing production above consumption growth is becoming more and more difficult. The most recent assessment of prospects for feeding the world in the 1990s by the Worldwatch Institute, a group renowned for its pessimism, asserts, "Growth in world food output is being slowed by environmental degradation, a worldwide scarcity of cropland and irrigation water, and a diminishing response to the use of additional chemical fertilizer" (Brown and Young 1990, 59).

This group's opinion on the continued momentum of the Green Revolution is equally pessimistic: "To be sure, there will be some further gains in output from high-yielding crop varieties, but they are not likely to make the impressive jumps registered from the mid-sixties to the mid-eighties" (Brown and Young 1990, 77).

Perceiving limited promise for future crop production gains from biotechnology and holding low expectations that agricultural reforms will quickly end the USSR's dependence on grain imports, these "futurists" conclude,

> If the world continues with business-as-usual policies in agriculture and family planning, a food emergency within a matter of years may be inevitable. . . . Soaring grain prices and ensuing food riots could both destabilize national governments and threaten the integrity of the international monetary system (Brown and Young 1990, 77).

World Agricultural Trade and National Policy Reforms

The apocalyptic food perspective described above stands in sharp contrast to the one implicit in the debate over the reform of protectionist agricultural policies in industrial market countries. Many studies have quantified the burdens of domestic agricultural support that are borne by consumers and taxpayers, which in most countries far outweigh benefits to producers. Multicommodity, multicountry models have revealed sizable potential gains in real income, globally and for individual countries, that would result from multilateral liberalization of agricultural trade.

High government outlays, in the face of government budget pressures, have created strong motivation for the United States and countries of the European Community—the world's largest agricultural exporters—to move in the direction of coordinated policy reforms. Policy measures in these countries have also imposed severe losses on other countries heavily dependent on agricultural exports. Importing countries, however, have received immediate benefits from the commodity bargains emanating from the subsidized farm sectors of industrial countries but doubt the wisdom of basing their plans for future food and feed supplies on a continuation of those conditions. Not only is there understandable concern in these countries about the long-term availability of such cut-rate priced commodities, but there is also the important question of the need for an agriculturally-led growth strategy in most of them—especially in Africa—that have been left behind economically in the 1980s.

Present efforts for multilateral agricultural policy reforms are taking place in the framework of the Uruguay Round of trade negotiations under the General Agreement on Tariffs and Trade (GATT). The conditions leading to these reforms have resulted in great costs to the industrial and developing countries alike. Recent U.S. and EC policies have limited the markets of competing exporters and undercut incentives of food-importing developing countries to accelerate their own agricultural output.

Trade in agricultural commodities across national boundaries has long been an important feature of the world economy. Differences in resources, climate, technology, and economic institutions lead to significant differences in costs of producing food and fiber commodities from country to country. From the beginning of economics, agriculture has provided important examples of international trade that benefit consumers through expansion of output by lower-cost producers. Recent estimates show that about 17 percent of world production of goods and services is traded across national boundaries. For agriculture, the figure is a surprising 30 percent: some 12 percent of total trade is in agricultural products (Jones 1983-84). The latter figure, however, keeps falling as nonagricultural trade grows faster than agricultural trade.

Changes in the internal economic structures of nations are mirrored in their trade relations with other countries. Development economists have documented the pattern of internal shifts in the agricultural sector as countries grow: an increase in marketed production; a declining share of overall national production and labor force; and increased production, yields, and labor productivity based, in part, on inputs purchased from the nonagricultural sector. These changes, nonetheless, do not appear to have often been linked to the displacement of imports and the expansion of exports of agricultural products. Rather, rapid economic growth, even when accompanied by increased agricultural production, has most often been associated with rising rather than falling agricultural imports. Domestic demand for foodstuffs has often expanded faster than domestic production, leading countries to depend upon growing imports from world markets. Becoming richer, their populations turn from traditional food staples to more consumption of animal products, fruits, and vegetables causing growing imports of grains, oilseeds, and oilseed cake for animal feed. As a result, the internationally traded share of world grain and oilseed production has risen: grains alone account for some 20 percent of world agricultural trade. More and more, richer urban populations in both developing and industrialized socialist countries are consuming animal products fattened on feedstuffs imported largely from the handful of industrial and developing countries whose production exceeds domestic consumption.

Two quite different implications for food trade and aid policies emerge. First, many of the poorer countries, particularly in sub-Saharan Africa, have lagged economically in the 1980s. These countries face the continuing problems of dependence on traditional crop exports, declining terms of trade, widespread poverty, rising food imports, and reliance on food aid. Foreign assistance policies need to focus on the development of these countries, but commodity pricing and trade policies are generally a weak instrument for that purpose. Second, shifts in trade patterns are bringing new pressures to resolve agricultural commodity trade issues. Importing countries are now more exposed to commodity cost fluctuations and the impacts of domestic policies in major exporting countries. High levels of agricultural protection in industrialized countries restrict trade and limit the opportunities for developing countries to utilize new agricultural technology without imposing painful adjustments in agricultural income and employment on rich and near-rich countries. Further attempts to reduce barriers to trade are needed for both industrial and agricultural products. In this process, developing countries should participate more actively. The current GATT negotiations in the Uruguay Round offers an opportunity.

Most of the support given to crop producers in the Organization for Economic Cooperation and Development (OECD) countries is directly tied to production. The resulting price incentives have increased output while world effective demand has grown slowly. When consumer prices are maintained through government purchase programs, large stocks of surplus commodities can be acquired. The costs of carrying excess stocks and subsidies to dispose of them in international markets are additional sources of social losses to the producing countries, their international competitors, and possibly the importing countries as well. In addition, the domestic structural problems of industrial countries are, to a degree, a direct consequence of government programs linked to production that provide continuing incentives to maintain excess resources in agricultural production.

The policies underlying these distortions are fashioned through domestic political processes in pursuit of national objectives. They exist primarily to increase incomes of domestic farmers and in some cases promote national self-sufficiency. Policies to raise domestic prices above world levels require control of imports and, if the country is already self-sufficient, stock accumulation, exports, or some other form of surplus disposal. Excess incentives given to domestic production shrink markets and reduce the gains from trade. Importing countries may even be turned into net exporters. The EC, for example, used to be a large net importer of grains. By 1985, the EC was exporting 16 million metric tons (mmt), a reduction in the market for other exporters of 35 mmt within a decade. Similar net-trade reversals have also occurred in sugar and meat markets.

These strong reversals in the international market position of the EC have been bought with expensive export subsidies. But the EC is by no means the only subsidizer of agricultural exports. The United States, using marketing loans under the Food Security Act of 1985, is subsidizing exports of cotton and rice—a policy that may be extended to other major crops, such as soybeans. The act also provided for an "export enhancement program," which allows the U.S. Department of Agriculture (USDA) to use subsidies in specific markets against countries deemed to be engaging in unfair trade. So far this program has mainly been applied against the EC in grains and a few other products. In the case of rice, U.S. subsidies are having a clearly negative effect on Thailand, the other major rice exporter.

Sugar is a striking example in which all important OECD sugar producers maintain domestic price supports protected by border measures. This approach has resulted in a situation in which prices in the freely traded world market have on occasion fallen as low as one-fourth of those in the protected domestic markets, creating income losses for traditional developing-country sugar exporters. Another feature of the sugar market is the extreme fluctuations that commonly occur in international prices, an instability that reflects the residual character of the world market in contrast to the comparative stability of prices within the insulated domestic markets of the protectionist countries. Moreover, domestic supply responses to supported prices and competition from other sweeteners have eroded markets for tropical cane sugar producers.

Other factors have also affected world commodity markets. Debt and balance-of-payments deficits have combined with low-income growth to depress imports in countries where they might otherwise have grown rapidly. Production increases in India and China have kept those huge countries essentially self-sufficient. Where agricultural and economic growth are not associated with significant gains in employment and income for the poorer groups, a country may become an exporter of agricultural products even when the food and nutritional needs of its own population are far from satisfied. India and Brazil provide contrasting examples, with China illustrating how more equitable distribution can absorb large food production increments and even imports when production growth slows.

Agricultural Policy Reforms in Industrialized Market Countries

A number of studies have evaluated the potential economic implications of agricultural policy reform in industrial countries. In one of the most recent, Economic Research Service (ERS) staff used a multicommodity, multicountry world model to show the magnitude and distribution of benefits from agricultural trade liberalization (Roningen and Dixit 1989). The model included 22 commodities, which together make up almost 90 percent of the total value of U.S. agricultural production. It did not include tropical or beverage products other than sugar, although those products account for the majority of exports by developing countries. The results indicated that world agricultural prices overall would increase by 22 percent if industrial countries simultaneously eliminated all assistance to agriculture. The simulated rise in world prices was greatest for dairy products (65 percent) and next greatest for sugar (53 percent). World prices for food grains, feed grains, and meat also rose (wheat—37 percent, rice—26 percent, coarse grains—26 percent, red meat—21 percent, other meat—12 percent). Only prices of oilseeds and products rose less than 10 percent.

The study documented gains and losses to producers, consumers, and taxpayers, and overall efficiency gains, that would come from multilateral trade liberalization. Aggregate gains to liberalizing industrial countries were estimated at $35 billion annually, about 10 percent of their combined agricultural gross domestic product but less than 0.5 percent of their total gross domestic product.

Trade liberalization would cause production of most agricultural commodities to fall in the protectionist industrial countries due to declines in domestic producer prices. Total farm output would fall in the United States and Canada by 11 and 2 percent, respectively. In the EC and Japan, it would decline by 7 and 32 percent, respectively. Farm output would increase in Australia and New Zealand because their producers would receive higher prices since increases in world prices would more than offset declines in their domestic assistance.

These results are qualitatively consistent with a recent OECD study also based on a multicommodity, multicountry model that incorporated a multisector analytical capability (OECD 1989-90). The model was used to see what would happen if OECD agricultural support based on 1986-88 average levels were to be eliminated. It also showed prices would rise and agricultural output in the OECD would fall, the latter by 13.6 percent, according to the model. Gains in output in Australia and New Zealand would be more than offset by declines in other countries: by 24 percent in Japan, 19 percent in the EC, 17 percent in Canada, and 7 percent in the United States. The resources released would expand industrial and service output and raise real household income everywhere in the OECD. The average rise of 1 percent in real household income implies that agricultural protection currently costs the OECD countries as much as $72 billion (in 1988 prices) in lost income by diverting resources from more productive uses in other sectors.

Both of these studies confirm that agricultural production would contract in Japan, Canada, the EC, and the United States if subsidies were eliminated. The OECD study shows a larger production decline overall, and even a surprising 17 percent fall in Canada.

Much less attention has been given to the potential effects on developing and socialist industrial countries. In general, the studies undertaken so far have shown that the impacts of total agricultural trade liberalization by the OECD countries on other countries differ depending on whether the country is a net importer or exporter of a given product. Exporters of commodities, or close substitute commodities, that are in surplus supply at depressed prices are the most vulnerable. Thailand, an exporter of rice, has already been identified as a good example.

In contrast, net food importers now receive immediate benefit from low world prices caused by current policies. Thus it would appear at first glance that they would lose from liberalization. They would respond to higher prices by importing less. Tighter domestic supplies, especially if accompanied by higher domestic prices, would make it more difficult for poorer groups in those countries to meet their minimum food needs. Hunger and malnutrition would increase. But the idea that they would lose may well be only a short-term view. If they improve their own policies, and make required investments in production technology and services, they could become more efficient producers—if they are not already—and decrease their imports or perhaps become net exporters.

Access to markets in the West for all developing countries would also be improved. Even when industrial countries appear to provide developing countries with exporting opportunities, their scope may be limited by other policies. High grain prices in the EC created an attractive market for feed grain substitutes, such as cassava, corn gluten, and citrus pulp. But China, Indonesia, and Thailand, all cassava producers, have had to accept "voluntary export restraints" that limit their access to this market.

Reducing all protection in industrial countries would also directly benefit developing countries through increases in prices of their tropical exports. These gains could be multiplied if escalating tariffs (higher tariffs on processed forms of raw commodities), which are common in industrial countries, were removed. As goods become more highly processed—and incorporate more domestic labor and capital inputs—developing countries face rising barriers to entering markets of the industrial countries. This system blocks first and often efficient steps toward industrialization through forward linkages in the form of further processing of raw products.

In the ERS study, the effects on developing countries of agricultural trade liberalization by industrial market economies are created by changes in world market prices. As would be expected, the comparative-statics results revealed that food-importing countries (Nigeria, Korea, Taiwan) would lose because the increases in costs of imported food, feed, and fiber products would more than offset income gains to their domestic producers. On the other hand, developing-country exporters (Brazil, Argentina, Thailand) would gain because increases in incomes for their producers from higher agricultural exports would more than offset the higher prices to their consumers. Since developing countries overall were net importers of the agricultural products included in the model, they would on balance suffer modest welfare losses of about $5 billion from the policy reforms.

As net importers, centrally planned economies would also experience net welfare losses under trade liberalization by western industrial countries. The reason is the same: higher prices for their food, feed, and fiber imports.

The results of both studies depend on assumptions in the models about two crucial sets of responses. One is the "price transmission elasticities" for the centrally planned and developing countries. This example of professional jargon deals with the important issue of whether policymakers in those countries permit domestic prices to change in accordance with world prices or insulate their domestic consumers and producers from world price changes. The model results are based on "moderate to low" price transmission elasticities of 0.5 and 0.2 for developing and centrally planned economies, respectively. These vales are regarded as "probably larger than those that exist with current policies in place but much smaller than those that would exist in a free trade environment" (Roningen and Dixit 1989, 12).

Supply elasticities are the second set of crucial response parameters. These are meant in the models as measures of medium-term production responses to price changes. They range between 0.35 and 0.5 for industrial countries, and 0.27 and 0.33 for developing countries. Their values are justified on the reasonable grounds that while resources can be shifted somewhat among alternative products, sector-level constraints on inputs, like land, limit aggregate output responses. The supply elasticities in the models determine output responses along given aggregate and static supply curves as prices change in response to trade liberalization.

The authors note that estimated gains to the industrial market economies depend "to a large extent" on assumed price transmission elasticities for the centrally planned and developing countries. Were smaller elasticities assumed, then increases in world prices following multilateral liberalization would be larger and the gains to liberalizing countries would be higher. Conversely, if the centrally planned and developing countries were to "take advantage" of the incentives inherent in the increases in world prices and transmit all of them to their domestic producers, then income gains to the industrial market economies would most likely be smaller. In much the same way, the results also depend on the assumed supply elasticities. Static inelastic supply curves in the model restrict output responses in the non-OECD countries and thus preserve the gains from higher prices for the liberalizing countries.

In terms of food security, the developing countries might receive some benefits if world food, feed, and fiber markets became more stable after trade liberalization by the industrial market economies. But prices would be more stable around a higher level, higher even than the prices caused by the 1988-89 droughts if the studies reviewed are to be believed.

Food importers, especially the indebted, low-growth, food-short countries, would face higher import prices and most likely a reduction in concessional or free supplies from food aid donors. Their internal policy reforms would become more painful and difficult to maintain. However, as noted earlier, they would also have greater incentives to undertake policy actions and investments to increase their own agricultural production, reduce imports, and possibly even become exporters. Their success would mainly be reflected in outward supply-shifting improvements in their domestic agricultural productivity rather than price-induced movements along static supply curves. This is the main inadequacy of the reviewed studies, which generally fail to capture the dynamic processes of agricultural growth. Yet productivity growth based on new technology and inputs is the essence of agricultural development and the main source of future output growth in developing and industrialized countries alike.

Foreign Aid, Economic Growth, and Agricultural Exports

In recent years, U.S. commodity organizations have become more vociferous opponents of aid to lower-income countries to develop those countries' own agriculture. This may be one reason why the United States has reduced its share of GNP devoted to foreign aid. Twenty years ago the United States gave up to 0.6 percent of its GNP every year to development aid. Today that figure has declined by more than half and the United States has become one of the lowest of western aid-giving countries. Some would say this retreat should be lamented by all who wish to expand U.S. agricultural exports.

Research has shown that it is no accident that some of today's largest developing-country agricultural importers were once recipients of generous quantities of foreign aid. The mechanism has already been explained. Where foreign aid was associated with rapid growth, including agricultural growth, increasing incomes led to growing quantities of imported food, especially feedstuffs to increase the meat content of the diet in the then more prosperous countries. No longer recipients of foreign aid inflows, these countries then began to purchase their growing imports on straight commercial terms. Taiwan and South Korea, despite their relatively small population size, together import more wheat and feed grains now than all the poorer, more populous, low-growth nations of sub-Saharan Africa combined. Contrary to the implications of trade and policy reforms, this line of reasoning shows that U.S. agricultural export interests would be among the first to benefit if Third World development could be accelerated. For their own long-term best interests, they should therefore be leading rather than impeding efforts to stimulate agriculturally led overall economic growth in the Third World. Both trade and aid should play important roles in that process.

A comparable argument has been used to claim that previous recipients of food aid are now among the top purchasers of U.S. farm commodities. Specifically, it is pointed out that of the 50 or so largest importers of U.S. agricultural products, 30 are developing countries and 21 of these are former food aid beneficiaries. Indeed, 7 of the 10 leading importers of U.S. commodities in 1986 were former food aid recipients. Again, Korea is often cited as an example, since its annual imports of U.S. agricultural products now have a higher value than all U.S. food aid provided to that country in the late 1950s.

The problem with this argument is that actual contributions of food aid to the recipients' development have never been made clear. Obviously, Korea, Taiwan, and some other former food aid recipients have grown economically and are now commercial food importers. These countries, as well as Western Europe, were also recipients of large amounts of financial foreign aid. A number of studies have presented evidence of the beneficial effects of the large foreign aid transfers for the recipients' development. In the case of food aid, the claim is mainly based on the observed pattern whereby some former large recipients have undeniably developed and become importers on commercial terms. Nevertheless, this pattern neither proves cause and effect nor establishes that food aid was as effective as other forms of aid would have been.

While developing and socialist industrial countries are now the most important markets for U.S. agricultural exports, success in internal policy reforms in both groups of countries may well reduce the growth in those markets and even result in new export competition. Both the USSR and Eastern Europe could emerge from their expected conversion to market economies as net exporters of agricultural products. While sub-Saharan Africa sorely needs to increase its agricultural exports, most of those exports will be tropical and beverage products that do not directly compete with western exports.

Yet the long-term perspective study of development in sub-Saharan Africa by the World Bank (1989) argues for a targeted agricultural growth goal of 4 percent per year for the African region. This rate of increase would apply to both food production and export crops. The rationale is that then African countries not only could meet their own food requirements, but also could generate the foreign exchange needed for development. The proposed growth rate is termed "ambitious but not impossible."

The World Bank report indicates that the agricultural growth target could be attained by expanding the area under cultivation by not more than 1 percent per year and raising the productivity of cultivated land by around 3 percent per year. This report provides relevant and pertinent insight about prospects for sub-Saharan agriculture: "This rate of growth would be enough to feed the growing population (2.75 percent a year), improve nutrition (1 percent a year), and progressively eliminate food imports (0.25 percent a year) between 1990 and 2020."

World food demand is rising on a secular basis and thereby creating continuing pressure for technical change and other means to increase food production. World grain demand is growing somewhat faster than population, largely because developing countries with rapid economic growth are both consuming more food and shifting their diets toward grain-fed animal products. These changes are concentrated in Asia where several countries enjoy rapidly increasing per capita incomes. Examples include Taiwan, South Korea, Malaysia, and Thailand.

The food policy situation in many developing countries is much different from that in industrial countries. Despite the spread of policy reforms under which a growing number of developing countries are paying producer prices roughly equivalent to world prices, many developing countries continue economic policies biased against their domestic agricultural sectors. Overvalued exchange rates, food price controls, and government marketing monopolies are examples of policies responsible for this bias. Even with the recent trend toward policy reforms, a large number of countries continue to subsidize the consumption of cereals (e.g., wheat and rice) as a key domestic food policy instrument, and this tendency is often abetted by export subsidies and food aid conferred by major industrial food exporters.

As its first objective the workshop explored these developments and, focusing on the next decade, projected the likely organization and operation of international food markets in the 1990s within anticipated macroeconomic and policy environments.

U.S. Economic Assistance to Developing Countries

U.S. foreign economic assistance on a large and sustained scale began after World War II with the Marshall Plan. In the 1950s and 1960s, foreign aid was gradually extended to Third World countries and concentrated on infrastructure investments. These efforts were further institutionalized in 1961 by the Foreign Assistance Act and the creation of the Agency for International Development (AID). The "new directions" legislative initiative of 1973 emphasized U.S. foreign aid for the rural poor, connecting concerns about income distribution with an emphasis on small-farm production. More recently development economists have stressed the need for enlightened trade, macroeconomic, and investment policies—both in donor and recipient countries. They argue that developing countries can advance through growth-oriented economic policies based on market forces reflecting international trading opportunities. At the same time, more U.S. foreign aid has been allocated for foreign policy/strategic objectives, reducing funding for traditional technological and institutional approaches to agricultural development in the poorer countries.

As various ideas regarding agricultural development and food security evolved, in the 1980s the U.S. agricultural industry became increasingly opposed to foreign aid programs. The growing dependence of U.S. agriculture on exports and stiffer competition in international commodity markets led to questions about the compatibility of food and agricultural foreign assistance with the interests of American farmers. The response to this challenge was to show that (1) agricultural development is often the first key step in generating economic growth, and (2) demand for more and different foodstuffs has grown more rapidly than food production in high-growth less-developed countries (LDCs). Where income-based food demand has risen more rapidly than food production, the United States and other agricultural exporters have enjoyed expanded sales (Angel et al. 1989). Nevertheless, as pointed out earlier, increased agricultural exports from developing countries may be both essential for those countries to earn foreign exchange in the short run and efficient if their resource endowments and technology adoption make them low-cost producers in the longer run.

As a second objective, the workshop considered the most appropriate role for U.S. economic assistance for food security within the changing global food system and the changing macroeconomic and policy environments in industrialized and developing countries.

Food Aid

There is a lack of consensus on the actual and potential role of food aid in international food trade and in the LDC development process. There are also serious questions about the compatibility of food aid with other development assistance directed at agricultural growth and food security.

The development literature devotes little attention to the role of food aid in the evolving world food trading system and has given very little attention to the positive or negative effects of the food trading system on LDC food security concerns. What food trade patterns benefit or harm LDC food security concerns? How can food aid programs better fit into the system and act as more positive influences?

U.S. food aid now involves only 8 percent of total U.S. grain exports (in the 1960s it represented 40 to 60 percent), and total world food aid represents less than 5 percent of total world food grain trade. Food aid's trade distorting and trade promotion potential and its surplus disposal utility are far less important today than 35 years ago when Congress first passed PL 480 legislation. On the other hand, recent U.S. price policies and export subsidy programs, and parallel efforts to reduce agricultural trade subsidies through the GATT, raise questions about the future of the entire food aid program, particularly that part supporting domestic supply management and trade promotion efforts.

Although recent food aid levels remain significant in relation to total U.S. development assistance, historically food aid has been considered a second-best resource that may keep assistance levels up but is really not central to legitimate development efforts. While the general public thinks of food aid in terms of hunger, famine, and emergency needs, many food aid allocations are not closely related to need, greater food production, or even food security. Large portions of the food aid budget are more directly connected to macroeconomic objectives (foreign exchange and government budget support for recipients), foreign policy objectives, and private charitable programs. In other contexts food aid is seen as promoting U.S. agricultural trade, foreign policy, and the particular interests of commodity producers, value-added processors, and shippers. There is, however, a growing disenchantment with the conflicting objectives of the legislation and the numerous management inefficiencies and administrative restrictions that limit the effectiveness of the overall program to promote hunger reduction, food security, and long-term development in recipient developing countries.

Recent efforts to design reforms of foreign assistance legislation and adjust food and agriculture development strategies have included suggestions that the food aid legislation receive similar fundamental reform treatment in the 1990 Farm Bill or in later legislation. This nexus of concerns and possibilities was explored as the third objective of the workshop. If basic changes in the legislation do occur, given the projected world food situation in the 1990s, what revisions in PL 480 would be in the U.S. interest? Should the program's overall purposes continue to include market development, trade promotion, and support for U.S. agriculture? Should the U.S. government attempt to integrate food aid in its economic support fund (ESP) and development assistance programs or treat it as a separate and unique development resource? These are among the questions discussed in the following chapters of this book.

References

Angel, Bruna, Tom Harrington, W. H. Meyers, and S. R. Johnson. 1989. *Economic Growth and Agricultural Trade of Less-Developed Countries: Summary Report.* CARD Staff Report 89-SR37. Ames, Iowa: Center for Agricultural and Rural Development.

Brown, Lester R., and John E. Young. 1990. "Feeding the World in the Nineties." In Linda Starke, ed., *State of the World 1990; Worldwatch Institute.* New York: W. W. Norton.

Jones, W. I. 1983-84. "Agriculture's Changing Role in International Trade and Aid: Tastes and Techniques." *Annales d'Etudes Internationales* 13:53-68.

Organization for Economic Cooperation and Development. 1989-90. "Modelling the Effects of Agricultural Policies." *Economic Studies* (Winter):131-72.

Roningen, Vernon O., and Praveen M. Dixit. 1989. *Economic Implications of Agricultural Policy Reforms in Industrial Market Economics.* USDA/ERS Staff Report No. AGES 89-136. Washington, D.C.: Government Printing Office.

World Bank. 1989. *Sub-Saharan Africa: From Crisis to Sustainable Growth.* Washington, D.C.: World Bank.

PART I

The Global Setting:
Economic Growth and International
Markets in the 1990s

The most common perception of international trade is that developing countries export agricultural products and raw materials in exchange for manufactured goods from industrial countries. This perception underlies the identification of commodity terms-of-trade issues as crucial for developing countries and has often been used as justification for the costly import-substitution industrialization policies many of those countries adopted in the 1950s and 1960s. In those decades the identification of primary exports with developing countries was broadly appropriate. But in the 1970s and 1980s rapid changes in trade patterns took place.

Total world trade values multiplied more than fivefold in the decade from 1970-72 to 1980-82.[1] The rate of trade growth slowed after 1980 and became negative in 1982 as a result of the world recession. Recovering in 1983, world trade growth has since consistently exceeded overall production growth.[2] In this period since 1983, developing countries have increased their share of total exports, accounting for about one-fourth of world export values in recent years.

The overall export performance of developing countries was propelled by the large increase in petroleum export earnings during the 1970s, of which developing countries accounted for approximately two-thirds. Fuels aside, however, the developing countries' export share in the most rapidly growing world market of goods increased, while their export share in manufacturing agricultural raw materials and foods declined.

In 1970-72, agricultural and mineral products made up 61 percent of nonpetroleum export earnings of developing countries compared to 37 percent for manufactures. Within primary products, agricultural commodities accounted for 53 percent of all exports. After a decade, manufactures had risen to 55 percent of export earnings, while agricultural products had fallen to 37 percent and total primary products to 43 percent. By this measure, developing countries in 1980-82 had a greater stake in export markets for manufactured goods than in world markets for primary products. To this extent they now share the interests of industrial country groups that also slightly increased their concentration on manufactured exports while reducing their dependence on primary product exports. These data at least raise the interesting possibility that declining relative prices for primary products now offer net benefits to all major country groups, though obviously not to all industrial countries nor to all producer groups within a given country.

It should be remembered that vast differences among countries and geographic regions are concealed by using the broad developing and industrial country groupings. Not all developing countries possess oil resources nor share in the strong export performance of the few newly industrializing countries. Furthermore, agricultural and other primary exports remain important for both the OECD and Eastern European/USSR industrial country groups. Nevertheless, it is increasingly less accurate to identify interests of developing countries with the export of primary products and developed countries with manufactures.

In 1970-72, export earnings were rather evenly distributed across groupings of developing countries by the four major geographic regions. A decade later, the Near East had outstripped other regions, largely due to oil exports. Removing fuel export earnings gives a clearer picture of structural changes in regional exports. Africa and Latin America have generally retained heavy dependence on primary product exports. Manufactured exports remain relatively low in Africa and Latin America but have reached well over 60 percent of total exports in the Near East and almost 70 percent in the Far East. The Far East region is now as dependent on manufactures as Africa is on primary products.

In 1982, developing countries were net importers of agricultural products. This compares to agricultural exports that were about twice as large annually as imports in the 1969-71 period. While agricultural exports were marginally larger than imports both in 1979-81 and 1983, the surplus was small. In terms of regional patterns, only Latin America remains a significant surplus producer of agricultural products among developing countries. The Far East region remained a small net exporter but both Africa and the Near East moved sharply from agricultural export surpluses to deficits. The shift in Africa primarily reflected a fall in agricultural export volumes while the Near East showed sharply higher agricultural imports based on income gains from oil exports.

The size and scope of international agricultural trade are truly a triumph of factor endowments and economic forces over policy interferences. It has grown despite protectionist domestic policies of the United States, the European Community, and Japan and efforts of developing countries to promote industry at the expense of agriculture. Its recent evolution strongly reflects heavy policy interventions by governments as well as economic and technical factors. Ironically, both of the policy orientations have to some extent increased trade, through surplus disposal by the industrial exporters and growing food imports of industry-promoting developing countries.

The net result of the links between domestic agricultural policies and world commodity markets is that the gaps between world prices and the prices received by domestic producers in given countries are often substantial and occasionally outrageous. Japanese rice producers are paid four to six times the world price for the rice they produce, and they produce an excess over domestic consumption. U.S. and EC producers receive as much as four times the world price for sugar and nearly three times the world price for butter. European beef producers receive more than double the world price for their product. Before recent international price increases, wheat support prices for the EC were about twice the world price, while U.S. wheat target prices were about 50 percent above the world price. In many developing countries, in contrast, prices to producers are held below world market levels by subsidized imports.

The agricultural policies of the United States and other industrialized market economies may be designed to benefit their own producers but their effects spill out on the rest of the world, as shown by expanded output and reduced and destabilized world prices described in Chapter 1.

Price support policies for agricultural commodities in the United States, EC, and Japan provide clear examples of the linkages between domestic policies and world agricultural trade. Problems arise when countries encourage excess production behind protective barriers, with surpluses then stored or exported into international markets. These policies also impose costs on the countries' consumers who pay higher domestic prices and are prevented by tariffs, variable levies, quotas, or other border restrictions from importing the commodities at lower prices. It is through these divergences of domestic and world market prices—as well as through direct budgetary outlays—that large income transfers to agricultural producers are achieved. Dismantling the domestic policies and their supporting border measures requires a reassessment of the quantities of land, labor, and capital resources committed to crop and livestock production in the industrial countries.

World agricultural markets are also affected by the economic and agricultural growth of developing countries and their external trade and payments balances. Falling food production per person in sub-Saharan African has created pressures for higher food imports but low growth and poor export performance have generated insufficient income and foreign exchange to pay for them. Food aid has filled some of the gap especially in response to African droughts, civil wars, and refugee movements. Highly indebted countries have been forced to run current account surpluses to service their debts. These surpluses have been secured to some extent by export expansion but substantial import reductions have also been necessary. In recent years, the merchandise trade surplus of the 15 highly indebted developing countries has reached $26 billion, most of which represents foregone imports of consumption and capital goods including food and fiber commodities.

The premise underlying the two chapters in Part I is that foreign agricultural assistance and food security for developing countries are best viewed in the context of the evolving global world trade and food system. Moreover, world food trade itself is affected not only by its own supply, demand, and policy variables but also by the distribution of global economic growth and income among industrialized and developing countries in the world economy.

Lehman B. Fletcher

Notes

1.   Data in this and the following paragraphs on the volume and pattern of international trade are from FAO as summarized in T. Josling (1987), "The Changing Role of Developing Countries in International Trade," Chapter 3 of E. Clay and J. Shaw, eds., *Poverty, Development and Food* (London: Macmillan Press).

2.   *IMF Survey,* April 16, 1990, pp. 118-19. Washington, D. C.: International Monetary Fund.

2

Global Reach of Economic Growth and Prosperity in the 1990s: Trends and Issues

Lawrence R. Klein

Appraisals of the Economic State of the World

Recent reports of several international organizations, especially those featuring projections for the major industrial nations, present a picture of great optimism. An economic expansion is underway and has been joined in greater force by Western Europe, which had been a somewhat lagging area. The expansion dates back to the end of 1982 for the United States and to 1983 or 1984 for other countries. In many cases there is a feeling that record prosperity is imminent, with consequent improvements in material living standards.

While the reports of the Organization for Economic Cooperation and Development (OECD), International Monetary Fund (IMF), and General Agreement on Tariffs and Trade (GATT), individual governments, and private research institutes generally describe this prosperous environment, the report of the United Nations Commission on Trade and Development (UNCTAD), whose main constituency is the Third World, starts on a very sour note and gives the impression that the world is not in such good economic condition.

The facts show that global macroeconomic indicators are unquestionably good and are generally projected to remain strong. However, a more in-depth analysis of statistics shows that there are some very poor nations who have not been part of this world prosperity. Many developing countries and many socialist countries are not making satisfactory economic progress at the present time; some are actually on the decline. Major debtor countries of Latin America are experiencing severe hardship. They have low or negative growth and often experience apparently uncontrollable inflation. African countries, apart from South Africa and the countries along the northern coast, are in a period of long-term stagnation. There is lack of sufficient food in some cases and poor growth prospects in others. And South Africa has economic trouble in addition to political problems. War-torn countries of the Middle East and Central America are also in bad shape. It is not difficult to find exceptions to the unparalleled prosperity of the industrial world.

Southeast Asian and Pacific Basin countries that are not members of OECD have been outstanding performers in the world economic scene and remain so, but their margins of superiority have been somewhat reduced.

The most aggregative figures, the macroeconomic magnitudes for the global economy, look extremely good but are marred by poor distribution of world prosperity among nations. Not only is there a distribution problem across countries, but also across people within countries—even those countries that are supposedly best off. Indeed, there has been a tendency for a number of years for income to be distributed even more unevenly in the United States, or, to put the matter differently, families living below the poverty line have increased in both absolute numbers and in percentage terms. Homelessness and substance abuse among lower income groups have increased at an alarming rate. Within Third World countries, income distribution remains as inequitable as ever, shows little sign of improving, and has worsened in those countries suffering economic setbacks because of debt problems.

Some Problem Countries and Regions

Latin America

In Latin America, the countries that now face the most difficult economic prospects are Peru, Brazil, Argentina, Venezuela, Mexico, and some of the war-disrupted states of Central America. It is not just a question of poor growth in many of these countries—for 1989 as a whole, there was very significant negative growth.

Brazil and Mexico are the two largest economies of Latin America, together accounting for more than 50 percent of the region's gross domestic product (GDP). For 1989, Brazil showed negative growth, as low as 5 percent. Mexico just achieved positive growth by about 0.5 percent.

Whatever the final figures, there is no doubt that both major countries are in very difficult economic situations and will improve only gradually. There have been troubles for some time, in the form of low income with hyperinflation, and belt-tightening in the foreign sector. Both countries must restrain imports and export a great deal just to cover high debt-service burdens. Brazil ran a large current account surplus in 1989. Through restructuring of debt, discounted swaps for equity, and other makeshift devices, both countries have learned to live with the debt situation or slightly reduce outstanding obligations.

Debt problems and hyperinflation also plague Argentina, Venezuela, and Peru. They, too, experienced large declines in GDP in 1989, and were unable to hold inflation in check. Earlier in 1989, these perverse economic pressures brought about riots in Venezuela, a country that was once considered stable, free of extreme inflation, and rich in natural resources. Its position deteriorated significantly in a period of about three years.

Africa

A different class of problems appears in Africa. A poor infrastructure, political instability, corruption, and low levels of expertise hold back economic progress. Some of the countries below the Sahara are growing moderately, and some are declining, but for the region as a whole, per capita GDP is falling. Population growth is high in Africa, as in Latin America.

Debt burdens in Africa do not add up to the enormous amounts found in some Latin American nations, but the modest-appearing numbers are very burdensome in relation to GDP or other overall measures of economic strength. However, the economic problems of Africa go far beyond poor GDP figures. Measures of public health, such as infant mortality totals, are discouraging, as are figures for food production. Economists have often scoffed at Malthus's poor predictions of growing food/population imbalances, but in Africa the Malthusian principles seeming to apply.

Eastern Europe and the USSR

A third area of economic difficulty is the socialist block—Council for Mutual Economics Assistance (CMEA)—encompassing six countries of Eastern Europe plus Yugoslavia and the USSR. For some time this group constituted a solid, slow moving buffer that did not fluctuate with the same cyclical rhythm that was found in the OECD areas. The late 1980s saw these economies deteriorate badly. Poland, first of the fallen debtors of the 1970s and 1980s, bears many of the same problems as the Latin American countries, and has also shown similar mismanagement along with its partners in CMEA. But all the countries in this group, whether more liberal and market oriented, as Hungary, or tightly controlled, as the USSR, are having economic difficulties. Growth is slow or negative, inflation is picking up (accelerated, in Poland), and trade deficits are growing. Restructuring and disarmament are the principal routes by which the CMEA countries intend to recover to a positive growth path and to raise the quality of their production.

China

In some respects, China's economic problems are like those of the CMEA bloc. It was making excellent progress along a path of economic reform, and there can be no doubt that material living conditions improved markedly over the past decade, but political unrest, corruption, and other societal ills have now upset progress. It is too early to say what the outcome in China will be, but growth in 1989 fell by 50 percent or more from the pace of 1988, and the trade deficit grew. Inflation was rising in 1988-89 but was not yet at the hyperinflation stage. More prudent decentralization and use of external resources will have to be introduced in the Chinese restructuring program. This will keep growth on a much lower path than was realized prior to 1989.

Problem Issues

Another way of looking behind the strong figures of world aggregate performance is to consider economic issues. These cut across regional lines and appear in both prosperous and depressed countries.

Strong growth in world trade and world production produces a set of export/import balances that vary from country to country. By accounting principles, world exports and world imports must balance, apart from measurement discrepancies. A good result for world stability is one in which small trade imbalances are widely distributed over many countries, with only temporary departures from this pattern. For several years, we have had major departures with a large deficit in the U.S. current account being offset by large surpluses in Germany and Japan. This situation does not seem to be getting better at a reasonable rate, and in recent years South Korea's and Taiwan's surpluses have been added to the picture, while troublesome deficits have been built up in the United Kingdom, France, Italy, and Spain.

Some people think that this series of offsetting large imbalances is not a cause for concern because, if world prosperity has been achieved in their presence, it is evidence that we can live with these surplus and deficit balances. The trouble is that the world economy is seriously exposed. If unforeseen large shocks occur, countries with big deficits can have unusually serious difficulties making adjustments. Large, persistent deficits are indications of large debt accumulations with significant interest burdens that are extremely hard to bear during periods of recession or other economic adversity.

A related issue is the existence of large debts owed by several developing countries. They are among the countries that do not enjoy world prosperity at the present time. The debt issue, whether it is the sizable U.S. foreign debt or the LDC debt, is a matter that deserves examination, but obviously it is detracting from the good economic performance of the world economy.

In reality, the two issues—large current account deficits and LDC debt service burdens—are interrelated. For one thing, U.S. exports to LDC debtor countries, as well as those of some other large deficit countries, have decreased greatly since 1982. Currency adjustments, the striving for efficiency gains, and other changes are working very slowly toward restoring a healthier export/import balance and, it can be argued, that balance will not be restored soon unless stronger trading relations are restored between some large industrial countries and their traditional partners in the Third World. For example, U.S. exports to Mexico and Brazil are still below their 1982 levels.

There are many reasons for this inability of the United States to turn around the current account deficit, but one that often escapes policymakers is the connection between U.S. domestic fiscal deficit and the current account deficit. This connection is intricate and will not be revealed by a simple bivariate correlation. Suffice it to say at this point, that credit market conditions are affected by the U.S. deficit and keep interest rates higher than they otherwise would be, thus adding to the serious burden of the U.S. budget deficit, the current account deficit, and the LDC debt service burden.

This is not meant as a full assessment of global issues. Inadequate or poor anti-inflation policy in developing countries, low U.S. savings rates, and persistently high West European unemployment rates are other issues that make the present economic environment highly unsatisfactory.

Cyclical Versus Trend Issues

The poor performance of the Latin American countries is probably not going to last for a long time. These are vital countries with dynamic populations that are steadily improving in training, skills, and education. The region's resource base is excellent. Some countries already do well in medium- or high-technology manufacturing, while virtually all have capabilities in low-technology manufacturing. They can compete in many service sectors. Eventually, they should bring inflation under control. Some have already done so, and they can start to grow again at their historical growth rates, of 5 percent or more.

The debt problem of Latin America and many other developing countries has diverse roots. Some steps to resolve the problem are being taken, but they are not adequate and the heavily burdened countries will not grow out of their servicing difficulties, en masse, by natural development. There will have to be much more debt forgiveness in order to solve the problem in a complete sense.

One condition that will have to be fulfilled is that the basic world interest rate (U.S. prime or LIBOR) and an accepted risk premium should be less than the current dollar growth rate of exports from debtor nations. This will approximately stabilize the debt-export ratio. In addition, there must be a net financial capital inflow from the industrial countries to the developing countries.

In Africa, poor economic performance is not cyclical. These countries are in an unfortunate trend depression. A long-term policy of investment in human and fixed capital is necessary in order to initiate good economic performance there.

The slowing down of expansion in the Asia-Pacific region is mainly cyclical. There are exceptions in Burma, Bangladesh, and other Asian countries, but in mainstream countries there is every reason to be optimistic that the tendency for the world's economic center of gravity to continue to shift to this region will continue. China also should start restructuring again, although not along the very rapid path that it followed during the last decade.

It remains to be seen how restructuring will proceed in the CMEA bloc. It can be done: the socialist countries can become more efficient, but they are getting a poor start amidst a very uncertain political climate. They have grown at impressive rates in the past, and there is no reason to think that they cannot regain some of that momentum.

Successful *perestroika* will be essential for establishing efficiency gains. It appears that it is to be accompanied by disarmament. The two together, to a stronger degree than has been suggested by top

U.S. experts, will have a fair chance for improving the economic climate in Eastern Europe and the USSR.

An Optimistic Outlook for the 1990s

In an outlook conference at the end of the "Fabulous Fifties," a speaker projected the "Soaring Sixties." Ten years later, at a recent conference there were some similar judgments about prospects for the 1970s. The decade did start off briskly, was set back by food, fuel, and other shocks, and did not turn out well, as far as the main aggregates of the world economy are concerned. Then the 1980s got off to a very poor start, with severe recessions in the industrial world, followed by the debt crisis of the early 1980s.

But we ended the 1980s on a strong note, subject to the problem of maldistribution that was pointed out at the beginning of this paper. Perhaps these problems will not be overcome. That could induce sluggish performance; and we could call it an underachieving world. Or the great crash of the 1990s could be building up before our eyes without our being able to see it.

A popular forecast is that some of the expansionary power of the 1950s and 1960s is being put into place. World trade growth, which reached very high rates at the end of the 1960s, was not seen again in the figures until 1988 and 1989. Now, we appear to have had two successive years at 7 to 8 percent growth, very high figures, but not as high as those from the 1960s.

Trend extrapolation from the last two decades will not produce high growth and the problems cited earlier are still with us. What are some of the reasons for looking forward to good performance in the 1990s? Some positive elements are:

1. Economic exploitation of many new technologies. We always have new developments in science and technology, but the pace is rapid now and some things are only in the early stages of commercialization. Biotechnology has been relatively slow in fully reaching the market. New metals and materials, telecommunications, sophisticated service delivery,

and microelectronics are all developing very fast but seem to be far from mature. Much of the painful shift from older technologies has been accomplished.

2. Efforts to improve efficiency in the United States and other industrial countries. Productivity was definitely hurt by the disturbances of the 1970s. Some progress in restoring productivity growth has been realized in the United States and in other OECD countries. In addition, there have been significant productivity gains among the newly industrialized countries. This process should continue. If it can be accelerated, the technical base for a strong expansion in the 1990s can be realized.

3. Establishment of a single market in the European Economic Community (EC). Some of the spurt in economic growth that has taken place in Western Europe during 1988-89 is attributed to the carrying out of plans for a single market by January 1, 1993. Investment has been particularly strong in Europe during these two years. It is not assured that the new Common Market will be a success, and its possible effects are not yet fully understood, but the concept has created an air of economic enthusiasm that is likely to carry forward for some time. The best forecast now is that the single market will have a strong positive effect both for the EC and the world.

4. Market liberalization, domestic and international. The extension of the European Common Market is itself a program of liberalization, at least for a good part of the world economy. Not only are trade flows to be free, but the whole European economic superstructure—laws, currency systems, movement of people—is being harmonized. The institutional process is also moving towards economic policy coordination in Europe.

Apart from this European movement towards international liberalization, there is very significant movement toward domestic economic liberalization in many countries. This can be positive but has to be carefully monitored. In China, inflation, excessive use of exchange reserves, and other bad effects of improperly controlled liberalization caused the economic and political situation to get out of control. The Chinese must find a way back to constructive liberalization. The U.S. crisis among thrift institutions and general financial volatility owes much to careless deregulation or inadequate regulation in this atmosphere of liberalization. It is obvious that unfettered liberalization is not the way to generate stable and equitable growth. This difficulty has created problems for Eastern Europe and the USSR, who must develop manageable, sustainable programs for liberalization.

Conditions and opportunities are at hand for accelerating economic growth and development in the 1990s. In the short run, opinions and forecasts sometimes swing rapidly and wildly. A few years ago, this optimistic kind of prognosis was generally dismissed as implausible. It has met with both receptivity and disdain over the past several months. But at present, I believe things are working out to make an optimistic projection credible.

To illustrate the points made in this chapter, a series of tables and graphs containing aggregate values for country groups are provided in Appendix 2.A. They deal with the 1989 outlook from Project LINK and show the world summary as well as performance in specific countries or areas of the world.

Appendix 2.A: Definitions of Aggregates and Project LINK Data

North America
  Canada, United States
Developed East Asia
  Australia, Japan, New Zealand.
EC
  Belgium/Luxembourg, Denmark, France, Germany (F.R.),
  Greece, Ireland, Italy, Netherlands, Portugal, Spain,
  United Kingdom
Other Industrialized Market Economies
  Austria, Cyprus, Finland, Iceland, Malta, Norway, South Africa,
  Sweden, Switzerland, Turkey, Yugoslavia.
OPEC
  Algeria, Ecuador, Gabon, Indonesia, Iran, Iraq, Kuwait, Libya,
  Nigeria, Other West Asia sil exporters, Saudi Arabia,
  Venezuela.
Africa
  Ethiopia, Ghana, Kenya, Morocco, Sudan, Tunisia,
  Other Africa, Africa Least Developed.
Asia
  China, Hong-Kong, India, Korea, Malaysia, Other Southeast
  Asia, Pakistan, Philippines, Singapore, Southeast Asia Least
  Developed, Taiwan, Thailand.
Middle East nonoil
  Egypt, Israel, West Asia Oil Importers.
Western Hemisphere Developing
  Argentina, Bolivia, Brazil, Caribbean, Chile, Colombia, Mexico,
  Paraguay, Peru, Uruguay.
Centrally Planned Economies
  Bulgaria, Czechoslovakia, Germany (GDR), Hungary, Poland,
  Romania, USSR.

Note: Regions are defined in the respective country tables.

Table 2.A.1. World exports, imports, and trade balances (f.o.b.), Project LINK—United Nations/DIESA, premeeting forecast, Fall 1989 ($ US billions)

	1988	% change	1989	% change	1990	% change	1991	% change	1992	% change	1993	% change
INDUSTRIALIZED COUNTRIES												
Exports	2013.73	14.90	2197.17	9.10	2429.69	10.60	2650.63	9.10	2900.16	9.40	3160.79	9.00
Imports	2030.49	13.90	2212.27	9.00	2430.45	9.90	2650.55	9.10	2899.96	9.40	3166.54	9.20
Balance	-16.75		-15.10		-0.76		0.08		0.20		-5.75	
NORTH AMERICA												
Exports	432.19	25.40	490.49	13.50	541.63	10.40	596.00	10.00	653.38	9.60	715.01	9.40
Imports	549.99	10.80	592.22	7.70	627.73	6.00	673.34	7.30	722.38	7.30	779.93	8.00
Balance	-117.79		-101.73		-86.11		-77.34		-69.00		-64.92	
DEVELOPED EAST												
Exports	298.70	15.40	328.94	10.10	358.69	9.00	379.41	5.80	407.27	7.30	434.40	6.70
Imports	202.43	25.80	234.73	16.00	261.33	11.30	285.99	9.40	310.61	8.60	338.98	9.10
Balance	96.27		94.21		97.36		93.42		96.66		95.42	
EUROPEAN COMMUNITY												
Exports	1049.29	11.90	1129.20	7.60	1252.92	11.00	1366.73	9.10	1499.01	9.40	1639.33	9.40
Imports	1037.07	14.20	1133.55	9.30	1257.50	10.90	1375.33	9.40	1515.29	10.20	1661.80	9.70
Balance	12.22		-4.35		-4.58		-8.60		-16.28		-22.47	
OTHER INDUSTRIALIZED												
Exports	233.55	10.20	248.54	6.40	276.45	11.20	308.49	11.60	340.50	10.40	372.05	9.30
Imports	241.00	10.90	251.76	4.50	283.88	12.80	315.89	11.30	351.69	11.30	385.84	9.70
Balance	-7.45		-3.22		-7.44		-7.40		-11.18		-13.79	
DEVELOPING COUNTRIES												
Exports	607.42	15.90	694.93	14.40	756.63	8.90	832.54	10.00	919.69	10.50	1016.17	10.50
Imports	575.95	20.70	644.08	11.80	711.56	10.50	787.43	10.70	867.38	10.20	961.56	10.90
Balance	31.46		50.86		45.07		45.11		52.32		54.61	

OPEC												
Exports	125.45	-1.00	150.74	20.20	156.45	3.80	166.95	6.70	180.59	8.20	194.16	7.50
Imports	101.57	7.10	105.44	3.80	114.79	8.90	124.10	8.10	133.72	7.80	144.04	7.70
Balance	23.88		45.30		41.65		42.85		46.87		50.12	
AFRICA												
Exports	28.66	12.10	31.05	8.40	33.64	8.30	36.65	9.00	40.05	9.30	43.74	9.20
Imports	36.07	10.30	38.23	6.00	41.69	9.10	45.47	9.10	49.67	9.20	54.39	9.50
Balance	-7.41		-7.17		-8.06		-8.82		-9.62		-10.66	
ASIA (Including China)												
Exports	342.25	24.30	393.11	14.90	440.25	12.00	492.34	11.80	549.95	11.70	615.48	11.90
Imports	334.52	30.50	392.99	17.50	439.76	11.90	492.85	12.10	551.59	11.90	617.35	11.90
Balance	7.73		0.13		0.49		-0.50		-1.63		-1.88	
MIDDLE EAST (Nonoil)												
Exports	15.23	8.00	16.67	9.50	17.97	7.80	19.26	7.10	20.73	7.70	22.32	7.60
Imports	29.71	7.10	31.33	5.40	33.45	6.80	35.62	6.50	37.94	6.50	41.13	8.40
Balance	-14.48		-14.65		-15.47		-16.36		-17.20		-18.82	
WESTERN HEMISPHERE												
Exports	95.82	16.10	103.35	7.90	108.32	4.80	117.33	8.30	128.37	9.40	140.48	9.40
Imports	74.08	12.70	76.10	2.70	81.86	7.60	89.40	9.20	94.47	5.70	104.64	10.80
Balance	21.74		27.26		26.46		27.94		33.90		35.84	
CPE (Excluding China)												
Exports	217.65	3.50	230.55	5.90	247.98	7.60	270.85	9.20	290.36	7.20	313.64	8.00
Imports	208.05	3.80	228.14	9.70	247.23	8.40	268.99	8.80	290.03	7.80	311.73	7.50
Balance	9.60		2.41		0.75		1.87		0.33		1.91	
Statistical Discrepancy	-23.52		-37.26		-44.03		-46.00		-51.73		-49.58	
World Exports	2836.09	14.10	3119.56	10.00	3431.30	10.00	3750.75	9.30	4106.71	9.50	4486.56	9.20
World Export Price	3.71	6.00	3.84	3.40	4.06	5.80	4.27	5.20	4.47	4.60	4.70	5.10
World Export Real Price	764.29	7.70	813.01	6.40	844.86	3.90	878.16	3.90	919.25	4.70	955.41	3.90

SOURCE: Project LINK, "Project LINK World Outlook" (Philadelphia: University of Pennsylvania, Department of Economics/New York: United Nations, Department of International Economic and Social Affairs, 1989).

Table 2.A.2. World gross national product (1970 $ US), Project LINK—
United Nations/DIESA, premeeting forecast, Fall 1989: growth rates (percent)

	1988	1989	1990	1991	1992	1993	Mean
INDUSTRIALIZED COUNTRIES	4.00	3.00	2.50	2.80	3.00	2.90	3.00
North America	4.40	2.40	2.20	2.90	3.20	3.20	3.00
Developed East	5.40	4.60	3.40	3.60	3.60	3.70	4.10
EC	3.50	3.40	2.70	2.50	2.60	2.50	2.80
Other Industrialized	1.70	1.80	2.20	2.20	2.40	2.30	2.10
DEVELOPING COUNTRIES	5.70	3.40	4.80	5.10	4.80	5.30	4.90
OPEC	4.00	1.20	2.80	3.40	3.80	3.90	3.20
Africa	3.10	2.50	3.30	3.70	3.60	3.20	3.20
Asia (including China)	10.10	6.50	6.40	6.30	6.30	6.70	7.10
Middle East (nonoil)	2.00	2.40	2.80	3.40	3.50	3.20	2.90
Western Hemisphere	-0.20	-1.30	3.20	3.80	2.40	3.60	1.90
CPE (excluding China)	1.80	1.30	0.90	1.50	2.00	2.40	1.60
WORLD TOTAL	3.90	2.80	2.60	2.90	3.10	3.30	3.10

SOURCE: Project LINK, "Project LINK World Outlook" (Philadelphia:
University of Pennsylvania, Department of Economics/New York: United Nations,
Department of International Economic and Social Affairs, 1989).

Table 2.A.3. Per capita gross national product (1970 $ US), Project LINK—
United Nations/DIESA, premeeting forecast, Fall 1989: growth rates (percent)

	1988	1989	1990	1991	1992	1993	Mean
INDUSTRIALIZED COUNTRIES	3.50	2.50	2.00	2.30	2.50	2.40	2.50
North America	3.50	1.50	1.30	2.00	2.40	2.40	2.20
Developed East	4.80	4.00	2.80	3.00	3.00	3.10	3.50
EC	3.50	3.30	2.60	2.50	2.50	2.40	2.80
Other industrialized	1.40	1.40	1.70	1.50	1.80	1.40	1.50
DEVELOPING COUNTRIES	4.00	1.70	3.00	3.40	3.10	3.60	3.10
OPEC	1.30	-1.30	0.10	0.80	1.20	1.20	0.50
Africa	0.20	-0.40	0.40	0.80	0.80	0.30	0.40
Asia (including China)	8.60	5.00	4.90	4.90	4.90	5.30	5.60
Middle East (nonoil)	-0.30	0.20	0.70	1.40	1.40	1.10	0.70
Western Hemisphere	-2.20	-3.20	1.20	1.90	0.60	1.70	0.00
CPE (excluding China)	1.10	0.50	0.20	0.80	1.30	1.70	0.90
WORLD TOTAL	3.20	2.00	1.90	2.20	2.40	2.50	2.40

SOURCE: Project LINK, "Project LINK World Outlook" (Philadelphia:
University of Pennsylvania, Department of Economics/New York: United Nations,
Department of International Economic and Social Affairs, 1989).

Table 2.A.4. OECD unemployment rate, Project LINK—
United Nations/DIESA, premeeting forecast, Fall 1989 (percent)

	1988	1989	1990	1991	1992	1993	Mean
OECD	7.10	7.10	7.20	7.10	7.00	7.10	7.10
North America	5.60	5.60	5.90	5.60	5.60	5.70	5.70
Developed East	3.20	3.20	3.30	3.50	3.60	3.90	3.50
EC	11.10	10.60	10.50	10.40	10.20	10.20	10.50
Rest of OECD	13.10	13.50	13.90	14.00	14.00	14.80	13.90

SOURCE: Project LINK, "Project LINK World Outlook" (Philadelphia:
University of Pennsylvania, Department of Economics/New York:
United Nations, Department of International Economic and Social
Affairs, 1989).

Note: Excluding Greece, Iceland, Netherlands, and Switzerland.

Table 2.A.5. OECD private consumption deflator (inflation rate in
local currency weighted with GNP in current $ US), Project
LINK—United Nations/DIESA, premeeting forecast, Fall 1989

	1988	1989	1990	1991	1992	1993	Mean
OECD	2.90	5.80	4.20	3.80	3.00	3.00	3.80
North American	4.00	5.10	4.60	5.10	4.70	4.60	4.70
Developed East	1.60	3.30	2.30	2.40	2.50	2.70	2.50
EC	1.80	3.50	3.20	3.20	2.40	2.40	2.80
Rest of OECD	31.30	91.50	42.10	19.00	14.30	12.90	32.80

SOURCE: Project LINK, "Project LINK World Outlook" (Philadelphia:
University of Pennsylvania, Department of Economics/New York:
United Nations, Department of International Economic and Social
Affairs, 1989).

3

Changing International Food Markets in the 1990s: Implications for Developing Countries

Bruna Angel and S. R. Johnson

Many of the fundamental assumptions about foreign economic assistance and food aid, and the programs through which they are implemented, are being questioned. In part, these programs are conditioned by information on agriculture and the food supplies of nations perceived to be in deficit. If this information is systematically developed and progressive, it can be used to improve the positioning of these programs and anticipate problems that will require alternative forms of intervention.

As background for the discussion of agricultural policy reforms and to identify possible problems implied by a continuation of current foreign assistance and food aid policies, projections of per capita grain production, consumption, and trade for selected countries and regions have been developed. The projections are for the period 1988-89 to 1997-98 and from a modeling system maintained by the Food Agriculture Policy Research Institute (FAPRI). (FAPRI is funded by a U.S. special congressional grant and provides analysis of trade and domestic agricultural policy. FAPRI has university centers that conduct this analysis at Iowa State University and at the University of Missouri-Columbia.)

The projections reflect market conditions and policies in place during the spring of 1989. These projections, the technology assumptions from which they are developed, and the macroeconomic, trade, and agricultural policy implications provide a context for assessing agricultural policy, foreign assistance, and food aid initiatives of the United States.

The FAPRI modeling system is multinational and multi-commodity, including five major crop submodels for wheat, coarse grains, soybean and related products, rice, and cotton. Each submodel has behavioral relations for domestic supply and demand of major importers and exporters. Factors such as macroeconomic performance and agricultural and trade policies, which condition output and domestic demand, are incorporated and assessed for their market and trade impacts.

The focus of the analysis is on wheat and coarse grains, which are staple foods in many food deficit nations, and on the importance and likely changes in food deficits if current macro-economic conditions, technology trends, and agricultural trade and food policies are continued.

A brief introduction to the FAPRI trade models and macro-economic, policy, and technology assumptions for the spring 1989 outlook in the next section is followed by country- and region-specific per capita projections for wheat and coarse grains production, consumption, and trade in the third section. The analysis emphasizes developing nations and regions. The fourth section provides observations on the food supply and use trends for developing countries and regions. Concluding comments suggest implications for the U.S. foreign assistance and aid programs.

International Commodity Market Projections

This summary of FAPRI projections for the United States and international commodity markets provides the basis for the analysis of supply and use in developing nations and regions. For background the FAPRI modeling system is described along with the assumptions that condition the projections. The projections were completed in early 1989. The summary of these projections concludes with updating comments using more recently available information.

FAPRI Trade Models

The FAPRI agricultural trade models are dynamic, nonspatial, partial equilibrium, and econometric. The commodities represented are wheat, coarse grains (corn, sorghum, barley, and oats), rice, cotton, and the soybean complex (soybean, soybean meal, and soy oil). All five models were used for the current analysis; however, detailed results are presented only for wheat and coarse grains, major staples in many of the aid-recipient countries.

Individual commodity models are integrated into a system through price linkages that admit cross-country and cross-commodity interactions. These linkages reflect the interactions among agricultural commodity markets in the price determination processes. The multimarket equilibrium for the modeling system is obtained by imposing market clearing identities for the five commodities.

The models include domestic supply and demand functions for major trading and producing countries and regions. Parameters for these equations are estimated from historical data, roughly for the period 1965 through 1988. Equilibrium prices, quantities, and net trade are determined by equating country and regional excess demands and supplies, and explicitly linking domestic and world prices. Except where set by government, domestic prices are related to world prices through estimated linkage equations that incorporate bilateral exchange rates, transfer service margins, and (implicitly) trade barriers not directly specified.

Figure 3.1 describes the five trade models and their regional and country detail. Documentation for each of the trade models and the U.S. crop and livestock models is available from CARD (FAPRI 1989). The country and regional detail of the modeling system has recently been extended to more fully represent the developing nations (FAPRI 1988).

Conditioning Assumptions

The FAPRI U.S. and World Agricultural Outlook (1989), the

source of the wheat and coarse grains projections in this chapter, contains a detailed description of its underlying macroeconomic and policy assumptions. To p are briefly summarized. The FAPRI trade models are solved on a "satellite basis" with the world macroeconomy. This means that there is no feedback between macroeconomic conditions and commodity market outcomes.

Macroeconomic Conditions. The macroeconomic setting for the projection period was developed from the WEFA Group (1988-89) and Project LINK (1989) forecasts. These macroeconomic forecasts, in most cases, extend only to 1993. The projections used for the period 1994-98 are based on a continuation of the macroeconomic conditions during the 1991-93 period and supporting data sources.

Key components of the domestic and foreign macroeconomic forecasts are presented in Table 3.1. The outlook for the agriculture commodity markets is sensitive to the values of these variables from the general economy (FAPRI 1989). In developing countries more than elsewhere, demand for agricultural commodities is sensitive to income and prices as impacted by exchange rates.

The WEFA Group forecasts show slower U.S. and world economic growth in 1989 and 1990, following a slightly stronger performance in the out years. Lower growth rates, at around 2 percent, are projected in the early 1990s for the United States, reflecting policies yielding higher domestic interest rates. World economic growth averages around 3 percent over the forecast period. No recession is indicated. Generally, while world economic performance is improved over that of the early 1980s, it is not as robust as in the 1970s (FAPRI 1989). Economic growth in most other developed-country market economies follows the U.S. pattern, slowing in 1989 and 1990 and recovering somewhat thereafter in response to policies that lower interest rates and increase investment.

The projected economic growth patterns vary widely in the developing world (Figure 3.2). The most rapid economic growth is in the Pacific Basin and China, with rates well above the world average. Latin America and African nations are shown as growing more rapidly than in recent years. Growth potential in these countries is severely constrained by heavy debt burdens, limited access to credit, and a likely continuation of the same kind of management of the economies that resulted in these problems. The WEFA forecasts presume that most of these countries will somehow muddle through their debt problems, a major source of uncertainty for the projections.

Economic reforms in the Soviet Union and other countries in Eastern Europe also introduce uncertainty into the macroeconomic forecast. Success with reforms could lead to higher economic growth rates. However, short-run disruptions caused by adjustments to reforms could seriously limit economic growth potential for these nations. The WEFA forecast for the USSR and Eastern Europe takes a middle position on the reform-growth issue, showing 2 to 3 percent per year economic growth over the projection period.

Population. The source used for historical and projected populations is the FAO/ESSA Population Long-term Projections (UN 1988). The underlying data are from the United Nations Population Division. Four projections are supplied: high, medium, low, and constant variants. The variant used for this analysis includes medium-growth assumptions for fertility, mortality, and international migration. Even with this medium variant, the implied growth rates in many of the Latin American and African nations are at high levels relative to the developed world.

Policy Environment. The FAPRI projections are conditioned on the assumption that the major provisions of the Food Security Act of 1985 (FSA85) will be continued in the 1990 legislation. However, reduced crop inventories and increased commodity prices resulting from the 1988 drought in North America have changed the commodity programs. Most important, idled acres for coarse grains and wheat have been reduced and remain low during the projection period (FAPRI 1989). For the 1990 U.S. Agricultural Act, target prices are anticipated to be at 1990 levels and loan rates will be adjusted using the same formulas as in FSA85.

The Export Enhancement Program (EEP), authorized by FSA85 to combat "unfair trade" practices of competitors, reached a funding level of $1.2 billion in fiscal 1988. Spending on EEP is assumed to be reduced in fiscal 1989 to $775 million and held at this level through fiscal 1991. The EEP funding is assumed to fall by $125 million per year over the remaining projection period, due to budgetary concerns and declining stocks and increased exports that make the program less attractive (FAPRI 1989).

The EEP has accounted for large percentages of wheat imports of many developing countries, as well as the USSR, with subsidies of up to $39.85 per metric ton in 1987-88 and even $22.48 in 1988-89. Brooks et al. (1989) show that importer responses to the EEP depend greatly on the country-specific transmission elasticity; that is, the linkage of the domestic to the import price. Simulations assuming no EEP for 1986-87 to 1988-90 resulted in only moderate response of wheat import to the implied change in import price: ranging from zero for Egypt, Mexico, Eastern Europe, and the USSR to a 30 percent reduction for India in 1988-89. Total trade was estimated to have increased by 0.7 million metric tons (mmt) in 1986-87 and 1.7 mmt in 1987-88 and 1988-89 due to the EEP. Most developing countries with policies subsidizing food consumption have very low price transmission elasticities and will experience significant increases in costs if the EEP program is phased out and they continue to import at the same levels.

Other countries are also assumed to continue current agricultural policies. In particular, domestic support prices of the European Community (EC) remain constant at current nominal levels. The FAPRI projections do not incorporate policy changes that may result from the current GATT Round. While policy changes that would deregulate agriculture in the developed nations are likely to occur relatively slowly over time, their cumulative effect could be significant. The GATT Round is scheduled to conclude in 1990 and likely changes will include reduced agricultural subsidies.

Technology Assumptions. The projected supply and use situation, especially for the developing nations, is highly dependent upon assumptions about technical progress. In the FAPRI models, these assumptions are reflected in yield trends. First average yields are used, limiting the variability of the projections. Second, the technical change assumptions are from base trends, in most cases the last 15 years. These technology trends are generally increasing yields between 1 and 2 percent per year.

Commodity Markets

Table 3.2 summarizes the supply, use, and trade results from the FAPRI projections (FAPRI 1989). Crop prices for wheat, coarse grains, and soybeans fell when the FSA85 was implemented and they remained low until the North American drought of 1988. The drought caused sharp increases in market prices and dramatic reductions in crop inventories. The lower carryover levels will likely make commodity prices rise more in the projection period than in the recent past. Commodity prices fall in 1989 and 1990, assuming normal weather and no export demand shocks. A small increase in prices is anticipated after 1990-91, due primarily to an increasing export demand driven by macroeconomic conditions. In real terms, however, prices of these commodities are stable throughout the projection period (Figure 3.3).

World import growth for the commodities included in the analysis is particularly strong in the second part of the projection period (Figures 3.4 and 3.5). Much of this growth originates in the developing countries and is due to forecasted higher income (especially for the Asian nations). This aspect of the projections emphasizes the importance of continued economic growth in the developing countries to the maintenance of stable real commodity prices, and the sensitivity of agricultural trade to macroeconomic and financial policy (FAPRI 1989).

In recent years, even with large areas of cropland idled, the United States has carried larger reserve commodity supplies in inventory than in idled production capacity. However, the combination of FSA85 programs to reduce stock levels and the North American drought of 1988 have sharply reduced crop inventories. Projected ending stocks for wheat and coarse grains are lower than in the recent past, except for the mid-1970s. These low stock levels, along with the change for program idled acres from annual to multiyear contracts (the Conservation Reserve of 40 million acres), signal the potential for price volatility during the projection period (FAPRI 1989).

Near-term Adjustments

The FAPRI outlook used macroeconomic forecasts from October 1988 and information on agricultural markets available by mid-January 1989. USDA updates on supply and use levels suggest several short-term changes. Continuing effects of drought in North America and Asia, and stronger than expected import demand for the USSR and China, imply higher than projected grain prices for 1989-90. The U.S. and world stocks should remain low compared to recent years (Meyers 1989). However, the medium-term outlook is not altered significantly by results from the agricultural commodity markets between 1989 and 1990.

Fall 1989 Project LINK forecasts for real U.S. and world GDP growth rates are slightly more optimistic than in the WEFA fall 1988 forecasts (WEFA Group 1988). Project LINK fall 1989 projections of real GDP growth rates are also more optimistic, in particular, for Thailand, Argentina, Egypt, and Morocco. However, they are significantly more pessimistic for the centrally planned economies including China, Brazil, and Mexico. They are marginally lower for Algeria, Tunisia, India, and Saudi Arabia.

In general, WEFA fall 1989 forecasts indicate slightly higher economic growth than the WEFA fall 1988 forecasts for Africa and the Pacific Basin. Also, they are practically unchanged for Western Europe and are more pessimistic for Latin America. In a broad sense the more recent macroeconomic projections imply higher growth in import demand for grains from Africa and Asia and lower growth in impact demand from Latin America and the centrally planned economies.

In summary, the FAPRI projections of supply, use, and trade for wheat and coarse grains over the next decade, even as modified by this more recent information, imply a relatively optimistic future for the exporting nations. World trade grows faster than either consumption or production, and stocks are reduced from the oppressive levels of the early and mid-1980s. This growth in trade comes primarily from impressive import demand increases in the developing countries as real incomes recover in Africa and Latin America and continue to grow in the Pacific Basin (Table 3.2). The combination of lower stock levels and strong import demand leads to rising nominal prices for wheat and coarse grains, stable real prices over the projection period, and lower subsidies for agriculture in the developed exporting countries.

Implications for Developing Countries

Implications of the world commodity market outlook for the developing countries and regions are of importance as a backdrop for assessments of foreign assistance and food aid policies. Converting these projections to a per capita basis is helpful in understanding the food situation for developing nations. The FAPRI trade models are not general equilibrium in nature. Thus, they cannot provide information on resource market adjustment and impacts and responses to changes in other sectors of the economy that could be offset by agricultural sector and food market performance. However, the projections provide indicators of conditions that may affect future food aid policy.

The supply, use, and trade projections for each nation and region, as well as income, are divided by the FAO population projections to make the per capita conversion. Of course, the resulting per capita trends do not reflect distributional changes that could be important for food consumption and dietary status. That is, the distribution of the food supply and income is assumed unchanged. Each region—Latin America, Africa and the Middle East, and Asia—is assessed in turn. The overall situation for the region is described, followed by a detailed analysis for a representative country.

Latin America

For the Latin America region, Mexico, Brazil, and Argentina are individually modeled in the FAPRI system. The other nations in Latin America are aggregated and represented as a single region. Figures 3.6 and 3.8 present the per capita supply and use projections for wheat for the Other Latin America region and Mexico. Figures 3.7 and 3.9 provide similar information for coarse grains. Historical data from crop year 1980-81 are included to provide perspective.

Detailed summaries of the commodity market, income, and population data are in Appendix Tables 3.A.1. to 3.A.4. Similar tabular information is available for Brazil and Argentina but was not included.

Population growth rates in Latin America fall over the evaluation period, to average annual rates of around 1.3 percent in Argentina, 1.8 percent in Brazil, and 2.1 percent in Mexico and Other Latin America between 1993-94 and 1997-98. However, despite the reduced population growth rates and increases in overall grain production, per capita production actually declines for coarse grains in Other Latin America and Mexico, and for wheat and coarse grains in Brazil.

The situation that emerges, with few exceptions, for the Latin American wheat and coarse grains importers, is one of declining per capita consumption and declining production but increasing per capita imports. In the Other Latin America region, wheat imports are approximately 80 percent of use. Over the projection period, imports decrease; but this decrease is not offset by the slight upward trend in domestic production. The result is a small decline in per capita consumption. The decline in per capita consumption of coarse grains is even more pronounced, resulting from more than a 2 percent decline in per capita domestic production, which is not offset by the small rise in imports. Per capita use for both commodities is significantly lower by the end of the projection period than at any time during the 1980s.

In Mexico, per capita consumption of wheat increases over the projection period after falling in the late 1980s. Per capita production also increases, but not as fast as consumption, resulting in rising per capita imports. Per capita coarse grain consumption remains relatively stable over the projection period, but at levels significantly lower than in the early 1980s. Production and imports also remain stable in per capita terms. In Brazil, wheat per capita consumption rises, mainly due to increased imports. Per capita coarse grain consumption shows a slight downward trend as imports are not sufficient to make up per capita production shortfalls relative to past consumption levels.

The declining levels of per capita consumption and production in Latin America are indicative of the severe recession experienced in this region in the 1980s and of population growth rates that are not sustainable at a constant real income given the projected rates of economic and agricultural growth. Per capita income growth in the Other Latin America region remains negative into the early 1990s and turns only moderately positive after 1992-93. In Mexico, per capita incomes declined throughout the 1980s and start to increase in the early 1990s. Argentina also experiences very low per capita income growth rates over the projection period. The macroeconomic projections are somewhat more optimistic for Brazil.

The debt overhang in Latin America casts considerable uncertainty about even these forecasted low income growth rates, except perhaps for Brazil, given its natural resource potential and diversified industrial base. During the 1980s, the Latin American region as a whole had debt service to export ratios of about 20 percent, reaching 30.6 percent in 1986. Individual countries continue to experience deficits in their current accounts and high debt service ratios, albeit down from 50.4 for Argentina and 33.2 in Brazil in 1986.

Unilateral debt moratorium, with the consequence of reduced access to credit markets, continues as an option for many of these countries. Brazil took this step in 1984, reducing its debt service ratio from 43.1 percent in 1982 to 23.7 percent. Another option is continued negotiation of debt service. Mexico has followed this path and has managed to contain its debt service ratio at 30 to 40 percent despite having one of the largest debt to GNP ratios, 84 percent in 1986.

The negative capital flows experienced by many Latin American nations may jeopardize future growth by reducing investment in development and critically reducing human capital. For countries that depend on imports for staple commodities, the shortage of foreign exchange is a symptom of even more serious problems. As evidenced by wheat supply and use in the Other Latin America region, when production decreases occur, the option of turning to world markets to make up the shortfall is not available or increasingly difficult and per capita consumption declines. These declines are likely magnified for the lower income populations, suggesting concerns for food and policy change, or among the donor nations.

Africa and the Middle East

The trade models for this region include Egypt, Algeria, Morocco, Tunisia, and an Other Africa and Middle East region for wheat. For the coarse grains model, Egypt and Saudi Arabia are modeled individually and the other countries are represented as an aggregate region. Figures 3.10 and 3.11 and Appendix Tables 3.A.5 and 3.A.6 report results for the Other Africa and Middle East region. Figures 3.12 and 3.13 and Appendix Tables 3.A.7, 3.A.8, and 3.A.9 present the results of the per capita calculations for Egypt and Morocco.

The Other Africa and Middle East region for both grain models include the vast majority of the population. Growth rates of population from the medium projection are high, averaging 3 percent from 1993-94 to 1997-98. For the individually modeled countries, population growth rates are similarly high, from around 1.8 percent in Tunisia to nearly 3.6 percent in Nigeria over the last part of the projection period.

In aggregate, wheat and coarse grains production and consumption are generally rising in this period for these nations. However, consumption rises faster than production, leading to projections of large increases in imports. Wheat imports rise at an average annual rate of 4.7 percent between 1993-94 and 1997-98 in the Other Africa and Middle East region, while coarse grains imports rise at an average annual rate of 6.6 percent over this same period.

On a per capita basis, the situation in this region is very different. Production of wheat and coarse grains in the Other Africa and Middle East region rises by only about 1.6 percent over the last part of the projection period, mainly attributable to increases in area cultivated. However, with population growth rates of around 3 percent, per capita consumption declines at more than 1 percent per year. The rise in per capita imports, although rapid (and even questionable on the basis of the financial balances of the nations), cannot sustain consumption or use at current levels, resulting in decreased per capita consumption of all grains. This same picture emerges in Egypt, Algeria, Saudi Arabia, and Nigeria. For Egypt, per capita consumption of wheat and coarse grains falls at annual average rates of 1.2 and 1.4 percent per year, respectively, over the 1993-94 to 1997-98 period.

Morocco and Tunisia present a slightly different situation. While domestic production also falls in per capita terms, import growth more than makes up the difference, resulting in a small upward trend in per capita consumption. Thus, the general condition is one of decreased per capita availability of food and coarse grains in Africa over the next decade, coupled with increased use of world markets to supplement domestic production. This is especially evident in those countries least able to pay for imports. According to the modeling system, unless policies or other factors change, consumption per capita will drop.

In both of the aggregated regional specifications, while real per capita incomes do not fall as fast as in the decade of the 1980s, they continue their downward trend. The debt service to export ratio for all of the Africa and Middle East region was more than 20 percent over the early 1980s and reached 32.8 percent in 1986 (World Bank 1988). And, foreign exchange receipts from exports of goods and services continue to be dwarfed by the value of imports. The prospect of an economic recovery in those countries with population growth rates currently outstripping real income growth is not good. Moreover, shortages of foreign exchange over the 1980s and high debt service ratios have probably reduced the rate of investment in infrastructure and other projects important for agricultural and general economic development. Lack of investment and even disinvestment, in agricultural and other primary sectors, such as education, health, and a lack of diversity in the economic base for many of these countries may limit potential economic growth. Future income growth is already compromised, and the foreign exchange necessary for the projected levels of imports may not be available.

Asia

The wheat model for the Asia region includes China, High Income East Asia (Singapore, Taiwan, Hong Kong, and Korea), India, and an aggregate region, Other Asia. The coarse grains model includes China, Thailand, High Income East Asia, and an aggregate

region, Other Asia. Figures 3.14 through 3.17 show per capita
production and use projections for Other Asia and China for wheat
and coarse grains and Appendix Tables 3.A.10 through 3.A.13 give
additional country detail for the per capita calculations during the
1980s and for the projection period.

In contrast to Africa, average annual population growth rates
over the 1993-94 period do not exceed 2 percent. In fact, over this
period average population growth rates are generally between 1.2
percent and 1.6 percent for the individual countries, and slightly
higher for the aggregate region.

The general theme emerging from the Asian calculations is for
rapid growth in per capita consumption of both wheat and coarse
grains. In the Other Asia and High Income East Asia regions this
growth is chiefly satisfied by increased imports. In India, self-
sufficiency policies lead to growth in domestic wheat production
and decreasing imports, and stable per capita wheat consumption
over the projection period.

Highlighting the Other Asia region, per capita consumption of
both grains is increasing although at low levels compared to
consumption in the remaining Asian countries. This indication of
food supply is more limited for Asia, however, since the staple in
most cases is rice. Per capita coarse grains production falls slightly
over the period while per capita consumption rises at an average
annual rate of almost 1 percent over the last five years of the
projection. Per capita wheat production is up slightly, and per capita
consumption rises at an average annual rate of about 1.5 percent.

The High Income East Asia countries have small domestic
production bases for wheat and coarse grains. Thus, growth in per
capita use, rising at an average annual rate of 3.5 percent for wheat
and 4.5 percent for coarse grains by the end of the evaluation period,
is satisfied by increased imports. This growth in per capita
consumption and especially the growth in imports for the region
and the individual countries is supported by rising per capita
incomes. Average annual growth rates for GDP for the countries in
this region range from around 3 percent to almost 7 percent in the
1993-94 to 1997-98 period.

Debt service to export ratios for the Asia region did not exceed 20 percent until 1986, and have generally been between 10 percent and 15 percent in the 1980s (World Bank 1988). For the region as a whole, revenues from the export of goods and services have not covered import costs, but the deficit is not as wide as it is for Africa and the Middle East or Latin America. And selected countries, like those on the Pacific Basin and Thailand, are experiencing a small but growing trade surplus.

While these aggregate results may mask disparities due to the income distribution among and within countries, the calculations based on the projections for the 1990s do not suggest major food supply problems for Asia. Asia as a whole is not burdened by heavy external debt, and positive income growth in the 1980s has stimulated investment and economic development while population growth rates have fallen to levels that do not swamp the associated income gains. Asia is a region likely to have rapid growth in grains imports and increasing dependence on commercial markets to satisfy higher per capita consumption levels.

The Outlook and Current Policy

What does the outlook for international commodity markets and for supply and use systems in the developing economies suggest for U.S. agriculture and foreign assistance policies? The outlook is for increasing nominal prices of agricultural commodities, increased total trade, and reductions in subsidies for agriculture in developed countries. The trend toward deregulation of domestic and international markets, perhaps accelerated by the GATT Round, will likely result in even higher prices and increased volume in international markets for major agricultural commodities.

For the developing nations, the impacts of these outcomes are varied. The modeling system used for the outlook is partial and cannot fully capture adjustments to major economic dislocations. Still, the per capita trends in consumption of major food commodities, trade, and production, particularly for Africa and Latin

America, imply problems and hardships. The major source of growth in the export market is from Asian nations.

The lack of focus for current U.S. food policies and the outlook suggest a number of observations.

Market Development

Opportunities for market development suggested by the outlook are for the Asian countries. These are the countries responsible for most of the recent growth in the export markets. For many Latin American, African, and Middle East nations, foreign exchange availability is likely to limit possibilities for commercial imports.

Foreign Policy

The outlook for food production and distribution systems in Latin America, Africa, and selected Middle East nations suggest a major crisis at hand. Food consumption levels in many of these countries are low by dietary standards. And they are projected to decrease. Moreover, the countries have little capacity to import or invest to alleviate the implied food shortages.

Development Assistance

Particularly for Africa, the Middle East, and Latin America significant opportunities exist for development assistance. For food aid historically delivered, however, the situation appears almost overwhelming. The debt overload for these countries is staggering. Agricultural production systems are not projected to generate the food increases to support the likely population increases. The higher prices in international commodity markets and concerns for political stability in these low-income countries may lead to use of available foreign exchange for food imports, reducing opportunities for domestic investment and growth. There is a growing disparity between the haves and have-nots in terms of national food supplies.

Disposal of Surplus

In the future, agricultural surplus problems are not indicated for the developed economies. Stocks are low. Policies for the United States and the European Community contributing to these surpluses are being changed. There are likely to be few surplus commodities, and budget pressures to dispose of surpluses will be a less important factor for U.S. food aid policy.

Budget Cost

Budget costs for food aid will reflect the higher nominal agricultural prices. Nominal costs of holding U.S. food aid at constant quantity levels will increase. But real prices of the agricultural commodities are flat, even falling in the out period. Thus, the real budgetary implication of holding the U.S. food aid program to current quantity levels is neutral.

Humanitarian Cost

Calculations using the current outlook show that the hungry population, however defined, was, at best, constant as a share of the world population during the 1970s and 1980s. The commodity market projections show a likely deterioration in this situation. The countries with the highest rates of population growth are generally the poorest. Famines, serious food shortages, and other emergencies are likely to become more frequent.

Concluding Observations

Generally, the outlook suggests favorable conditions for agriculture, trade in agricultural commodities, and developed nations. The situation is quite the reverse for many of the countries in Africa, the Middle East, and Latin America. For these countries, the decline in food use per capita from already low levels is alarming. Significant reforms in food aid and other policies, domestically and internationally, may be required to deal with these problems. The food situation for these disadvantaged populations has not improved in the last 10 years and, based on the outlook, it is likely to deteriorate.

Perhaps the most significant single piece of information from the outlook suggesting a priority for policy reform is that the share of the world population with inadequate food supplies, however defined, is likely to increase significantly over the next five to 10 years.

The concluding observations based on the FAPRI outlook specialized to the developing nations and U.S. foreign aid and food aid policies are twofold. First, the food deficit/availability problem for low-income nations is likely to get more severe if current macroeconomic, agricultural, and technology policies continue. Population growth is outstripping income growth and the increases in domestic production in these nations, and the nominal price of importing food will increase, recognizing the low average availabilities and the importance of wheat and coarse grains to the food supplies in these nations. Major problems are indicated for the populations that are at the low end of countries' income distributions. These problems are of such magnitude that it is unlikely, given the situation for agriculture, governments budget, and other factors in developed nations, that these food needs can be serviced by concessionary sales or donations.

Second, the secular trends in the food supplies must be addressed by other policy measures. These policy measures must address the sources of food availability problems. In fact, the food deficit problems are symptoms of other nonsustainable economic and political policies and institutions. Research to uncover the sources of the problems and, more important, how to make changes in these nations that can result in adequate food supplies, will be required. As well, a commitment to solving these problems is needed, reflecting that the measures will likely go to the very basics of the political and economic structures of the developed and developing nations.

Table 3.1. Domestic and foreign economic projections

	1985	1986	1987	1988	1989	1990	1991	1992	1993	Average 1994-98
UNITED STATES										
Real GDP (percent change)	3.60	3.10	3.50	4.10	2.00	2.00	3.30	2.80	2.50	2.60
GDP Deflator (percent change)	2.40	3.10	3.00	3.70	4.20	4.70	4.50	4.30	4.10	4.30
Civilian Unemployment Rate (percent)	7.20	7.00	6.20	5.40	5.60	6.20	5.80	5.60	5.60	5.10
Three-Month T. Bill Rate (percent)	7.50	6.00	5.80	6.60	8.00	7.00	6.20	6.10	6.10	6.20
Moody's AAA Corporate Bond Rate (percent)	11.40	9.00	9.40	9.90	10.70	9.80	9.00	8.90	9.00	9.20
Federal Budget Surplus ($ US billions)	-196.90	-205.60	-157.80	-141.30	-158.80	-139.60	-87.80	-84.80	-83.20	-35.40
Current Account ($ US billions)	-116.40	-141.40	-160.70	-140.50	-141.20	-138.60	-156.20	-156.90	-160.90	-158.20
FOREIGN AND DOMESTIC										
Saudi Light ($ US per barrel)	27.80	14.00	16.70	14.70	14.70	14.90	15.90	17.40	19.40	24.70
EFFECTIVE EXCHANGE RATE										
MERM United States (percent change)	4.20	-18.20	-11.70	-5.80	-1.30	-0.60	-2.00	-1.90	-0.80	-1.60
REAL GDP (percent change)										
World	3.20	3.20	3.10	3.50	2.70	2.80	3.30	3.10	3.10	3.20
Africa	3.40	-0.90	0.80	2.00	2.10	2.30	2.80	2.80	3.10	2.90
Latin America	3.80	4.20	1.80	0.00	1.40	4.00	4.70	4.60	4.30	4.50
Pacific Basin	2.00	7.30	8.80	7.30	6.00	4.50	5.30	5.60	6.10	5.70
Western Europe	2.60	2.70	2.60	3.20	2.30	2.60	2.80	2.80	2.80	2.80
Centrally Planned	3.30	4.90	3.00	3.10	3.20	3.70	3.10	3.40	3.60	3.40
FOREIGN CURRENCY/$ (percent change)										
Argentina	788.90	56.70	136.70	305.90	450.00	307.00	296.00	312.00	302.00	303.00
Brazil	235.50	120.20	187.40	600.00	779.50	464.90	196.60	261.90	242.30	234.00
Canada	5.40	1.80	-4.00	-7.40	1.30	1.20	-0.60	-0.60	2.10	-0.10
Australia	25.50	4.50	-4.30	-9.30	-0.90	5.20	4.40	3.70	1.90	0.60
Thailand	14.90	-3.20	-2.20	-1.40	-2.10	-4.40	-0.60	0.10	0.10	-0.10
Japan	-0.20	-29.30	-13.90	-11.10	-3.70	-2.90	-4.20	-4.80	-3.20	-4.00
EC	3.60	-22.30	-15.00	-0.50	-2.40	-0.10	-1.80	-1.70	-1.70	-1.50
S. Korea	7.90	1.30	-6.70	-11.70	-9.80	-5.40	-3.10	1.10	1.30	-1.00
Taiwan	0.60	-5.00	-15.80	-10.40	-7.40	-6.70	-4.30	-3.90	-3.40	-3.90

SOURCE: FAPRI U.S. and World Agricultural Outlook.

Table 3.2. FAPRI April 1989 baseline projections of wheat and coarse grains supply, use, and trade

	Actual 86/87	Projected 89/90	90/91	91/92	92/93	93/94	Average 93/97
Nominal prices ($ US/mt)							
Wheat (a)	109.00	158.00	142.00	136.00	147.00	147.00	160.00
Corn (b)	74.00	98.00	95.00	95.00	97.00	97.00	105.00
Real prices (1980 $/mt)							
Wheat	82.00	105.00	90.00	82.00	84.00	81.00	81.00
Corn	56.00	65.00	61.00	57.00	56.00	54.00	53.00
Wheat (mmt)							
World production	530.20	534.28	553.92	566.19	575.52	586.87	607.03
World consumption	523.00	534.57	548.52	561.59	573.37	584.48	606.43
World stocks	175.10	112.51	117.91	122.51	124.66	126.05	127.14
Net exports							
Industrial	72.64	76.92	78.52	80.25	83.08	85.37	89.33
Developing Countries	-55.09	-60.83	-62.16	-63.92	-67.12	-69.59	-74.10
CPE (ex. China)	-17.50	-16.09	-16.35	-16.30	-15.97	-15.78	-15.24
Coarse Grains (mmt) (c)							
World Production	771.90	766.68	777.26	794.66	808.87	823.03	855.29
World Consumption	742.52	761.23	777.13	794.03	807.73	824.11	856.94
World Stocks	201.44	89.87	90.00	90.63	89.76	88.69	85.18
Net exports (d)							
Industrial	39.60	45.05	45.55	47.39	50.44	53.52	59.98
Developing Countries	-25.11	-28.33	-26.65	-27.95	-29.48	-32.85	-38.10
CPE (ex. China)	-10.66	-18.76	-18.22	-18.79	-19.44	-20.09	-21.37

Wheat use and imports by importing countries							
Developing Use (mmt)	154.12	161.27	166.58	171.62	176.82	181.24	190.27
Net imports (mmt)	59.49	65.21	67.01	68.77	71.98	74.67	79.61
Import cost ($ US billions)	5.60	9.62	8.83	8.78	10.16	10.76	12.94
Import share (percent)	38.60	40.40	40.20	40.10	40.70	41.20	41.80
CPE (ex. China)							
Use (mmt)	243.80	248.61	255.07	260.94	266.59	272.14	282.89
Net imports (mmt)	17.50	16.09	16.35	16.30	15.97	15.78	15.24
Import cost ($ US billions)	1.30	2.13	1.91	1.88	2.09	2.16	2.41
Import share (percent)	7.20	6.50	6.40	6.20	6.00	5.80	5.40
Coarse grain use and imports by importing countries							
Developing Use (mmt)	191.17	195.55	200.12	204.19	209.12	213.84	223.82
Net imports (mmt)	35.13	38.74	37.91	40.11	42.17	45.89	52.02
Import cost ($ US billions)	2.49	3.80	3.63	3.84	4.09	4.47	5.47
Import share (percent)	18.40	19.70	18.90	19.60	20.20	21.50	23.20
CPE (ex. China)							
Use (mmt)	156.35	161.31	166.77	172.02	172.12	182.13	192.11
Net imports (mmt)	10.66	18.76	18.22	18.79	19.44	20.09	21.37
Import cost ($ US billions)	0.75	1.84	1.74	1.80	1.88	1.96	2.25
Import share ($ US billions)	6.80	11.60	10.90	10.90	11.00	11.00	11.10

SOURCE: FAPRI U.S. and World Agricultural Outlook 1989.

(a) **Wheat: FOB Gulf #2 Winter, ordinary protein.**
(b) **Corn: FOB Gulf #3 yellow.**
(c) **Coarse Grains: corn, sorghum, barley, and oats.**
(d) **Total trade may not balance due to timing, unreported data, and grain in transport.**

Note: **The abbreviation *mt* is defined as metric tons; *mmt* is million metric tons.**

Sorghum

Exporters	Importers
U.S., Australia, Argentina, S. Africa	Japan, Mexico, Nigeria, India, ROW

Soybeans

Exporters	Importers
U.S., Brazil, Argentina, China	Japan, EC-12, E Europe, USSR, Mexico, Other Latin America, S. Korea, Taiwan, ROW

Price

Rice

Exporters	Importers
Burma, China, India, Pakistan	EC-12, Japan, Saudi Arabia, Indonesia, ROW

Feed Grains (Corn, Barley, Oats)

Exporters	Importers
U.S., EC-12, Australia, Canada, S. Africa, Thailand, Argentina, China	Japan, USSR, E. Europe, Brazil, Mexico, Other Latin America, Egypt, Saudi Arabia, Nigeria, Other Africa & Mid East, High Income E. Asia, China, India, Other Asia, ROW

Wheat

Exporters	Importers
U.S., EC-12, Australia, Canada, Argentina	Other W. Europe, USSR, E. Europe, Japan, Brazil, Mexico, Other Latin America, Egypt, Tunisia, Algeria, Morocco, Other Mid. East & Africa, India, High Income E. Asia, China, Other Asia, ROW

Figure 3.1. CARD/FAPRI world agricultural trade models (annual econometric system)

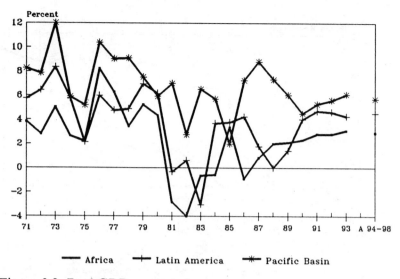

Figure 3.2. Real GDP percent change

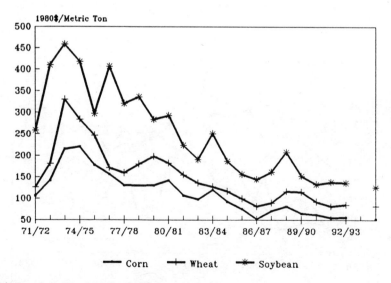

Figure 3.3. Real U.S. Gulf Port prices

NOTE: Figures 3.2 - 3.17 are from the 1989 FAPRI U.S. and World Agricultural Outlook. Published by the Food and Agricultural Policy Research Institute, Iowa State University and University of Missouri - Columbia.

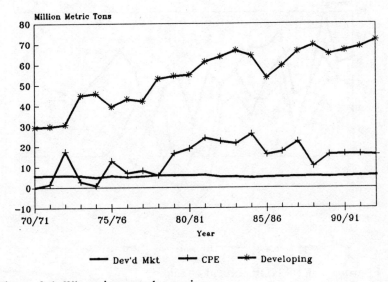

Figure 3.4. Wheat imports by region

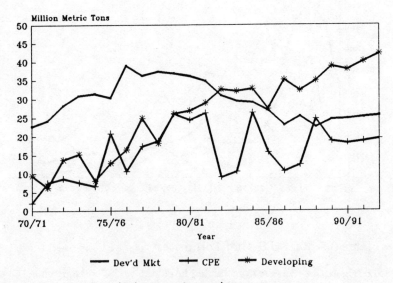

Figure 3.5. Feed grain imports by region

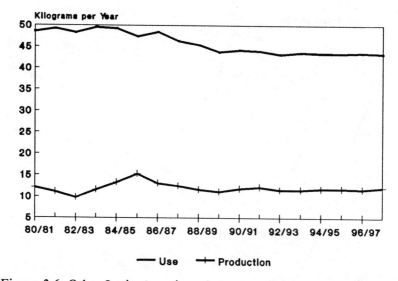

Figure 3.6. Other Latin America wheat, per capita production and use

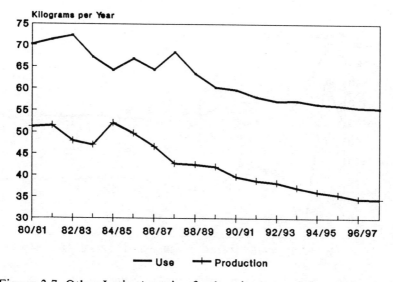

Figure 3.7. Other Latin America feed grains, per capita production and use

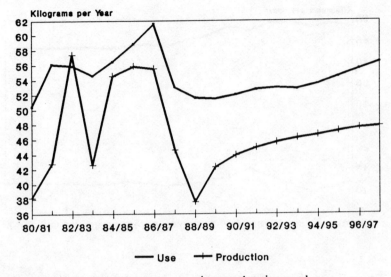

Figure 3.8. Mexico wheat, per capita production and use

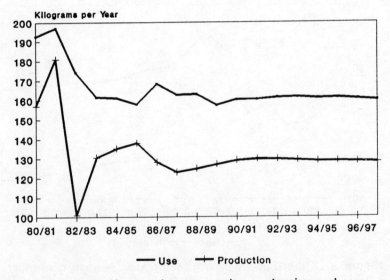

Figure 3.9. Mexico feed grains, per capita production and use

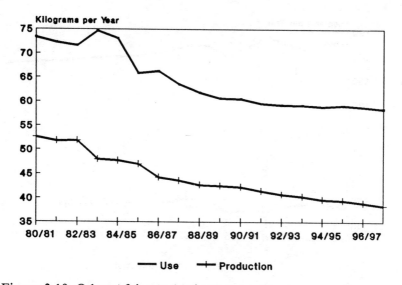

Figure 3.10. Other Africa and Middle East wheat, per capita
production and use

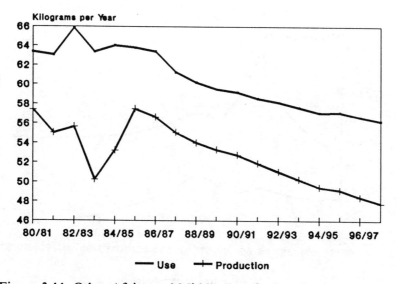

Figure 3.11. Other Africa and Middle East feed grains, per capita
production and use

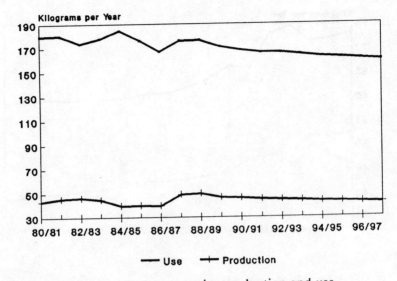

Figure 3.12. Egypt wheat, per capita production and use

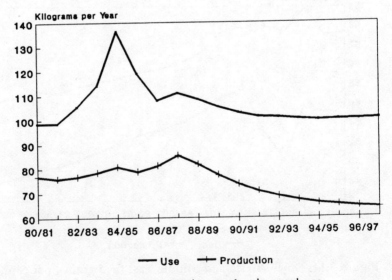

Figure 3.13. Egypt corn, per capita production and use

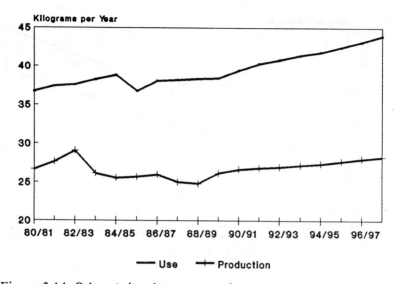

Figure 3.14. Other Asia wheat, per capita production and use

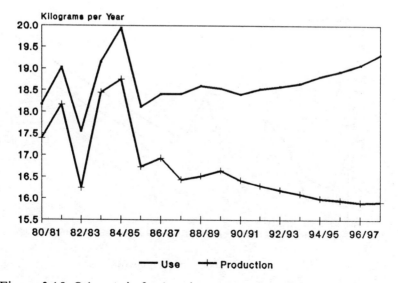

Figure 3.15. Other Asia feed grains, per capita production and use

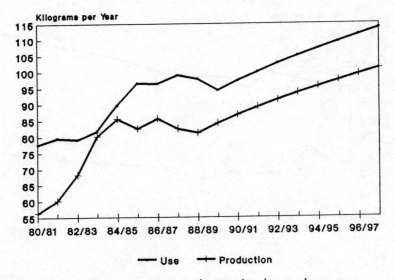

Figure 3.16. China wheat, per capita production and use

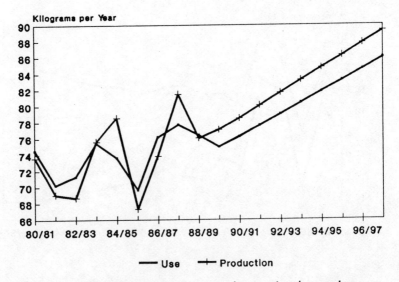

Figure 3.17. China feed grains, per capita production and use

APPENDIX 3.A:
COMMODITY, MARKET, INCOME, AND POPULATION DATA

Tables 3.A.1 - 3.A.17 contain data on the U.S. agricultural outlook as implied by a continuation of policies current in 1989, domestically and internationally. The outlook is prepared annually by the Food and Agricultural Policy Research Institute (FAPRI), Iowa State University and University of Missouri - Columbia. Funded by the U.S. Congress, FAPRI develops the most widely circulated and publicly available outlook for U.S. agriculture.

Table 3.A.1. Other Latin America wheat supply, use, and trade

	Year					
	81/82	82/83	83/84	84/85	85/86	86/87
WHEAT						
Production (mmt)	1.51	1.38	1.68	1.97	2.32	2.03
3-year avg. annual growth (percent)		-8.97			18.92	
Domestic use (mmt)	6.70	6.83	7.17	7.30	7.19	7.52
3-year avg. annual growth (percent)		2.14			1.76	
Net imports (mmt)	5.02	5.39	5.66	5.36	4.95	5.53
3-year avg. annual growth (percent)		3.69			-2.65	
Per capita imports (kg)	37.00	38.00	39.00	36.00	33.00	36.00
3-year avg. annual growth (percent)		1.27			-4.89	
Per capita use (kg)	49.00	48.00	50.00	49.00	47.00	48.00
3-year avg. annual growth (percent)		-0.22			-0.58	
Per capita prod. (kg)	11.00	10.00	12.00	13.00	15.00	13.00
3-year avg. annual growth (percent)		-11.07			16.18	
Annual real per capita growth rate (percent)	-5.60	-6.81	0.99	6.16	2.26	4.93
Annual real GDP growth rate (percent)	-4.77	-3.21	3.38	8.68	4.63	7.40
Population (000)	136,156.00	141,424.00	144,777.00	148,220.00	151,659.00	155,225.00
3-year avg. annual growth (percent)		2.38			2.36	

(continues)

Table 3.A.1. (cont.)

	Year 87/88	Projection by Year				
		88/89	89/90	90/91	91/92	92/93
WHEAT						
Production (mmt)	2.00	1.93	1.92	2.10	2.21	2.14
3-year avg. annual growth (percent)		-5.83			4.70	
Domestic use (mmt)	7.44	7.56	7.58	7.86	8.00	8.04
3-year avg. annual growth (percent)		1.71			1.91	
Net imports (mmt)	5.43	5.65	5.66	5.78	5.81	5.90
3-year avg. annual growth (percent)		4.65			0.94	
Per capita imports (kg)	34.00	34.00	33.00	33.00	32.00	32.00
3-year avg. annual growth (percent)		1.46			-1.97	
Per capita use (kg)	46.00	45.00	44.00	44.00	44.00	43.00
3-year avg. annual growth (percent)		-1.41			-1.02	
Per capita prod. (kg)	12.00	12.00	11.00	12.00	12.00	12.00
3-year avg. annual growth (percent)		-8.75			1.70	
Annual real per capita growth rate (percent)	-2.57	-0.89	-1.60	1.19	-0.48	-0.87
Annual real GDP growth rate (percent)	0.80	2.80	2.40	3.80	1.80	1.40
Population (000)	160,587.00	166,568.00	173,337.00	177,812.00	181,883.00	186,055.00
3-year avg. annual growth (percent)		3.18			2.98	

(continues)

Table 3.A.1. (cont.)

| | 93/94 | Projection by Year | | | | Average 1993-97 |
		94/95	95/96	96/97	97/98	
WHEAT						
Production (mmt)	2.19	2.29	2.33	2.36	2.50	2.33
3-year avg. annual growth (percent)		1.25			2.99	
Domestic use (mmt)	8.30	8.46	8.60	8.81	8.97	8.63
3-year avg. annual growth (percent)		1.89			1.97	
Net imports (mmt)	6.14	6.19	6.28	6.47	6.49	6.31
3-year avg. annual growth (percent)		2.14			1.60	
Per capita imports (kg)	32.00	32.00	32.00	32.00	31.00	32.00
3-year avg. annual growth (percent)		-0.15			-0.42	
Per capita use (kg)	44.00	43.00	43.00	44.00	43.00	43.00
3-year avg. annual growth (percent)		-0.40			-0.05	
Per capita prod. (kg)	12.00	12.00	12.00	12.00	12.00	12.00
3-year avg. annual growth (percent)		-1.03			0.95	
Annual real per capita growth rate (percent)	1.96	0.19	0.71	0.35	0.35	0.71
Annual real GDP growth rate (percent)	4.30	2.50	2.50	2.50	2.50	2.86
Population (000)	190,331.00	194,713.00	198,166.00	202,409.00	206,753.00	198,474.00
3-year avg. annual growth (percent)		2.30			2.02	

Note: The abbreviation *mmt* is defined as million metric tons.

Table 3.A.2. Other Latin America coarse grain supply, use, and trade

	Year					
	81/82	82/83	83/84	84/85	85/86	86/87
COARSE GRAINS (a)						
Production (000 mt)	7,014.00	6,789.00	6,811.00	7,722.00	7,545.00	7,242.00
3-year avg. annual growth (percent)		-2.04			3.80	
Domestic use (000 mt)	9,720.00	10,233.00	9,738.00	9,518.00	10,142.00	9,979.00
3-year avg. annual growth (percent)		4.61			-0.18	
Net imports (000 mt)	2,597.00	3,083.00	2,860.00	1,881.00	2,428.00	2,842.00
3-year avg. annual growth (percent)		20.57			-4.13	
Per capita imports (kg)	19.00	22.00	20.00	13.00	16.00	18.00
3-year avg. annual growth (percent)		17.62			-6.33	
Per capita use (kg)	71.00	72.00	67.00	64.00	67.00	64.00
3-year avg. annual growth (percent)		2.18			-2.48	
Per capita prod. (kg)	52.00	48.00	47.00	52.00	50.00	47.00
3-year avg. annual growth (percent)		-4.28			1.41	
Annual real per capita growth rate (percent)	-5.60	-6.81	0.99	6.16	2.26	4.93
Annual real GDP growth rate (percent)	-4.77	-3.21	3.38	8.68	4.63	7.40
Population (000)	136,156.00	141,424.00	144,777.00	148,220.00	151,659.00	155,225.00
3-year avg. annual growth (percent)		2.38			2.36	

(a) Includes corn, barley and oats.

(continues)

Table 3.A.2. (cont.)

	Year 87/88	Projection by Year				
		88/89	89/90	90/91	91/92	92/93
COARSE GRAINS (a)						
Production (000 mt)	6,867.00	7,082.00	7,285.00	7,056.00	7,047.00	7,119.00
3-year avg. annual growth (percent)		-2.02			-0.13	
Domestic use (000 mt)	10,987.00	10,554.00	10,444.00	10,612.00	10,571.00	10,637.00
3-year avg. annual growth (percent)		1.52			0.06	
Net imports (000 mt)	4,072.00	3,501.00	3,201.00	3,523.00	3,516.00	3,529.00
3-year avg. annual growth (percent)		15.44			0.43	
Per capita imports (kg)	25.00	21.00	18.00	20.00	19.00	19.00
3-year avg. annual growth (percent)		11.92			-2.43	
Per capita use (kg)	68.00	63.00	60.00	60.00	58.00	57.00
3-year avg. annual growth (percent)		-1.61			-2.82	
Per capita prod. (kg)	43.00	43.00	42.00	40.00	39.00	38.00
3-year avg. annual growth (percent)		-5.04			-3.03	
Annual real per capita growth rate (percent)	-2.57	-0.89	-1.60	1.19	-0.48	-0.87
Annual real GDP growth rate (percent)	0.80	2.80	2.40	3.80	1.80	1.40
Population (000)	160,587.00	166,568.00	173,337.00	177,812.00	181,883.00	186,055.00
3-year avg. annual growth (percent)		3.18			2.98	

(continues)

Table 3.A.2. (cont.)

				Projection by Year			Average
	93/94	94/95	95/96	96/97	97/98		1993-97
COARSE GRAINS (a)							
Production (000 mt)	7,065.00	7,040.00	7,033.00	6,996.00	7,133.00		7,053.00
3-year avg. annual growth (percent)		-0.03			0.44		
Domestic use (000 mt)	10,890.00	10,998.00	11,130.00	11,270.00	11,477.00		11,153.00
3-year avg. annual growth (percent)		1.33			1.43		
Net imports (000 mt)	3,818.00	3,952.00	4,095.00	4,267.00	4,367.00		4,100.00
3-year avg. annual growth (percent)		4.02			3.39		
Per capita imports (kg)	20.00	20.00	21.00	21.00	21.00		21.00
3-year avg. annual growth (percent)		1.69			1.34		
Per capita use (kg)	57.00	56.00	56.00	56.00	56.00		56.00
3-year avg. annual growth (percent)		-0.94			-0.58		
Per capita prod. (kg)	37.00	36.00	35.00	35.00	35.00		36.00
3-year avg. annual growth (percent)		-2.28			-1.55		
Annual real per capita growth rate (percent)	1.96	0.19	0.71	0.35	0.35		0.71
Annual real GDP growth rate (percent)	4.30	2.50	2.50	2.50	2.50		2.86
Population (000)	190,331.00	194,713.00	198,166.00	202,409.00	206,753.00		198,474.00
3-year avg. annual growth (percent)		2.30			2.02		

Note: The abbreviation *mt* is defined as metric tons.

Table 3.A.3. Mexico wheat supply, use, and trade

				Year		
	81/82	82/83	83/84	84/85	85/86	86/87
WHEAT						
Production (mmt)	3.05	4.20	3.20	4.20	4.41	4.49
3-year avg. annual growth (percent)		23.01			4.15	
Domestic use (mmt)	4.00	4.09	4.10	4.35	4.65	4.98
3-year avg. annual growth (percent)		6.49			4.41	
Net imports (mmt)	0.93	0.04	0.56	0.48	0.09	0.46
3-year avg. annual growth (percent)		-32.08			401.49	
Per capita imports (kg)	13.00	1.00	7.00	6.00	1.00	6.00
3-year avg. annual growth (percent)		-33.90			388.69	
Per capita use (kg)	56.00	56.00	55.00	56.00	59.00	62.00
3-year avg. annual growth (percent)		3.67			1.79	
Per capita prod. (kg)	43.00	57.00	43.00	55.00	56.00	55.00
3-year avg. annual growth (percent)		19.75			1.53	
Annual real per capita growth rate (percent)	-1.23	-6.56	-1.19	0.23	-3.37	-2.53
Annual real GDP growth rate (percent)	1.46	-4.07	1.41	2.82	-0.91	-0.18
Population (000)	71,281.00	73,184.00	75,103.00	77,040.00	78,996.00	80,905.00
3-year avg. annual growth (percent)		2.72			2.58	

(continues)

Table 3.A.3. (cont.)

	Year	Projection by Year				
	87/88	88/89	89/90	90/91	91/92	92/93
WHEAT						
Production (mmt)	3.70	3.20	3.69	3.91	4.09	4.25
3-year avg. annual growth (percent)		-9.76			8.63	
Domestic use (mmt)	4.40	4.39	4.49	4.63	4.80	4.93
3-year avg. annual growth (percent)		-1.59			3.02	
Net imports (mmt)	0.75	1.20	0.78	0.75	0.74	0.70
3-year avg. annual growth (percent)		178.05			-13.39	
Per capita imports (kg)	9.00	14.00	9.00	8.00	8.00	8.00
3-year avg. annual growth (percent)		171.37			-15.31	
Per capita use (kg)	53.00	52.00	51.00	52.00	53.00	53.00
3-year avg. annual growth (percent)		-3.99			0.72	
Per capita prod. (kg)	45.00	38.00	42.00	44.00	45.00	46.00
3-year avg. annual growth (percent)		-11.96			6.19	
Annual real per capita growth rate (percent)	-0.41	-1.40	-0.02	1.65	2.06	0.62
Annual real GDP growth rate (percent)	2.11	1.10	2.51	3.74	4.39	2.92
Population (000)	82,957.00	85,060.00	87,217.00	89,012.00	91,043.00	93,120.00
3-year avg. annual growth (percent)		2.50			2.29	

(continues)

Table 3.A.3. (cont.)

	Projection by Year					Average
	93/94	94/95	95/96	96/97	97/98	1993-97
WHEAT						
Production (mmt)	4.40	4.54	4.67	4.81	4.93	4.67
3-year avg. annual growth (percent)		3.54			2.79	
Domestic use (mmt)	5.03	5.21	5.40	5.61	5.82	5.41
3-year avg. annual growth (percent)		2.77			3.76	
Net imports (mmt)	0.65	0.70	0.76	0.82	0.91	0.77
3-year avg. annual growth (percent)		-1.62			9.15	
Per capita imports (kg)	7.00	7.00	8.00	8.00	9.00	8.00
3-year avg. annual growth (percent)		-3.81			7.06	
Per capita use (kg)	53.00	53.00	54.00	55.00	56.00	55.00
3-year avg. annual growth (percent)		0.48			1.78	
Per capita prod. (kg)	46.00	47.00	47.00	48.00	48.00	47.00
3-year avg. annual growth (percent)		1.23			0.82	
Annual real per capita growth rate (percent)	-0.01	1.70	2.19	1.96	1.96	1.56
Annual real GDP growth rate (percent)	2.27	4.02	4.02	4.02	4.02	3.67
Population (000)	95,244.00	97,417.00	99,165.00	101,168.00	103,211.00	99,241.00
3-year avg. annual growth (percent)		2.28			1.94	

Note: The abbreviation *mmt* is defined as million metric tons.

Table 3.A.4. Mexico coarse grains and sorghum supply, use, and trade

			Year			
	81/82	82/83	83/84	84/85	85/86	86/87
COARSE GRAINS (a)						
Production (000 mt)	12,890.00	7,390.00	9,810.00	10,420.00	10,910.00	10,372.00
3-year avg. annual growth (percent)		-3.70			14.56	
Domestic use (000 mt)	14,043.00	12,745.00	12,135.00	12,416.00	12,479.00	13,618.00
3-year avg. annual growth (percent)		-1.16			-0.65	
Net imports (000 mt)	681.00	4,005.00	2,544.00	1,768.00	1,692.00	3,403.00
3-year avg. annual growth (percent)		34.18			-23.76	
Per capita imports (kg)	10.00	55.00	34.00	23.00	21.00	42.00
3-year avg. annual growth (percent)		128.06			-25.67	
Per capita use (kg)	197.00	174.00	162.00	161.00	158.00	168.00
3-year avg. annual growth (percent)		-3.78			-3.15	
Per capita prod. (kg)	181.00	101.00	131.00	135.00	138.00	128.00
3-year avg. annual growth (percent)		-6.26			11.67	
Annual real per capita growth rate (percent)	-1.23	-6.56	-1.19	0.23	-3.37	-2.53
Annual real GDP growth rate (percent)	1.46	-4.07	1.41	2.82	-0.91	-0.18
Population (000)	71,281.00	73,184.00	75,103.00	77,040.00	78,996.00	80,905.00
3-year avg. annual growth (percent)		2.72			2.58	

(a) Coarse grains include corn, barley, and oats

(continues)

Table 3.A.4 (cont.)

	Year		Projection by Year			
	87/88	88/89	89/90	90/91	91/92	92/93
COARSE GRAINS (a)						
Production (000 mt)	10,204.00	10,620.00	11,084.00	11,491.00	11,814.00	12,080.00
3-year avg. annual growth (percent)		-0.82			3.62	
Domestic use (000 mt)	13,498.00	13,864.00	13,736.00	14,269.00	14,607.00	15,024.00
3-year avg. annual growth (percent)		3.65			1.78	
Net imports (000 mt)	3,195.00	3,305.00	2,757.00	2,881.00	2,879.00	3,015.00
3-year avg. annual growth (percent)		32.82			-4.05	
Per capita imports (kg)	39.00	39.00	32.00	32.00	32.00	32.00
3-year avg. annual growth (percent)		29.61			-6.18	
Per capita use (kg)	163.00	163.00	157.00	160.00	160.00	161.00
3-year avg. annual growth (percent)		1.13			-0.50	
Per capita prod. (kg)	123.00	125.00	127.00	129.00	130.00	130.00
3-year avg. annual growth (percent)		-3.24			1.30	
Annual real per capita growth rate (percent)	-0.41	-1.40	-0.02	1.65	2.06	0.62
Annual real GDP growth rate (percent)	2.11	1.10	2.51	3.74	4.39	2.92
Population (000)	82,957.00	85,060.00	87,217.00	89,012.00	91,043.00	93,120.00
3-year avg. annual growth (percent)		2.50			2.29	

(continues)

Table 3.A.4 (cont.)

		Projection by Year				Average 1993-97
	93/94	94/95	95/96	96/97	97/98	
COARSE GRAINS (a)						
Production (000 mt)	12,312.00	12,544.00	12,772.00	12,999.00	13,232.00	12,772.00
3-year avg. annual growth (percent)		2.02			1.80	
Domestic use (000 mt)	15,386.00	15,686.00	15,991.00	16,259.00	16,523.00	15,969.00
3-year avg. annual growth (percent)		2.40			1.75	
Net imports (000 mt)	3,135.00	3,201.00	3,277.00	3,317.00	3,350.00	3,256.00
3-year avg. annual growth (percent)		3.60			1.53	
Per capita imports (kg)	33.00	33.00	33.00	33.00	32.00	33.00
3-year avg. annual growth (percent)		1.29			-0.41	
Per capita use (kg)	162.00	161.00	161.00	161.00	160.00	161.00
3-year avg. annual growth (percent)		0.12			-0.19	
Per capita prod. (kg)	129.00	129.00	129.00	128.00	128.00	129.00
3-year avg. annual growth (percent)		-0.26			-0.15	
Annual real per capita growth rate (percent)	-0.01	1.70	2.19	1.96	1.96	1.56
Annual real GDP growth rate (percent)	2.27	4.02	4.02	4.02	4.02	3.67
Population (000)	95,244.00	97,417.00	99,165.00	101,168.00	103,211.00	99,241.00
3-year avg. annual growth (percent)		2.28			1.94	

(continues)

Table 3.A.4 (cont.)

| | | | Year | | | |
	81/82	82/83	83/84	84/85	85/86	86/87
SORGHUM						
Production (000 mt)	4,000.00	800.00	4,000.00	4,100.00	3,772.00	4,330.00
3-year avg. annual growth (percent)		21.75			12.45	
Domestic use (000 mt)	6,758.00	6,100.00	6,300.00	6,425.00	5,713.00	5,334.00
3-year avg. annual growth (percent)		13.91			-1.94	
Net imports (000 mt)	945.00	3,227.00	3,329.00	2,481.00	623.00	815.00
3-year avg. annual growth (percent)		70.17			-32.40	
Per capita imports (kg)	13.00	44.00	44.00	32.00	8.00	10.00
3-year avg. annual growth (percent)		65.70			-34.11	
Per capita use (kg)	95.00	83.00	84.00	83.00	72.00	66.00
3-year avg. annual growth (percent)		10.89			-4.41	
Per capita prod. (kg)	56.00	38.00	53.00	53.00	48.00	54.00
3-year avg. annual growth (percent)		18.51			9.62	

(continues)

Table 3.A.4 (cont.)

	Year		Projection by Year			
	87/88	88/89	89/90	90/91	91/92	92/93
SORGHUM						
Production (000 mt)	4,029.00	4,022.00	4,462.00	4,467.00	4,364.00	4,273.00
3-year avg. annual growth (percent)		2.56			2.92	
Domestic use (000 mt)	4,906.00	4,808.00	5,039.00	5,118.00	5,180.00	5,310.00
3-year avg. annual growth (percent)		-5.55			2.53	
Net imports (000 mt)	867.00	885.00	628.00	652.00	804.00	1,207.00
3-year avg. annual growth (percent)		13.09			-0.64	
Per capita imports (kg)	10.00	10.00	7.00	7.00	9.00	13.00
3-year avg. annual growth (percent)		10.34			-2.83	
Per capita use (kg)	59.00	57.00	58.00	57.00	57.00	57.00
3-year avg. annual growth (percent)		-7.85			0.23	
Per capita prod. (kg)	49.00	47.00	51.00	50.00	48.00	46.00
3-year avg. annual growth (percent)		0.06			0.60	

(continues)

Table 3.A.4 (cont.)

| | | Projection by Year | | | | Average |
	93/94	94/95	95/96	96/97	97/98	1993-97
SORGHUM						
Production (000 mt)	4,214.00	4,249.00	4,280.00	4,316.00	4,399.00	4,292.00
3-year avg. annual growth (percent)		-0.88			1.16	
Domestic use (000 mt)	5,293.00	5,379.00	5,473.00	5,537.00	5,537.00	5,444.00
3-year avg. annual growth (percent)		1.27			1.46	
Net imports (000 mt)	1,072.00	1,134.00	1,196.00	1,226.00	1,312.00	1,188.00
3-year avg. annual growth (percent)		14.91			5.00	
Per capita imports (kg)	11.00	12.00	12.00	12.00	13.00	12.00
3-year avg. annual growth (percent)		12.34			2.99	
Per capita use (kg)	56.00	55.00	55.00	55.00	54.00	55.00
3-year avg. annual growth (percent)		-0.99			-0.95	
Per capita prod. (kg)	44.00	44.00	43.00	43.00	43.00	43.00
3-year avg. annual growth (percent)		-3.09			-0.77	

Note: The abbreviation *mt* is defined as metric tons.

Table 3.A.5. Other Africa and Middle East wheat supply, use, and trade

	81/82	82/83	83/84	Year 84/85	85/86	86/87
WHEAT						
Production (mmt)	28.00	28.86	27.49	28.16	28.57	27.73
3-year avg. annual growth (percent)		2.25			-0.28	
Domestic use (mmt)	39.06	39.88	42.77	43.16	40.06	41.53
3-year avg. annual growth (percent)		2.94			0.33	
Net imports (mmt)	11.26	10.50	15.53	17.20	10.41	14.44
3-year avg. annual growth (percent)		-0.81			6.39	
Per capita imports (kg)	21.00	19.00	27.00	29.00	17.00	23.00
3-year avg. annual growth (percent)		-3.68			3.32	
Per capita use (kg)	72.00	72.00	75.00	73.00	66.00	66.00
3-year avg. annual growth (percent)		-0.03			-2.57	
Per capita prod. (kg)	52.00	52.00	48.00	48.00	47.00	44.00
3-year avg. annual growth (percent)		-0.71			-3.16	
Annual real per capita growth rate (percent)	-4.11	-5.28	-2.07	-3.33	-6.49	-2.69
Annual real GDP growth rate (percent)	-1.27	-2.48	0.83	-0.45	-3.70	0.27
Population (000)	540,745.00	556,747.00	573,251.00	590,329.00	607,946.00	626,456.00
3-year avg. annual growth (percent)		2.98			2.98	

(continues)

Table 3.A.5. (cont.)

	Year		Projection by Year			
	87/88	88/89	89/90	90/91	91/92	92/93
WHEAT						
Production (mmt)	28.27	28.68	29.60	30.23	30.60	31.06
3-year avg. annual growth (percent)		0.15			2.19	
Domestic use (mmt)	41.23	41.56	42.25	43.28	44.00	45.22
3-year avg. annual growth (percent)		1.25			1.92	
Net imports (mmt)	13.45	12.96	13.14	13.54	13.76	14.52
3-year avg. annual growth (percent)		9.40			2.02	
Per capita imports (kg)	21.00	19.00	19.00	19.00	19.00	19.00
3-year avg. annual growth (percent)		5.87			-1.15	
Per capita use (kg)	64.00	62.00	61.00	61.00	60.00	59.00
3-year avg. annual growth (percent)		-2.06			-1.25	
Per capita prod. (kg)	44.00	43.00	42.00	42.00	41.00	41.00
3-year avg. annual growth (percent)		-3.13			-0.99	
Annual real per capita growth rate (percent)	-2.09	-2.43	-0.98	0.04	-0.74	-0.80
Annual real GDP growth rate (percent)	1.36	1.08	2.66	2.72	2.53	2.46
Population (000)	648,549.00	671,856.00	696,560.00	715,214.00	738,717.00	763,026.00
3-year avg. annual growth (percent)		3.39			3.21	

(continues)

Table 3.A.5. (cont.)

	93/94	Projection by Year				Average 1993-97
		94/95	95/96	96/97	97/98	
WHEAT						
Production (mmt)	31.74	32.30	32.86	33.50	34.08	32.90
3-year avg. annual growth (percent)		1.82			1.80	
Domestic use (mmt)	46.66	47.92	49.21	50.55	51.88	49.24
3-year avg. annual growth (percent)		2.89			2.68	
Net imports (mmt)	15.38	16.07	16.79	17.52	18.25	16.80
3-year avg. annual growth (percent)		5.31			4.33	
Per capita imports (kg)	20.00	20.00	20.00	20.00	21.00	20.00
3-year avg. annual growth (percent)		1.95			1.37	
Per capita use (kg)	59.00	59.00	59.00	59.00	58.00	59.00
3-year avg. annual growth (percent)		-0.40			-0.23	
Per capita prod. (kg)	40.00	40.00	39.00	39.00	38.00	39.00
3-year avg. annual growth (percent)		-1.43			-1.08	
Annual real per capita growth rate (percent)	0.18	-0.48	0.51	-0.42	-0.43	-0.13
Annual real GDP growth rate (percent)	3.49	2.80	2.80	2.80	2.80	2.94
Population (000)	788,170.00	814,177.00	832,731.00	859,692.00	887,570.00	836,468.00
3-year avg. annual growth (percent)		3.30			2.92	

Note: The abbreviation *mmt* is defined as million metric tons.

Table 3.A.6. Other Africa and Middle East coarse grain supply, use, and trade

				Year		
	81/82	82/83	83/84	84/85	85/86	86/87
COARSE GRAINS (a)						
Production (000 mt)	30,121.00	31,357.00	29,138.00	31,763.00	35,340.00	35,879.00
3-year avg. annual growth (percent)		17.73			13.19	
Domestic use (000 mt)	34,497.00	37,088.00	36,745.00	38,231.00	39,218.00	40,152.00
3-year avg. annual growth (percent)		15.30			5.70	
Net imports (000 mt)	5,175.00	4,632.00	6,858.00	7,848.00	4,387.00	4,545.00
3-year avg. annual growth (percent)		-13.01			18.39	
Per capita imports (kg)	9.00	8.00	12.00	13.00	7.00	7.00
3-year avg. annual growth (percent)		-21.24			9.27	
Per capita use (kg)	63.00	66.00	63.00	64.00	64.00	63.00
3-year avg. annual growth (percent)		6.26			-3.06	
Per capita prod. (kg)	55.00	56.00	50.00	53.00	57.00	57.00
3-year avg. annual growth (percent)		8.62			4.21	
Annual real per capita growth rate (percent)	-4.33	-3.01	-2.03	-4.69	-2.57	-1.71
Annual real GDP growth rate (percent)	-1.51	-0.16	0.85	-1.87	0.32	1.27
Population (000)	547,294.00	563,376.00	579,947.00	597,084.00	614,752.00	633,356.00
3-year avg. annual growth (percent)		8.86			8.86	

(continues)

(a) Coarse grains include corn, barley, and oats

Table 3.A.6. (cont.)

	Year		Projection by Year			
	87/88	88/89	89/90	90/91	91/92	92/93
COARSE GRAINS (a)						
Production (000 mt)	36,097.00	36,664.00	37,508.00	38,119.00	38,717.00	39,334.00
3-year avg. annual growth (percent)		3.70			5.50	
Domestic use (000 mt)	40,147.00	40,870.00	41,862.00	42,757.00	43,684.00	44,795.00
3-year avg. annual growth (percent)		4.17			6.73	
Net imports (000 mt)	4,118.00	4,329.00	4,621.00	4,843.00	5,155.00	5,651.00
3-year avg. annual growth (percent)		-0.67			17.99	
Per capita imports (kg)	6.00	6.00	7.00	7.00	7.00	7.00
3-year avg. annual growth (percent)		-10.40			8.16	
Per capita use (kg)	61.00	60.00	59.00	59.00	59.00	58.00
3-year avg. annual growth (percent)		-5.73			-2.74	
Per capita prod. (kg)	55.00	54.00	53.00	53.00	52.00	51.00
3-year avg. annual growth (percent)		-6.18			-3.94	
Annual real per capita growth rate (percent)	-2.48	-0.61	-0.91	0.11	-0.80	0.35
Annual real GDP growth rate (percent)	0.94	2.94	2.71	2.78	2.42	3.62
Population (000)	655,539.00	678,935.00	703,727.00	722,476.00	745,931.00	770,184.00
3-year avg. annual growth (percent)		10.10			9.56	

(continues)

Table 3.A.6. (cont.)

	Projection by Year					Average 1993-97
	93/94	94/95	95/96	96/97	97/98	
COARSE GRAINS (a)						
Production (000 mt)	39,974.00	40,620.00	41,278.00	41,962.00	42,741.00	41,315.00
3-year avg. annual growth (percent)		4.84			5.13	
Domestic use (000 mt)	45,842.00	46,902.00	47,980.00	49,087.00	50,290.00	48,020.00
3-year avg. annual growth (percent)		7.19			7.06	
Net imports (000 mt)	6,066.00	6,481.00	6,901.00	7,319.00	7,781.00	6,910.00
3-year avg. annual growth (percent)		23.81			18.85	
Per capita imports (kg)	8.00	8.00	8.00	8.00	9.00	8.00
3-year avg. annual growth (percent)		13.60			9.95	
Per capita use (kg)	58.00	57.00	57.00	57.00	56.00	57.00
3-year avg. annual growth (percent)		-2.49			-1.52	
Per capita prod. (kg)	50.00	49.00	49.00	48.00	48.00	49.00
3-year avg. annual growth (percent)		-4.78			-3.39	
Annual real per capita growth rate (percent)	-0.34	-0.35	0.63	-0.27	-0.27	-0.12
Annual real GDP growth rate (percent)	2.90	2.90	2.90	2.90	2.90	2.90
Population (000)	795,263.00	821,196.00	839,753.00	866,438.00	894,022.00	843,335.00
3-year avg. annual growth (percent)		9.77			8.62	

Note: The abbreviation *mt* is defined as metric tons.

Table 3.A.7. Egypt wheat supply, use, and trade

	Year					
	81/82	82/83	83/84	84/85	85/86	86/87
WHEAT						
Production (mmt)	1.94	2.02	2.00	1.82	1.87	1.90
3-year avg. annual growth (percent)		2.92			-2.36	
Domestic use (mmt)	7.67	7.58	7.95	8.45	8.27	8.02
3-year avg. annual growth (percent)		1.94			3.01	
Net imports (mmt)	5.88	5.50	5.86	6.94	6.30	6.02
3-year avg. annual growth (percent)		4.14			5.25	
Per capita imports (kg)	138.00	126.00	131.00	152.00	134.00	125.00
3-year avg. annual growth (percent)		1.54			2.71	
Per capita use (kg)	180.00	174.00	178.00	185.00	176.00	167.00
3-year avg. annual growth (percent)		-0.60			0.53	
Per capita prod. (kg)	46.00	46.00	45.00	40.00	40.00	40.00
3-year avg. annual growth (percent)		0.36			-4.71	
Annual real per capita growth rate (percent)	3.00	6.38	0.61	-1.88	-0.68	-2.24
Annual real GDP growth rate (percent)	5.54	9.00	3.09	0.54	1.77	0.00
Population ('000)	42,546.00	43,597.00	44,674.00	45,778.00	46,909.00	47,984.00
3-year avg. annual growth (percent)		2.56			2.47	

(continues)

Table 3.A.7. (cont.)

	Year	Projection by Year				
	87/88	88/89	89/90	90/91	91/92	92/93
WHEAT						
Production (mmt)	2.40	2.50	2.39	2.41	2.41	2.43
3-year avg. annual growth (percent)		10.70			-1.19	
Domestic use (mmt)	8.66	8.89	8.82	8.84	8.92	9.11
3-year avg. annual growth (percent)		2.54			0.11	
Net imports (mmt)	6.43	6.40	6.42	6.43	6.51	6.69
3-year avg. annual growth (percent)		0.63			0.57	
Per capita imports (kg)	131.00	127.00	125.00	122.00	121.00	122.00
3-year avg. annual growth (percent)		-1.69			-1.57	
Per capita use (kg)	176.00	177.00	171.00	168.00	166.00	166.00
3-year avg. annual growth (percent)		0.17			-2.01	
Per capita prod. (kg)	49.00	50.00	46.00	46.00	45.00	44.00
3-year avg. annual growth (percent)		8.14			-3.28	
Annual real per capita growth rate (percent)	-1.37	0.40	0.60	0.93	1.02	2.16
Annual real GDP growth rate (percent)	0.99	2.81	3.01	2.92	3.19	4.35
Population (000)	49,135.00	50,314.00	51,521.00	52,536.00	53,664.00	54,817.00
3-year avg. annual growth (percent)		2.36			2.17	

(continues)

Table 3.A.7. (cont.)

			Projection by Year			Average 1993-97
	93/94	94/95	95/96	96/97	97/98	
WHEAT						
Production (mmt)	2.46	2.47	2.49	2.51	2.53	2.49
3-year avg. annual growth (percent)		0.82			0.80	
Domestic use (mmt)	9.22	9.31	9.42	9.54	9.67	9.43
3-year avg. annual growth (percent)		1.44			1.27	
Net imports (mmt)	6.76	6.85	6.94	7.04	7.14	6.95
3-year avg. annual growth (percent)		1.71			1.39	
Per capita imports (kg)	121.00	120.00	119.00	119.00	118.00	119.00
3-year avg. annual growth (percent)		-0.42			-0.49	
Per capita use (kg)	165.00	163.00	162.00	161.00	160.00	162.00
3-year avg. annual growth (percent)		-0.70			-0.61	
Per capita prod. (kg)	44.00	43.00	43.00	42.00	42.00	43.00
3-year avg. annual growth (percent)		-1.30			-1.07	
Annual real per capita growth rate (percent)	0.75	0.75	1.18	0.92	0.92	0.90
Annual real GDP growth rate (percent)	2.92	2.92	2.92	2.92	2.92	2.92
Population (000)	55,994.00	57,197.00	58,178.00	59,331.00	60,506.00	58,241.00
3-year avg. annual growth (percent)		2.15			1.89	

Note: The abbreviation *mmt* is defined as million metric tons.

Table 3.A.8. Egypt corn supply, use, and trade

			Year			
	81/82	82/83	83/84	84/85	85/86	86/87
CORN						
Production (000 mt)	3,232.00	3,347.00	3,509.00	3,698.00	3,699.00	3,900.00
3-year avg. annual growth (percent)		4.52			3.42	
Domestic use (000 mt)	4,200.00	4,600.00	5,100.00	6,247.00	5,587.00	5,181.00
3-year avg. annual growth (percent)		7.27			7.60	
Net imports (000 mt)	1,344.00	1,215.00	1,563.00	1,722.00	1,870.00	1,604.00
3-year avg. annual growth (percent)		46.20			15.80	
Per capita imports (kg)	32.00	28.00	35.00	38.00	40.00	33.00
3-year avg. annual growth (percent)		42.50			13.01	
Per capita use (kg)	99.00	106.00	114.00	136.00	119.00	108.00
3-year avg. annual growth (percent)		4.60			5.00	
Per capita prod. (kg)	76.00	77.00	79.00	81.00	79.00	81.00
3-year avg. annual growth (percent)		1.91			0.93	
Annual real per capita growth rate (percent)	3.00	6.38	0.61	-1.88	-0.68	-2.24
Annual real GDP growth rate (percent)	5.54	9.00	3.09	0.54	1.77	0.00
Population (000)	42,546.00	43,597.00	44,674.00	45,778.00	46,909.00	47,984.00
3-year avg. annual growth (percent)		2.56			2.47	

(continues)

Table 3.A.8. (cont.)

	Year		Projection by Year			
	87/88	88/89	89/90	90/91	91/92	92/93
CORN						
Production (000 mt)	4,200.00	4,118.00	3,990.00	3,872.00	3,799.00	3,768.00
3-year avg. annual growth (percent)		3.72			-2.65	
Domestic use (000 mt)	5,449.00	5,454.00	5,429.00	5,413.00	5,442.00	5,541.00
3-year avg. annual growth (percent)		-0.67			-0.07	
Net imports (000 mt)	1,305.00	1,238.00	1,519.00	1,578.00	1,640.00	1,780.00
3-year avg. annual growth (percent)		-12.67			10.17	
Per capita imports (kg)	27.00	25.00	29.00	30.00	31.00	32.00
3-year avg. annual growth (percent)		-14.68			7.81	
Per capita use (kg)	111.00	108.00	105.00	103.00	101.00	101.00
3-year avg. annual growth (percent)		-2.96			-2.20	
Per capita prod. (kg)	85.00	82.00	77.00	74.00	71.00	69.00
3-year avg. annual growth (percent)		1.33			-4.72	
Annual real per capita growth rate (percent)	-1.37	0.40	0.60	0.93	1.02	2.16
Annual real GDP growth rate (percent)	0.99	2.81	3.01	2.92	3.19	4.35
Population (000)	49,135.00	50,314.00	51,521.00	52,536.00	53,664.00	54,817.00
3-year avg. annual growth (percent)		2.36			2.17	

(continues)

Table 3.A.8. (cont.)

| | Projection by Year | | | | | Average |
	93/94	94/95	95/96	96/97	97/98	1993-97
CORN						
Production (000 mt)	3,757.00	3,765.00	3,788.00	3,820.00	3,869.00	3,800.00
3-year avg. annual growth (percent)		-0.30			0.91	
Domestic use (000 mt)	5,620.00	5,715.00	5,825.00	5,945.00	6,083.00	5,838.00
3-year avg. annual growth (percent)		1.65			2.10	
Net imports (000 mt)	1,890.00	1,981.00	2,067.00	2,140.00	2,253.00	2,066.00
3-year avg. annual growth (percent)		6.51			4.38	
Per capita imports (kg)	34.00	35.00	36.00	36.00	37.00	35.00
3-year avg. annual growth (percent)		4.27			2.45	
Per capita use (kg)	100.00	100.00	100.00	100.00	101.00	100.00
3-year avg. annual growth (percent)		-0.49			0.21	
Per capita prod. (kg)	67.00	66.00	65.00	64.00	64.00	65.00
3-year avg. annual growth (percent)		-2.39			-0.96	
Annual real per capita growth rate (percent)	0.75	0.75	1.18	0.92	0.92	0.90
Annual real GDP growth rate (percent)	2.92	2.92	2.92	2.92	2.92	2.92
Population (000)	55,994.00	57,197.00	58,178.00	59,331.00	60,506.00	58,241.00
3-year avg. annual growth (percent)	2.92	2.15	2.92	2.92	1.89	2.92

Note: The abbreviation *mt* is defined as metric tons.

Table 3.A.9. Morocco wheat supply, use, and trade

	Year					
	81/82	82/83	83/84	84/85	85/86	86/87
WHEAT						
Production (mmt)	0.89	2.18	1.97	1.99	2.05	3.32
3-year avg. annual growth (percent)		31.59			-1.91	
Domestic use (mmt)	3.10	3.78	4.13	4.22	4.25	4.58
3-year avg. annual growth (percent)		4.76			4.05	
Net imports (mmt)	2.23	1.33	2.12	2.45	2.02	1.50
3-year avg. annual growth (percent)		-1.61			19.14	
Per capita imports (kg)	112.00	65.00	102.00	114.00	92.00	67.00
3-year avg. annual growth (percent)		-3.94			16.22	
Per capita use (kg)	156.00	186.00	198.00	197.00	194.00	204.00
3-year avg. annual growth (percent)		2.27			1.50	
Per capita prod. (kg)	45.00	107.00	94.00	93.00	93.00	148.00
3-year avg. annual growth (percent)		28.43			-4.31	
Annual real per capita growth rate (percent)	0.33	1.93	-0.77	1.05	2.12	0.69
Annual real GDP growth rate (percent)	2.85	4.49	1.72	3.59	4.68	3.03
Population (000)	19,869.00	20,368.00	20,879.00	21,404.00	21,941.00	22,452.00
3-year avg. annual growth (percent)		2.44			2.51	

(continues)

Table 3.A.9. (cont.)

	Year	Projection by Year				
	87/88	88/89	89/90	90/91	91/92	92/93
WHEAT						
Production (mmt)	2.47	3.02	2.79	2.82	2.83	2.84
3-year avg. annual growth (percent)		19.54			-2.06	
Domestic use (mmt)	4.43	4.54	4.65	4.82	5.02	5.17
3-year avg. annual growth (percent)		2.32			3.41	
Net imports (mmt)	1.90	1.51	1.87	2.02	2.20	2.34
3-year avg. annual growth (percent)		-6.53			13.59	
Per capita imports (kg)	83.00	64.00	77.00	82.00	88.00	91.00
3-year avg. annual growth (percent)		-8.73			11.17	
Per capita use (kg)	193.00	193.00	193.00	196.00	200.00	202.00
3-year avg. annual growth (percent)		-0.07			1.22	
Per capita prod. (kg)	107.00	128.00	116.00	115.00	113.00	111.00
3-year avg. annual growth (percent)		16.75			-4.13	
Annual real per capita growth rate (percent)	1.01	1.81	0.15	1.07	1.80	1.50
Annual real GDP growth rate (percent)	3.47	4.29	2.59	3.09	3.91	3.59
Population (000)	22,999.00	23,560.00	24,135.00	24,616.00	25,125.00	25,645.00
3-year avg. annual growth (percent)		2.40			2.17	

(continues)

Table 3.A.9. (cont.)

| | Projection by Year | | | | | Average 1993-97 |
	93/94	94/95	95/96	96/97	97/98	
WHEAT						
Production (mmt)	2.86	2.87	2.89	2.90	2.71	2.85
3-year avg. annual growth (percent)		0.47			-1.84	
Domestic use (mmt)	5.32	5.47	5.61	5.75	5.90	5.61
3-year avg. annual growth (percent)		2.90			2.55	
Net imports (mmt)	2.47	2.61	2.74	2.86	3.00	2.74
3-year avg. annual growth (percent)		5.86			4.75	
Per capita imports (kg)	94.00	98.00	101.00	104.00	107.00	101.00
3-year avg. annual growth (percent)		3.72			2.99	
Per capita use (kg)	203.00	205.00	207.00	208.00	210.00	207.00
3-year avg. annual growth (percent)		0.82			0.83	
Per capita prod. (kg)	109.00	107.00	106.00	105.00	96.00	105.00
3-year avg. annual growth (percent)		-1.57			-3.49	
Annual real per capita growth rate (percent)	1.28	1.28	1.68	1.62	1.62	1.49
Annual real GDP growth rate (percent)	3.37	3.37	3.37	3.37	3.37	3.37
Population (000)	26,175.00	26,717.00	27,162.00	27,632.00	28,110.00	27,159.00
3-year avg. annual growth (percent)		2.07			1.71	

Note: The abbreviation *mmt* is defined as million metric tons.

Bruna Angel and S. R. Johnson

Table 3.A.10. Other Asia wheat supply, use, and trade

			Year			
	81/82	82/83	83/84	84/85	85/86	86/87
WHEAT						
Production (mmt)	16.83	16.93	18.24	16.80	17.26	17.85
3-year avg. annual growth (percent)		4.73			0.85	
Domestic use (mmt)	22.93	23.59	24.58	25.52	24.72	26.15
3-year avg. annual growth (percent)		2.31			1.63	
Net imports (mmt)	6.38	6.93	7.40	8.13	8.16	8.23
3-year avg. annual growth (percent)		-2.01			5.67	
Per capita imports (kg)	10.41	11.04	11.52	12.36	12.14	11.98
3-year avg. annual growth (percent)		-4.29			3.29	
Per capita use (kg)	37.00	38.00	38.00	39.00	37.00	38.00
3-year avg. annual growth (percent)		-0.06			-0.66	
Per capita prod. (kg)	28.00	29.00	26.00	26.00	26.00	26.00
3-year avg. annual growth (percent)		4.81			-3.92	
Annual real per capita growth rate (percent)	2.98	2.58	1.31	-0.11	0.00	1.68
Annual real GDP growth rate (percent)	5.45	5.02	3.71	2.22	2.21	3.90
Population (000)	613,070.00	627,707.00	642,576.00	657,537.00	672,084.00	686,748.00
3-year avg. annual growth (percent)		2.37			2.30	

(continues)

Table 3.A.10. (cont.)

	Year		Projection by Year			
	87/88	88/89	89/90	90/91	91/92	92/93
WHEAT						
Production (mmt)	17.57	17.83	19.22	19.95	20.51	21.04
3-year avg. annual growth (percent)		1.11			4.80	
Domestic use (mmt)	26.83	27.54	28.24	29.49	30.78	31.83
3-year avg. annual growth (percent)		3.68			3.78	
Net imports (mmt)	9.17	9.65	9.22	9.78	10.49	10.97
3-year avg. annual growth (percent)		5.84			2.96	
Per capita imports (kg)	13.06	13.43	12.55	13.07	13.73	14.06
3-year avg. annual growth (percent)		3.52			0.87	
Per capita use (kg)	38.00	38.00	38.00	39.00	40.00	41.00
3-year avg. annual growth (percent)		1.40			1.67	
Per capita prod. (kg)	25.00	25.00	26.00	27.00	27.00	27.00
3-year avg. annual growth (percent)		-1.11			2.66	
Annual real per capita growth rate (percent)	3.48	3.17	-1.50	6.55	2.60	2.39
Annual real GDP growth rate (percent)	5.83	5.51	0.75	8.52	4.78	4.56
Population (000)	702,334.00	718,301.00	734,660.00	748,234.00	764,085.00	780,283.00
3-year avg. annual growth (percent)		2.24			2.08	

(continues)

Table 3.A.10. (cont.)

| | | | Projection by Year | | | Average |
	93/94	94/95	95/96	96/97	97/98	1993-97
WHEAT						
Production (mmt)	21.66	22.27	22.91	23.60	24.30	22.95
3-year avg. annual growth (percent)		2.78			2.95	
Domestic use (mmt)	32.96	34.00	35.11	36.34	37.71	35.22
3-year avg. annual growth (percent)		3.37			3.51	
Net imports (mmt)	11.49	11.92	12.39	12.94	13.61	12.47
3-year avg. annual growth (percent)		4.35			4.52	
Per capita imports (kg)	14.42	14.65	14.97	15.35	15.84	15.05
3-year avg. annual growth (percent)		2.18			2.65	
Per capita use (kg)	41.00	42.00	42.00	43.00	44.00	43.00
3-year avg. annual growth (percent)		1.22			1.66	
Per capita prod. (kg)	27.00	27.00	28.00	28.00	28.00	28.00
3-year avg. annual growth (percent)		0.65			1.10	
Annual real per capita growth rate (percent)	1.84	1.84	2.27	2.07	2.07	2.02
Annual real GDP growth rate (percent)	4.00	4.00	4.00	4.00	4.00	4.00
Population (000)	796,837.00	813,754.00	827,488.00	843,161.00	859,141.00	828,076.00
3-year avg. annual growth (percent)		2.12			1.83	

Note: The abbreviation *mmt* is defined as million metric tons.

Table 3.A.11. Other Asia coarse grain supply, use, and trade

	Year					
	81/82	82/83	83/84	84/85	85/86	86/87
COARSE GRAINS (a)						
Production (000 mt)	23,031.00	21,040.00	24,412.00	25,345.00	23,090.00	23,817.00
3-year avg. annual growth (percent)		2.30			3.65	
Domestic use (000 mt)	24,113.00	22,733.00	25,343.00	26,951.00	24,998.00	25,900.00
3-year avg. annual growth (percent)		2.90			3.53	
Net imports (000 mt)	1,110.00	1,615.00	1,308.00	1,562.00	1,200.00	2,378.00
3-year avg. annual growth (percent)		24.86			-7.59	
Per capita imports (kg)	0.88	1.25	0.99	1.16	0.87	1.69
3-year avg. annual growth (percent)		22.20			-9.51	
Per capita use (kg)	19.02	17.55	19.15	19.94	18.12	18.41
3-year avg. annual growth (percent)		0.71			1.37	
Per capita prod. (kg)	18.16	16.24	18.45	18.75	16.74	16.93
3-year avg. annual growth (percent)		0.12			1.49	
Annual real per capita growth rate (percent)	2.94	3.18	2.32	1.29	2.87	1.44
Annual real GDP growth rate (percent)	5.17	5.41	4.53	3.45	5.01	3.42
Population (000)	1,267,946.00	1,295,364.00	1,323,263.00	1,351,509.00	1,379,600.00	1,406,610.00
3-year avg. annual growth (percent)		2.18			2.12	

(a) Coarse grains include corn, barley, and oats

(continues)

Table 3.A.11. (cont.)

	Year	Projection by Year				
	87/88	88/89	89/90	90/91	91/92	92/93
COARSE GRAINS (a)						
Production (000 mt)	23,587.00	24,186.00	24,875.00	24,953.00	25,231.00	25,547.00
3-year avg. annual growth (percent)		1.57			1.43	
Domestic use (000 mt)	26,433.00	27,239.00	27,705.00	27,976.00	28,695.00	29,324.00
3-year avg. annual growth (percent)		2.91			1.75	
Net imports (000 mt)	2,863.00	3,078.00	2,844.00	3,031.00	3,486.00	3,796.00
3-year avg. annual growth (percent)		42.02			4.66	
Per capita imports (kg)	1.99	2.10	1.90	1.99	2.25	2.41
3-year avg. annual growth (percent)		39.24			2.74	
Per capita use (kg)	18.42	18.60	18.54	18.41	18.53	18.59
3-year avg. annual growth (percent)		0.88			-0.12	
Per capita prod. (kg)	16.43	16.52	16.65	16.42	16.29	16.19
3-year avg. annual growth (percent)		-0.43			-0.45	
Annual real per capita growth rate (percent)	1.02	4.52	3.48	1.33	5.32	3.20
Annual real GDP growth rate (percent)	3.07	6.65	5.59	3.05	7.31	5.16
Population (000)	1,435,204.00	1,464,414.00	1,494,255.00	1,519,674.00	1,548,470.00	1,577,831.00
3-year avg. annual growth (percent)		2.01			1.88	

(continues)

Table 3.A.11. (cont.)

			Projection by Year			Average
	93/94	94/95	95/96	96/97	97/98	1993-97
COARSE GRAINS (a)						
Production (000 mt)	25,883.00	26,205.00	26,541.00	26,902.00	27,386.00	26,583.00
3-year avg. annual growth (percent)		1.27			1.48	
Domestic use (000 mt)	29,998.00	30,830.00	31,496.00	32,287.00	33,239.00	31,570.00
3-year avg. annual growth (percent)		2.42			2.54	
Net imports (000 mt)	4,135.00	4,547.00	4,978.00	5,409.00	5,882.00	4,990.00
3-year avg. annual growth (percent)		9.26			8.96	
Per capita imports (kg)	2.57	2.78	2.99	3.20	3.42	2.99
3-year avg. annual growth (percent)		7.23			7.20	
Per capita use (kg)	18.66	18.82	18.93	19.08	19.32	18.96
3-year avg. annual growth (percent)		0.51			0.88	
Per capita prod. (kg)	16.10	16.00	15.95	15.90	15.92	15.97
3-year avg. annual growth (percent)		-0.62			-0.16	
Annual real per capita growth rate (percent)	3.29	3.93	4.29	4.14	4.14	3.96
Annual real GDP growth rate (percent)	5.25	5.90	5.90	5.90	5.90	5.77
Population (000)	1,607,768.00	1,638,293.00	1,663,655.00	1,691,808.00	1,720,455.00	1,664,396.00
3-year avg. annual growth (percent)		1.90			1.64	

Note: The abbreviation *mt* is defined as metric tons.

           Bruna Angel and S. R. Johnson

Table 3.A.12. China wheat supply, use, and trade

	Year					
	81/82	82/83	83/84	84/85	85/86	86/87
WHEAT						
Production (mmt)	59.64	68.42	81.39	87.80	85.80	90.00
3-year avg. annual growth (percent)		3.59			8.18	
Domestic use (mmt)	78.84	79.42	83.00	92.18	100.40	101.50
3-year avg. annual growth (percent)		6.20			8.16	
Net imports (mmt)	13.20	13.00	9.60	7.40	6.60	8.50
3-year avg. annual growth (percent)		16.62			-19.96	
Per capita imports (kg)	13.00	13.00	9.00	7.00	6.00	8.00
3-year avg. annual growth (percent)		15.10			-20.94	
Per capita use (kg)	80.00	79.00	82.00	90.00	97.00	96.00
3-year avg. annual growth (percent)		4.83			6.84	
Per capita prod. (kg)	60.00	68.00	80.00	85.00	82.00	85.00
3-year avg. annual growth (percent)		2.27			6.86	
Annual real per capita growth rate (percent)	3.49	8.30	13.96	6.37	10.49	5.39
Annual real GDP growth rate (percent)	4.76	9.63	15.37	7.68	11.85	6.64
Population (000)	990,529.00	1,002,723.00	1,015,100.00	1,027,657.00	1,040,371.00	1,052,701.00
3-year avg. annual growth (percent)		1.30			1.24	

(continues)

Table 3.A.12. (cont.)

	Year		Projection by Year			
	87/88	88/89	89/90	90/91	91/92	92/93
WHEAT						
Production (mmt)	87.80	87.50	91.81	95.80	99.61	103.30
3-year avg. annual growth (percent)		0.70			4.42	
Domestic use (mmt)	105.50	105.50	102.95	107.48	111.74	116.05
3-year avg. annual growth (percent)		1.68			1.95	
Net imports (mmt)	15.00	15.01	11.13	11.68	12.12	12.74
3-year avg. annual growth (percent)		35.11			-5.71	
Per capita imports (kg)	14.00	14.00	10.00	11.00	11.00	11.00
3-year avg. annual growth (percent)		33.50			-6.83	
Per capita use (kg)	99.00	98.00	94.00	97.00	100.00	103.00
3-year avg. annual growth (percent)		0.47			0.77	
Per capita prod. (kg)	82.00	81.00	84.00	87.00	89.00	91.00
3-year avg. annual growth (percent)		-0.49			3.18	
Annual real per capita growth rate (percent)	7.31	7.38	9.08	7.93	6.93	8.13
Annual real GDP growth rate (percent)	8.62	8.68	10.40	9.24	8.18	9.40
Population (000)	1,065,477.00	1,078,409.00	1,091,497.00	1,104,744.00	1,117,668.00	1,130,744.00
3-year avg. annual growth (percent)		1.20			1.20	

(continues)

Table 3.A.12. (cont.)

	Projection by Year					Average 1993-97
	93/94	94/95	95/96	96/97	97/98	
WHEAT						
Production (mmt)	106.91	110.46	113.96	117.44	120.89	113.93
3-year avg. annual growth (percent)		3.51			3.05	
Domestic use (mmt)	120.11	124.12	128.09	132.05	135.98	128.07
3-year avg. annual growth (percent)		3.56			3.09	
Net imports (mmt)	13.20	13.66	14.13	14.61	15.09	14.14
3-year avg. annual growth (percent)		4.07			3.37	
Per capita imports (kg)	12.00	12.00	12.00	12.00	13.00	12.00
3-year avg. annual growth (percent)		2.87			2.22	
Per capita use (kg)	105.00	107.00	109.00	112.00	114.00	109.00
3-year avg. annual growth (percent)		2.37			1.93	
Per capita prod. (kg)	93.00	95.00	97.00	99.00	101.00	97.00
3-year avg. annual growth (percent)		2.31			1.90	
Annual real per capita growth rate (percent)	6.75	6.75	6.75	6.81	6.81	6.77
Annual real GDP growth rate (percent)	8.00	8.00	8.00	8.00	8.00	8.00
Population (000)	1,143,973.00	1,157,356.00	1,170,896.00	1,183,956.00	1,197,162.00	1,170,669.00
3-year avg. annual growth (percent)		1.17			1.13	

Note: The abbreviation *mmt* is defined as million metric tons.

Table 3.A.13. China coarse grain supply, use, and trade

				Year			
	81/82	82/83	83/84	84/85	85/86	86/87
COARSE GRAINS (a)						
Production (000 mt)	68,385.00	68,855.00	76,755.00	80,700.00	70,036.00	77,708.00
3-year avg. annual growth (percent)		-0.16			1.13	
Domestic use (000 mt)	69,585.00	71,505.00	76,561.00	75,650.00	72,459.00	80,203.00
3-year avg. annual growth (percent)		0.19			0.55	
Net exports (000 mt)	-1,200.00	-2,650.00	194.00	5,050.00	6,077.00	2,004.00
3-year avg. annual growth (percent)		41.07			805.37	
Per capita exports (kg)	-1.21	-2.64	0.19	4.91	5.84	1.90
3-year avg. annual growth (percent)		39.33			794.31	
Per capita use (kg)	70.00	71.00	75.00	74.00	70.00	76.00
3-year avg. annual growth (percent)		-1.10			-0.67	
Per capita prod. (kg)	69.00	69.00	76.00	79.00	67.00	74.00
3-year avg. annual growth (percent)		-1.45			-0.10	
Annual real per capita growth rate (percent)	3.49	8.30	13.96	6.37	10.49	5.39
Annual real GDP growth rate (percent)	4.76	9.63	15.37	7.68	11.85	6.64
Population (000)	990,529.00	1,002,723.00	1,015,100.00	1,027,657.00	1,040,371.00	1,052,701.00
3-year avg. annual growth (percent)		1.30			1.24	

(a) Include corn, barley, and oats

(continues)

Table 3.A.13. (cont.)

	Year		Projection by Year			
	87/88	88/89	89/90	90/91	91/92	92/93
COARSE GRAINS (a)						
Production (000 mt)	86,800.00	82,004.00	84,121.00	86,735.00	89,501.00	92,326.00
3-year avg. annual growth (percent)		5.71			2.96	
Domestic use (000 mt)	82,793.00	82,413.00	81,838.00	84,227.00	86,755.00	89,364.00
3-year avg. annual growth (percent)		4.49			1.74	
Net exports (000 mt)	3,007.00	3,091.00	2,282.00	2,508.00	2,746.00	2,962.00
3-year avg. annual growth (percent)		-4.73			-2.26	
Per capita exports (kg)	2.82	2.87	2.09	2.27	2.46	2.62
3-year avg. annual growth (percent)		-5.87			-3.42	
Per capita use (kg)	78.00	76.00	75.00	76.00	78.00	79.00
3-year avg. annual growth (percent)		3.24			0.54	
Per capita prod. (kg)	81.00	76.00	77.00	79.00	80.00	82.00
3-year avg. annual growth (percent)		4.45			1.74	
Annual real per capita growth rate (percent)	7.31	7.38	9.08	7.93	6.93	8.13
Annual real GDP growth rate (percent)	8.62	8.68	10.40	9.24	8.18	9.40
Population (000)	1,065,477.00	1,078,409.00	1,091,497.00	1,104,744.00	1,111,668.00	1,130,744.00
3-year avg. annual growth (percent)		1.20			1.20	

(continues)

Table 3.A.13. (cont.)

	93/94	94/95	Projection by Year 95/96	96/97	97/98	Average 1993-97
COARSE GRAINS (a)						
Production (000 mt)	95,184.00	98,069.00	100,978.00	103,911.00	106,867.00	101,002.00
3-year avg. annual growth (percent)		3.09			2.91	
Domestic use (000 mt)	92,003.00	94,675.00	97,383.00	100,129.00	102,914.00	97,421.00
3-year avg. annual growth (percent)		2.95			2.82	
Net exports (000 mt)	3,181.00	3,393.00	3,594.00	3,782.00	3,953.00	3,581.00
3-year avg. annual growth (percent)		7.31			5.23	
Per capita exports (kg)	2.78	2.93	3.07	3.19	3.30	3.06
3-year avg. annual growth (percent)		6.07			4.05	
Per capita use (kg)	80.00	82.00	83.00	85.00	86.00	83.00
3-year avg. annual growth (percent)		1.76			1.67	
Per capita prod. (kg)	83.00	85.00	86.00	88.00	89.00	86.00
3-year avg. annual growth (percent)		1.90			1.75	
Annual real per capita growth rate (percent)	6.75	6.75	6.75	6.81	6.81	6.77
Annual real GDP growth rate (percent)	8.00	8.00	8.00	8.00	8.00	8.00
Population (000)	1,143,973.00	1,157,356.00	1,170,896.00	1,183,956.00	1,197,162.00	1,170,669.00
3-year avg. annual growth (percent)		1.17			1.13	

Note: The abbreviation *mt* is defined as metric tons.

Table 3.A.14. Eastern Europe wheat supply, use, and trade

				Year			
	81/82	82/83	83/84	84/85	85/86	86/87	
WHEAT							
Production (mmt)	30.60	34.70	35.40	42.10	37.10	39.10	
3-year avg. annual growth (percent)		8.98			3.02		
Domestic use (mmt)	35.09	36.86	37.11	40.10	38.20	39.50	
3-year avg. annual growth (percent)		5.37			1.33		
Net imports (mmt)	4.30	2.20	1.50	-1.50	0.90	2.00	
3-year avg. annual growth (percent)		-18.12		-130.61		-37.89	
Per Capita Imports (kg)	32.00	16.00	11.00	-11.00	7.00	14.00	
3-year avg. annual growth (percent)		-18.60		-130.44		-38.20	
Per Capita Use (kg)	260.00	271.00	271.00	291.00	276.00	284.00	
3-year avg. annual growth (percent)		4.75			0.76		
Per Capita Prod. (kg)	226.00	255.00	259.00	306.00	268.00	281.00	
3-year avg. annual growth (percent)		8.33	5.17	4.74	2.44		
Annual real GDP growth rate (percent)	2.75	3.73			3.02	4.88	
Population (000)	135,191.00	135,993.00	136,795.00	138,311.00	139,035.00	139,825.00	
3-year avg. annual growth (percent)		0.59			0.57		

(continues)

Table 3.A.14. (cont.)

	Year 87/88	88/89	Projection by Year 89/90	90/91	91/92	92/93
WHEAT						
Production (mmt)	39.80	45.10	40.57	41.24	41.91	45.28
3-year avg. annual growth (percent)		6.83			-2.26	
Domestic use (mmt)	41.30	43.50	41.77	42.32	42.84	43.36
3-year avg. annual growth (percent)		4.43			-0.48	
Net imports (mmt)	1.41	-1.50	1.20	1.08	0.94	0.79
3-year avg. annual growth (percent)		-67.65		-17.89		-34.83
Per Capita Imports (kg)	10.00	-11.00	8.00	8.00	7.00	5.00
3-year avg. annual growth (percent)		-67.82		-18.31		-35.16
Per Capita Use (kg)	295.00	309.00	295.00	298.00	300.00	302.00
3-year avg. annual growth (percent)		3.85			-1.02	
Per Capita Prod. (kg)	285.00	321.00	287.00	290.00	293.00	296.00
3-year avg. annual growth (percent)		6.24			-2.79	
Annual real GDP growth rate (percent)	3.10	2.26	2.21	2.88	2.10	2.05
Population (000)	140,622.00	141,425.00	142,234.00	142,965.00	143,702.00	144,445.00
3-year avg. annual growth (percent)		0.55			0.55	

(continues)

Table 3.A.14. (cont.)

	Projection by Year					Average 1993-97
	93/94	94/95	95/96	96/97	97/98	
WHEAT						
Production (mmt)	43.25	43.92	44.59	45.26	45.93	44.59
3-year avg. annual growth (percent)		1.57			1.50	
Domestic use (mmt)	43.90	44.43	44.97	45.52	46.06	44.98
3-year avg. annual growth (percent)		1.22			1.21	
Net imports (mmt)	0.65	0.52	0.39	0.26	0.14	0.39
3-year avg. annual growth (percent)						
Per Capita Imports (kg)	4.00	4.00	3.00	2.00	1.00	3.00
3-year avg. annual growth (percent)						
Per Capita Use (kg)	304.00	306.00	308.00	310.00	312.00	308.00
3-year avg. annual growth (percent)		0.70			0.70	
Per Capita Prod. (kg)	299.00	302.00	306.00	309.00	312.00	306.00
3-year avg. annual growth (percent)		1.05			0.99	
Annual real GDP growth rate (percent)	2.30	2.30	2.30	2.30	2.30	2.30
Population (000)	145,192.00	145,891.00	146,648.00	147,409.00	145,917.00	
3-year avg. annual growth (percent)		0.52			0.51	

Note: The abbreviation *mmt* is defined as million metric tons.

Table 3.A.15. Eastern Europe feed grain supply, use, and trade

	81/82	82/83	83/84	84/85	85/86	86/87
				Year		
FEED GRAINS (a)						
Production (000 mt)	52,615.00	58,396.00	52,609.00	57,155.00	55,264.00	60,040.00
3-year avg. annual growth (percent)		3.04			-1.53	
Domestic use (000 mt)	56,765.00	58,506.00	54,563.00	57,239.00	59,036.00	59,623.00
3-year avg. annual growth (percent)		-1.48			0.43	
Net imports (000 mt)	4,683.00	784.00	1,067.00	1,371.00	3,423.00	619.00
3-year avg. annual growth (percent)		-39.03		71.42		
Per Capita Imports (kg)	35.00	6.00	8.00	10.00	25.00	4.00
3-year avg. annual growth (percent)		-39.39		70.48		
Per Capita Use (kg)	420.00	430.00	399.00	416.00	427.00	429.00
3-year avg. annual growth (percent)		-2.06			-0.13	
Per Capita Prod. (kg)	389.00	429.00	385.00	415.00	400.00	432.00
3-year avg. annual growth (percent)		2.44			-2.08	
Annual real GDP growth rate (percent)	2.75	3.73	5.17	4.74	3.02	4.88
Population (000)	135,191.00	135,993.00	136,795.00	137,599.00	138,311.00	139,035.00
3-year avg. annual growth (percent)		0.59			0.57	

(a) Feed grains include corn, barley and oats.

(continues)

Table 3.A.15. (cont.)

	Year	Projection by Year				
	87/88	88/89	89/90	90/91	91/92	92/93
FEED GRAINS (a)						
Production (000 mt)	50,097.00	48,604.00	56,646.00	58,260.00	59,681.00	61,083.00
3-year avg. annual growth (percent)		-3.63			7.28	
Domestic use (000 mt)	54,871.00	55,268.00	58,142.00	60,096.00	61,964.00	63,829.00
3-year avg. annual growth (percent)		-2.08			4.93	
Net imports (000 mt)	3,113.00	4,616.00	3,534.00	2,182.00	2,448.00	2,890.00
3-year avg. annual growth (percent)	123.09	123.09			-16.50	
Per Capita Imports (kg)	22.00	33.00	25.00	15.00	17.00	20.00
3-year avg. annual growth (percent)	121.83	121.83	-16.96		-16.96	
Per Capita Use (kg)	392.00	393.00	411.00	423.00	433.00	444.00
3-year avg. annual growth (percent)		-2.62			3.32	
Per Capita Prod. (kg)	358.00	346.00	401.00	410.00	417.00	425.00
3-year avg. annual growth (percent)		-4.16			6.69	
Annual real GDP growth rate (percent)	3.10	2.26	2.21	2.88	2.10	2.05
Population (000)	139,825.00	140,622.00	141,425.00	142,234.00	142,965.00	143,702.00
3-year avg. annual growth (percent)		0.55			0.55	

(continues)

Table 3.A.15. (cont.)

		Projection by Year				Average 1993-97
	93/94	94/95	95/96	96/97	97/98	
FEED GRAINS (a)						
Production (000 mt)	62,485.00	63,893.00	65,306.00	66,725.00	68,148.00	65,311.00
3-year avg. annual growth (percent)		2.30			2.17	
Domestic use (000 mt)	65,724.00	67,646.00	69,591.00	71,556.00	73,450.00	69,593.00
3-year avg. annual growth (percent)		2.92			-31.51	
Net imports (000 mt)	3,382.00	3,896.00	4,428.00	4,975.00	5,537.00	4,444.00
3-year avg. annual growth (percent)		16.76			12.43	
Per Capita Imports (kg)	23.00	27.00	30.00	34.00	38.00	30.00
3-year avg. annual growth (percent)		16.16			11.87	
Per Capita Use (kg)	455.00	466.00	477.00	488.00	498.00	477.00
3-year avg. annual growth (percent)		2.44			2.26	
Per Capita Prod. (kg)	433.00	440.00	448.00	455.00	462.00	448.00
3-year avg. annual growth (percent)		1.77			1.66	
Annual real GDP growth rate (percent)	2.30	2.30	2.30	2.30	2.30	2.30
Population (000)	144,445.00	145,192.00	145,891.00	146,648.00	147,409.00	145,917.00
3-year avg. annual growth (percent)		0.52			0.51	

Note: The abbreviation *mt* is defined as metric tons.

Bruna Angel and S. R. Johnson

Table 3.A.16. USSR wheat supply, use, and trade

		Year				
	81/82	82/83	83/84	84/85	85/86	86/87
WHEAT						
Production (mmt)	81.10	84.30	77.50	68.60	78.10	92.30
3-year avg. annual growth (percent)		-1.53			-1.90	
Domestic use (mmt)	104.90	100.60	93.00	91.20	91.60	102.80
3-year avg. annual growth (percent)		-4.27			3.02	
Net imports (mmt)	19.80	20.30	20.00	27.60	15.20	15.50
3-year avg. annual growth (percent)		21.18			-2.80	
Per capita imports (kg)	74.00	75.00	73.00	100.00	55.00	55.00
3-year avg. annual growth (percent)		20.05			-3.74	
Per capita use (kg)	391.00	372.00	340.00	330.00	329.00	366.00
3-year avg. annual growth (percent)		-5.17			-3.94	
Per capita prod. (kg)	314.00	286.00	251.00	248.00	280.00	328.00
3-year avg. annual growth (percent)		-5.34			-0.16	
Annual real per capita growth rate (percent)	0.23	3.17	0.44	0.15	1.42	1.38
Annual real GDP growth rate (percent)	1.22	4.19	1.43	1.14	2.32	2.34
Population (000)	268,118.00	270,769.00	273,446.00	276,149.00	278,617.00	281,258.00
3-year avg. annual growth (percent)		0.95			0.96	

(continues)

Table 3.A.16. (cont.)

	Year 87/88	Projection by Year				
		88/89	89/90	90/91	91/92	92/93
WHEAT						
Production (mmt)	83.30	88.00	89.00	90.00	91.00	92.00
3-year avg. annual growth (percent)		4.69			1.12	
Domestic use (mmt)	101.50	100.00	103.89	105.27	106.36	107.18
3-year avg. annual growth (percent)		3.16			2.08	
Net imports (mmt)	21.00	12.00	14.89	15.27	15.36	15.18
3-year avg. annual growth (percent)		-1.80			9.07	
Per capita imports (kg)	74.00	42.00	51.00	52.00	52.00	51.00
3-year avg. annual growth (percent)		-2.72			8.13	
Per capita use (kg)	357.00	349.00	359.00	361.00	362.00	361.00
3-year avg. annual growth (percent)		2.19			1.20	
Per capita prod. (kg)	293.00	307.00	308.00	308.00	309.00	310.00
3-year avg. annual growth (percent)		3.71			0.25	
Annual real per capita growth rate (percent)	0.95	1.37	1.47	1.44	1.51	1.62
Annual real GDP growth rate (percent)	1.90	2.30	2.43	2.32	2.32	2.44
Population (000)	283,924.00	286,615.00	289,332.00	291,822.00	294,161.00	296,519.00
3-year avg. annual growth (percent)		0.95			0.87	

(continues)

Table 3.A.16. (cont.)

		Projection by Year				Average 1993-97
	93/94	94/95	95/96	96/97	97/98	
WHEAT						
Production (mmt)	93.00	94.00	95.00	96.00	97.00	95.00
3-year avg. annual growth (percent)		1.09			1.05	
Domestic use (mmt)	108.13	109.05	109.86	110.64	111.56	109.85
3-year avg. annual growth (percent)		0.84			0.76	
Net imports (mmt)	15.13	15.05	14.86	14.64	14.56	14.85
3-year avg. annual growth (percent)		-0.68			-1.10	
Per capita imports (kg)	51.00	50.00	49.00	48.00	47.00	49.00
3-year avg. annual growth (percent)		-1.47			-1.82	
Per capita use (kg)	362.00	362.00	362.00	362.00	362.00	362.00
3-year avg. annual growth (percent)		0.03			0.02	
Per capita prod. (kg)	311.00	312.00	313.00	314.00	315.00	313.00
3-year avg. annual growth (percent)		0.28			0.31	
Annual real per capita growth rate (percent)	1.59	1.59	1.65	1.65	1.65	1.62
Annual real GDP growth rate (percent)	2.40	2.40	2.40	2.40	2.40	2.40
Population (000)	298,895.00	301,291.00	303,517.00	305,761.00	309,021.00	303,497.00
3-year avg. annual growth (percent)		0.80			0.74	

Note: The abbreviation *mmt* is defined as million metric tons.

Table 3.A.17. USSR feed grain supply, use, and trade

	Year					
	81/82	82/83	83/84	84/85	85/86	86/87
FEED GRAINS (a)						
Production (000 mt)	60,500.00	70,000.00	83,000.00	70,900.00	78,000.00	88,300.00
3-year avg. annual growth (percent)		-0.06			4.67	
Domestic use (000 mt)	83,100.00	79,300.00	91,500.00	93,900.00	90,372.00	96,727.00
3-year avg. annual growth (percent)		-3.74			4.75	
Net imports (000 mt)	21,600.00	8,300.00	9,500.00	25,000.00	12,373.00	10,039.00
3-year avg. annual growth (percent)		-10.41			42.37	
Per capita imports (kg)	81.00	31.00	35.00	91.00	44.00	36.00
3-year avg. annual growth (percent)		-11.25			40.99	
Per capita use (kg)	310.00	293.00	335.00	340.00	324.00	344.00
3-year avg. annual growth (percent)		-4.65			3.75	
Per capita prod. (kg)	226.00	259.00	304.00	257.00	280.00	314.00
3-year avg. annual growth (percent)		-1.00			3.68	
Annual real per capita growth rate (percent)	0.23	3.17	0.44	0.15	1.42	1.38
Annual real GDP growth rate (percent)	1.22	4.19	1.43	1.14	2.32	2.34
Population (000)	268,118.00	270,769.00	273,446.00	276,149.00	278,617.00	281,258.00
3-year avg. annual growth (percent)		0.95			0.96	

(a) Feed grains include corn, barley and oats.

(continues)

Table 3.A.17. (cont.)

	Year		Projection by Year			
	87/88	88/89	89/90	90/91	91/92	92/93
FEED GRAINS						
Production (000 mt)	91,690.00	80,411.00	87,939.00	90,635.00	93,715.00	96,740.00
3-year avg. annual growth (percent)		1.58				
Domestic use (000 mt)	100,031.00	100,517.00	103,163.00	106,670.00	110,053.00	113,292.00
3-year avg. annual growth (percent)		3.64				
Net imports (000 mt)	9,311.00	20,105.00	15,224.00	16,035.00	16,338.00	16,552.00
3-year avg. annual growth (percent)		29.94				
Per capita imports (kg)	33.00	70.00	53.00	55.00	56.00	56.00
3-year avg. annual growth (percent)		28.72				
Per capita use (kg)	352.00	351.00	357.00	366.00	374.00	382.00
3-year avg. annual growth (percent)		2.67				
Per capita prod. (kg)	323.00	281.00	304.00	311.00	319.00	326.00
3-year avg. annual growth (percent)		0.63				
Annual real per capita growth rate (percent)	0.95	1.34	1.47	1.44	1.51	1.62
Annual real GDP growth rate (percent)	1.90	2.30	2.43	2.32	2.32	2.44
Population (000)	283,924.00	286,615.00	289,332.00	281,822.00	294,161.00	296,519.00
3-year avg. annual growth (percent)		0.95				

(continues)

Table 3.A.17. (cont.)

| | | | Projection by Year | | | | Average |
	93/94	94/95	95/96	96/97	97/98	1993-97
FEED GRAINS						
Production (000 mt)	99,701.00	102,605.00	105,476.00	108,325.00	111,118.00	105,445.00
3-year avg. annual growth (percent)						
Domestic use (000 mt)	116,406.00	119,444.00	122,432.00	125,295.00	128,283.00	122,372.00
3-year avg. annual growth (percent)						
Net imports (000 mt)	16,705.00	16,839.00	16,955.00	16,970.00	17,165.00	16,927.00
3-year avg. annual growth (percent)						
Per capita imports (kg)	56.00	56.00	56.00	56.00	56.00	56.00
3-year avg. annual growth (percent)						
Per capita use (kg)	389.00	396.00	403.00	410.00	416.00	403.00
3-year avg. annual growth (percent)						
Per capita prod. (kg)	334.00	341.00	348.00	354.00	361.00	347.00
3-year avg. annual growth (percent)						
Annual real per capita growth rate (percent)	1.59	1.59	1.65	1.65	1.65	1.62
Annual real GDP growth rate (percent)	2.40	2.40	2.40	2.40	2.40	2.40
Population (000)	298,895.00	301,291.00	303,517.00	305,761.00	308,021.00	303,497.00
3-year avg. annual growth (percent)						

Note: The abbreviation *mt* is defined as metric tons.

References

Brooks, H. G., S. Devadoss, W. H. Meyers. 1989. "The Impact of the U.S. Export Enhancement Program on the World Wheat Market." Unpublished manuscript. Department of Economics, Iowa State University.

Chambliss, M. 1989. "PL 480 Food Aid Legislation." Discussion Paper. United States Department of Agriculture, Foreign Agricultural Service, Washington, D.C.

Christenson, P. L. 1989. "Food Aid Reforms Project." Report to the members of the DCC Subcommittee on Food Aid. Agency for International Development. Washington, D.C.

FAPRI. 1988. "Policy Scenarios with the FAPRI Commodity Models." Working Paper 88-WP 41. Food and Agricultural Policy Research Institute, University of Missouri-Columbia (CNFAP), Iowa State University (CARD).

FAPRI. 1989. *U.S. and World Agricultural Outlook, May 1989.* FAPRI Report 2-89. Ames: Iowa State University (CARD).

Fischer, G., K. Frohberg, K. S. Parikh, and F. Rabar. 1987. "The World Economy: Resilient for the Rich, Stubborn for the Starving." Center for Agricultural and Rural Development (CARD), Iowa State University. CARD Reprint Series 2.11. Reprinted by permission from *Agriculture in a Turbulent World Economy.* Proceedings of the Nineteenth International Congress of Agricultural Economists, pp. 259-65. New York: Gower.

Hanrahan, C. E. 1988. "Foreign Food Aid Programs: Effectiveness Issues." Environment and Natural Resources Policy Division, Congressional Research Service, The Library of Congress. Issue Brief Order Code IB88057.

_____. 1989. "Foreign Food Aid: Reauthorization Issues." Congressional Research Service, The Library of Congress. CRS Issue Brief Order Code IB89097.

Hopkins, R. F. 1989. "Reforming Food Aid for the 1990s." Statement before the House Select Committee on Hunger, Hearing on "Restructuring Food Aid: Time for a Change?"

House of Representatives. 1989. Report of the Task Force on Foreign Assistance to the Committee on Foreign Affairs, U.S. House of Representatives, February, 1989. 101st Congress 1st Session. Washington, D.C.: U.S. Government Printing Office.

Johnson, S. R. 1989. The Emerging Policy, Production, and Consumption Scenario. In *Food, Hunger, and Agricultural Issues: Proceedings of a Colloquium on Future U.S. Development Assistance.* Ed. D. Clubb and P.C. Ligon. Morrilton, Arkansas: Winrock International Institute for Agricultural Development.

Kramer, C. S. and L. M. Rubey. 1989. "A.I.D. Food Policy Programming: Lessons Learned; An Assessment of the 'Consumption Effects of Agricultural Policies' Project, 1977-1988." Washington, D.C.: National Center for Food and Agricultural Policy, Resources for the Future.

Mellor, J. W. 1989a. "From Hunger to Food Aid to Commercial Markets." International Food Policy Research Institute. Winrock Talk. Draft.

_____. 1989b. "Agricultural Development in the Third World: The Food, Poverty, Aid, Trade Nexus." *Choices* 4:4-8.

Meyers, W. H. 1989. "Near-Term Agricultural Outlook Update." Prepared for Project LINK Fall Conference, August 28-September 1, 1989. Paris, France.

Minear, L. 1989. "U.S. Food Aid: Give Priority to Human Needs." *Choices* 4:28-29.

OECD. 1986. *Annual Review on Development and Cooperation.* Paris, France: Organization for Economic Development and Cooperation.

The Phoenix Group. 1989. "Reforms Needed in U.S. Assistance to Developing Countries. The Convergence of Interdependence and Self-Interest." A review and recommendations by the Phoenix Group. International Trade and Development Education Foundation.

Project LINK. 1989. "Project LINK World Outlook, August 28, 1989." University of Pennsylvania, Department of Economics, Philadelphia; United Nations, Department of International Economic and Social Affairs, New York.

The WEFA Group. 1988. *October 1988 World Economic Outlook.* Bala Cynwyd, PA: Wharton Econometrics Forecasting Associates.
The WEFA Group. 1989. *July 1989 World Economic Outlook.* Bala Cynwyd, PA: Wharton Econometrics Forecasting Associates.

DISCUSSION OF CHAPTER 3
R. C. Duncan

Angel and Johnson discuss how the international food system will function over the next decade. Two considerations are important in any discussion of foreign assistance and food aid: (1) trends in the food system's performance and (2) shocks to which it may be subject.

I do not disagree with the authors' view of the future trends in world grain markets. The World Bank's macroeconomic assumptions are much the same as theirs and our trend forecasts for production, prices, and trade in these markets are much the same. The international food system has certainly improved its performance in the postwar period. The main areas of improvement have been those of productivity and quality, transport and distribution, and marketing. The area of least improvement has been trade policy—in both industrial and developing countries.

In the future, the food system will continue to improve most, I expect, in those areas where it has been improving. Greatest improvement most likely will be in the area of marketing and financial risk management; there has been substantial innovation in various kinds of financial instruments for hedging the financial risks in buying and selling primary commodities.

I expect least improvement in the trade area. I am not optimistic about reforms coming out of the GATT Uruguay Round, and I see little short-term prospect for changes in agricultural policies in the United States and the EC. The United States will reduce its export subsidies, but these were never intended to be permanent. They were put into place in the 1985 Farm Bill only to recover U.S. export markets lost due to the high loan rates adopted under the 1980 Farm Bill (and the subsequent dollar appreciation impact). I do not see the United States foregoing its long-term policy of attempting to manage the international grain and oilseed markets.

In the EC there is also no evidence of support for real reform (unlike recent changes in Japan). I expect to see only changes in

The remarks recorded here are the opinions of the author alone and do not reflect the opinions of the World Bank or of its member countries.

policy there to put more protection into the off-budget basket, as in the case of sugar and dairy products where country quotas are used to control production.

The developing countries are under considerable pressure to reform their agricultural policies because of their poor per-formance and external debt problems—reforms that are essentially aimed at their deriving greater benefit from participation in the international food system. It is hoped they will continue to increase their participation.

The kinds of model-based forecasts provided by Angel and Johnson are not terribly useful for the stated purposes of the conference. Of more use would have been an exploration of the impacts of various likely scenarios that could shock the international food system. Tracing through their impacts on various participants, particularly those in developing countries, would broaden the discussion usefully. I suggest several such scenarios that warrant contemplation:

1. Alternate scenarios for China and the USSR are possible—what one might describe as China's becoming more like the USSR or the USSR's becoming more like China. Will Chinese agricultural growth slow considerably, as is suggested by the performance of its wheat and feed grains sectors over the past four to five years (see Figures 3.16 and 3.17)? China could still be a substantial importer of grain under this scenario. On the other hand, through its reforms USSR agriculture might be able to speed up its productivity growth, in which case USSR imports of grain could decline substantially.

2. Developing countries' economic growth could suffer from a recession in the industrial countries in the next year or so. Those countries that have experienced several years of low or negative per capita income growth in the 1980s would experience further declines in grain consumption. Alternatively, industrial countries may continue their recent expansion, and economic growth in the developing countries may become more widespread than it has been in recent

years. In that case there could be a recovery in grains consumption in many developing countries.

3. There could be a new oil price boom. The sharp oil price increases in the 1970s had a substantial depressing impact on agriculture through fertilizer prices. With non-OPEC oil supplies growing more slowly, OPEC is getting a larger share of the market, so the probability exists for another sharp increase in prices.

In the final part of their chapter Angel and Johnson echo the introductory chapter's warning for food aid interests if agricultural trade liberalization in the major industrial producer countries, proposed to the current GATT Round by the United States, is achieved. Grain prices will rise on average and supplies will be lower and less available. This could mean less grain available for food aid and perhaps less interest by some groups, such as farmers, in backing food aid programs. Even so, higher and more stable grain prices, in the long run, may be a positive factor for the provision of food aid since this could yield a more rational approach wherein food aid supplies are not dependent on price-support policies and the ensuing surpluses.

PART II

International Agricultural Trade and Policy Reforms in Industrialized and Developing Countries

Medium-term prospects for world food and feed grain markets were assessed in Part I. Based on projected macroeconomic conditions, normal weather, and a virtual status quo policy environment, world effective demand is forecasted to just about balance world production at prevailing real price levels. No rapid or large buildup in carryover stocks is anticipated. Under this scenario, the center of gravity of agricultural and food concerns would likely shift to food-deficit importers. As pointed out in Chapter 3, the poor, indebted, low-growth, and food-scarce countries among them would face continuing declines in per capita consumption levels in a supply situation seemingly less conducive to subsidized sales or food aid.

If an agreement is reached in the GATT Uruguay Round to lower agricultural support in the industrialized exporting countries, the assumptions for these forecasts would be invalidated. Falling production in industrial exporters would bring higher nominal and real-world market prices, and probably even more pressure to curtail food aid. Thus, the likelihood of agricultural trade liberalization is closely related to the food trade and aid situation food-importing developing countries will face in the 1990s. Moreover, what developing countries can and are doing to reform their own internal macroeconomic and price policies to accelerate food and export production would then become even more critical for their future food security.

The two chapters in this part address these two interrelated issues. In Chapter 4 Paarlberg challenges much of the conventional thinking about the GATT negotiations on agricultural trade. First, he predicts they will fail. He bases this prediction on a loss of political will in the United States from the impact of higher market prices and lower stocks on the budget costs of federal farm support. Rising production, a buildup in stocks, further reductions in loan rates, and continued subsidization of sales could possibly rekindle political support in the future, although by then the present GATT opportunity will likely have been foreclosed.

Second, he argues that for the developing countries this anticipated failure really doesn't matter much. He examines several studies of liberalization very carefully for their measurements of magnitudes of impacts on developing countries. He finds evidence that open markets in industrial countries for tropical products, especially if processed, would significantly benefit tropical exporters. But that is not the focus of the current debate. For temperate food, feed, and fiber products he marshals evidence that net gains (to exporters) and losses (to importers) would be relatively small. He points out that gains from greater stability in world markets might even offset losses arising from a higher price level, and suggests that efforts to stabilize the extent of support should be emphasized over its reduction or elimination.

McCalla, in his discussion of Paarlberg's chapter, scrutinizes very closely its economic evidence and political prognoses. Suffice it to say that he fails to reject most of them. Readers will want to make their own evaluations.

Whatever the size of net losses to developing-country importers, there is no doubt that significant increases in world food price levels, if fully transmitted internally, will cause large transfers from domestic consumers to producers in those countries. If price changes are not transmitted, then the governments will necessarily face rising consumption subsidy costs and implicit taxation of production. How governments react to world price changes is an integral, but often neglected, part of their formulation of domestic price and market intervention policies.

Domestic policies of developing countries is the topic of the second chapter in Part II, in which Anne Krueger, Maurice Schiff, and Alberto Valdés preview forthcoming results of a large-scale comparative study. This chapter further documents what was already widely known—developing countries, with rare exception, have taxed agricultural exports and subsidized food imports through sector-specific policies. The chapter also shows what was less widely known, how currency overvaluation and industrial protection have generally intensified the negative effects of sector-specific price policies. In some cases, product and input price policies ostensibly favoring domestic producers are simply overwhelmed by the negative consequences of macroeconomic policies. Why these agriculturally adverse policies have come about, why they are maintained, and why they are not changed are key questions for policy reform process in developing countries.

In his discussion of Chapter 5, Roe criticizes some of the methodology used in the comparative study. His theoretical points will intrigue trade and development economists who wish to ruminate on concepts and measures. He also makes explicit a proposition that runs through this entire part. From the per-spective of import-substitution industrialization policies that transfer resources from agriculture to industry, he argues that the importance of removing price distortions is less to gain static efficiency than to propel the economy into efficient growth along a path of dynamic comparative advantage.

"Removing price distortions" is fundamentally a first-best ar-gument. It should not be blindly applied to sector-specific price interventions when the macroeconomic policies written about so eloquently by Krueger, Schiff, and Valdés are still largely in place. Moreover, the policy paradigm for some successful high-growth, export-led countries has been less the "open" economy than incentive-neutrality achieved by combining or sequencing protection of import substitutes with promotion of exports. The theoretical basis for connecting the absence of distortions to dynamic efficiency under technological change and instability is weaker than the connection to static efficiency. In reality, neither the research studies discussed by Paarlberg nor the measurements of distortions reported in Krueger, Schiff, and Valdés adequately address this issue. Governments may seek more price stability and food security than is offered by world markets. What are the most cost-effective policy options for them? Productive public investments and appropriate policies can cause supply functions to shift outward, thereby reducing imports or expanding exports. As Roe points out, "getting prices right" is at best only a partial prescription for how and where a country can most successfully seek its comparative advantage and also provide socially desired levels of price stability and food security.

Recognition of the consumption effects in poorer countries of agricultural trade liberalization by OECD countries raises ques-tions about assistance to help mitigate those effects (targeted subsidies possibly based on food aid) and increased development assistance to generate income growth to offset them. The central role of agricultural growth in the accelerated development of low-income countries brings the relationship between foreign assistance and agricultural development into focus. It will be discussed in Part III.

Lehman B. Fletcher

4

Agricultural Policy and Trade Reforms in Developed Countries: Projected Consequences for Developing Countries

Robert L. Paarlberg

How should the developing world—and the development assistance community—view the efforts currently underway in General Agreement on Tariffs and Trade (GATT) to negotiate a reduction in rich-country farm subsidies? It is widely presumed that developing countries that export temperate zone farm commodities, in competition with subsidized rich-country farmers, have a keen interest in seeing these negotiations succeed. At the same time, some fear that the developing countries that import such commodities may lose, because of the reduced supplies and the higher international prices that a successful reform might bring. Whatever the distribution of winners and losers, the significance of the current reform effort for the developing world is often taken as a given.

Here we shall question several parts of this standard analysis. The farm policy reform effort in GATT, on balance, is not of decisive significance to traders in the developing world. It lacks significance, first of all, because the current round of GATT negotiations on agriculture is scarcely more likely to produce sweeping change than previous rounds in the 1960s and 1970s. Second, even if a breakthrough is achieved, the impact on most countries in the developing world would be quite small. The biggest winners and losers from rich-country farm policy reform would be found within the rich countries themselves. And, within the developing world, the biggest winners and losers from reform would not be the "exporting" and "importing" countries overall, so much as individual producers and consumers within those countries. Even here, there is little to the fear that consumers would stand to lose more than producers would gain.

We conclude these qualifying arguments by observing that rich-country reforms that reduce the level of support provided to farmers may be of less value to the developing world than reforms that reduce the variability of that support. From the perspective of both citizens and officials in the developing countries—importers and exporters alike—this should be the objective most sought in what remains of the current GATT negotiations on temperate zone farm trade.

The Small Chance of a GATT
Breakthrough on Agriculture

We begin with an observation that the GATT talks on agriculture, which have now been officially underway since September 1986, are of questionable significance to the developing world because of the small likelihood that they will produce a significant result. Some developed country officials, hoping to build momentum, have consistently tried to project an optimistic view of the negotiations. They have at various times promised "early harvest" and "down payments" in the short run, and U.S. officials have even held out the long-run vision of total reform (the "zero option"). Developing-country officials should not be fooled. The current round of GATT negotiations is hardly more likely than past rounds to produce a significant rich-country farm policy reform.

GATT optimists have argued that there are two reasons why the current round can succeed where previous rounds failed. First, farm support policies are now so costly to rich-country governments, there is finally a "political will" on all sides to reform. Second, the current round—in contrast to previous rounds—finally makes domestic farm support measures an explicit part of the bargaining process. Officials with the political will to remove these domestic supports, it is said, will find it easiest to proceed by reaching a multilateral agreement in GATT rather than by moving unilaterally at their own pace (in what is called "unilateral disarmament" fashion). In retrospect, this optimism has been misplaced. From the vantage point of 1989, it is increasingly clear that the "political will" to embrace far-reaching reform has now mostly evaporated. Moreover, placing domestic support measures on the bargaining table seems to have blocked rather than facilitated the reform process.

Farm support policies in the industrial world did become far more costly for a time in the mid-1980s, particularly at the depths of the steep 1985-86 commodity price collapse. Increased farm budget costs, in combination with heightened trade frictions, did then inspire, for a brief time in 1986 and early 1987, a remarkable interlude of top-level political attention to the farm policy reform problem. In May 1986, the Tokyo G-7 economic summit conference devoted more time to agriculture than to any other single issue. In September 1986, the Punta del Este GATT ministerial meeting agreed that agriculture should be given highest priority in the Uruguay Round. In May 1987, an OECD ministerial session produced (in the words of Clayton Yeutter, then the U.S. trade representative) "the most comprehensive statement on agricultural policy reform that a group of ministers has ever made." It was at this point, when the momentum for multilateral reform seemed to be building, that the United States unveiled its dramatic "zero option" proposal to eliminate all production and trade distorting industrial country farm subsidies by the end of the century (Paarlberg 1988).

Unfortunately, almost from the moment the United States placed this far-fetched proposal on the table in Geneva, chances for a breakthrough on agriculture in the Uruguay Round negotiations began to decline. This occurred, first of all, because the extreme nature of the U.S. position provoked the European Community to respond, in kind, with a nonnegotiable proposal—to establish exporter cartels in international dairy, sugar, and cereals markets.

The result was a deadlock, which lasted for more than a year, right up through the failed "midterm review" conference in December 1988 in Montreal.

U.S. officials discovered in Montreal that their extreme zero option position was coming to be seen, even by the generally sympathetic Cairns group (the "nonsubsidizing" exporters), as a principal cause of the negotiating deadlock. They also recognized that this deadlock on agriculture was beginning to jeopardize the more substantial progress that had been made in other areas, such as tropical products, dispute settlement, and trade in services. Accordingly, in April 1989, the new U.S. administration reduced the priority that had earlier been assigned to agriculture in the Uruguay Round. It adjusted its official negotiating position to accept, as a new long-term objective, not a complete elimination but merely the "substantial progressive reduction" of agricultural support and protection (GATT Negotiating Group on Agriculture 1989).

This objective was left completely undefined, so the negotiation on agriculture was, in effect, back at its starting point. The parties agreed, in fact, to present to one another, before the end of the year, an entirely new set of formal negotiating proposals. In April 1989, the parties also embraced a "freeze" on supports for the duration of the negotiation, but then proceeded to declare most of their existing policy instruments exempt from this freeze. Asked what effect this freeze would have on European farm policies, the chief EC farm negotiator, Guy Legras, replied bluntly, "None."

These proposals are not likely to provide the basis for an agreement. The EC is expected to concentrate on seeking "credit" in the negotiations for the support reductions that it believes it has already made, and then on rebalancing, rather than reducing, the protection that remains. The United States, for its part, has proposed to seek reductions by first converting all protection instruments to import tariffs. This is a worthy idea, yet one that the EC has consistently rejected in the past, going all the way back to the 1963-67 Kennedy Round of GATT negotiations (Warley 1989).

Specific proposals aside, these negotiations have recently been faltering, in part because the political will of top leaders to pursue reform has diminished significantly since 1986-87. Inside the EC, the political impetus to embrace a difficult reform of the Common Agricultural Policy (CAP) disappeared following the successful February 1988 Brussels summit, which temporarily resolved the EC's farm budget crisis. The crisis was resolved partly through a modest stabilizer agreement (for which EC negotiators now want credit in GATT), which limits open-ended farm price supports, but mostly through a sizable increase (roughly 25 percent) in agreed member country financial contributions (Field, Hearn, and Kirby 1989).

Inside the United States, political interest in reform has also declined, in part because of enthusiasm among farm groups for the generous benefits they are receiving under the terms of current legislation, the 1985 U.S. Farm Bill. This legislation was at first greeted suspiciously by farmers, and it was extremely costly to taxpayers. Gradually, though, it managed to boost both exports and farm income. Then, following the 1988 summer drought—the worst in North America in half a century—U.S. crop production fell enough to boost short-term commodity prices, which sharply reduced budget costs. The higher international commodity prices that followed this drought also slowed the momentum of policy reform efforts in Europe. In Japan, meanwhile, a rash of political scandals, which led to a shocking defeat for the ruling Liberal-Democratic party in Upper House parliamentary elections in July 1989, left top leaders with less desire to challenge farmers.

So it was that the task of rich-country farm policy reform, by 1989, had lost almost all of its political urgency. President George Bush, conveniently forgetting promises he had made earlier to give top priority to agriculture at his first economic summit, scarcely mentioned the subject when he met with the other G-7 leaders in Paris in July. The lengthy (56-paragraph) summit communique devoted only one small part of one sentence—five words total—to "the pursuit of agricultural reform." The political will to reform, so much heralded by the GATT optimists, had thus disappeared.

Even in the unlikely event that top-level political interest in reform returns, there will be other reasons to doubt the likelihood of a significant GATT-brokered agreement to reduce industrial-country farm supports. GATT's much valued multilateral rule-making and negotiation procedures, far from being an impetus to reform, can perversely become—at least in the agricultural area—an inhibition to reform (Paarlberg 1989). This is because most agricultural support measures are primarily intranational rather than international in their operation. They operate more on national markets (which still dominate in the agricultural sector) than they do on international markets (which are still relatively thin). The primary political function of these policies is to accomplish an intranational transfer of income to farmers from consumers and taxpayers.

When these primarily domestic farm supports are put on the international bargaining table, unfortunate things can begin to happen. The political accountability of domestic farm groups, which is weak to begin with, is weakened further. Once a negotiation begins, these groups get a chance to represent their domestic rent-seeking behavior, erroneously, as part of an international contest with their "foreign competitors." In several ways, this can actually strengthen their political hand at home to demand more subsidies.

First, once multilateral negotiations begin abroad, farm groups are able to borrow a potent metaphor from the area of arms control. They begin to describe any reduction in their own domestic support as "unilateral disarmament." (When considering the reform of rent-seeking domestic farm support policies, a more exact metaphor would be to the problem of domestic gun control, a problem for which there is no easy internationally negotiated solution.) U.S. sugar growers seized upon this tactic, in 1989, to resist pressures from GATT itself to liberalize sugar quotas.

Second, the onset of an international negotiation gives domestic farm groups an excuse to demand more support measures at home, allegedly for use as bargaining chips to win a better agreement in Geneva. Farmers claim they must "arm in order to disarm." The continued use of U.S. export subsidies, even after the 1988 drought, has been defended by farm groups through recourse to this highly suspect bargaining chips argument. After first raising strong doubts about the cost effectiveness of export subsidies in 1989, even the Office of Management and Budget (OMB) finally endorsed a continuation of the program "as a tool for bringing about a successful conclusion to the GATT negotiations." Finally, if and when the GATT talks fail to produce significant reforms abroad, clever domestic farm lobbies will be able to ask for still more subsidies, this time as "compensation" for the intransigence shown by their foreign negotiating partners. U.S. farm groups have already made plans for this eventuality by writing into the 1988 trade bill a provision for automatically higher subsidies (a "triggered marketing loan") if the president cannot, by 1990, certify that the GATT talks have made progress. More recently, legislation was introduced in the U.S. Senate that would further tighten this linkage between failing GATT talks and still more protection for U.S. farmers. (The Agricultural Trade Act of 1990, introduced in 1989 by Sen. Max Baucus (D-MT), directs the Office of the U.S. Trade Representative to initiate unfair trade cases against the EC and Japan, under the Super 301 provision of the 1988 trade law, and directs the secretary of agriculture to expand the Export Enhancement Program (EEP), if support from these countries for the U.S. position in the Uruguay Round is not forthcoming by December 1990.)

In agriculture, therefore, the fact that multilateral negotiations are underway cannot be taken as a sign that reform is just around the corner. In the absence of sustained top-level attention, such negotiations probably do as much to retard as to stimulate the progress of domestic farm policy reform. It is no wonder that so many GATT negotiations in the past (Dillon Round, Kennedy Round, and Tokyo Round) produced such meager results. As advocates of reform, we are permitted to hope that the Uruguay Round will be different. As analysts, however, we are obliged to warn developing countries that a more likely outcome will be continued delay, and finally no dramatic change in the status quo.

The Small Consequences of a GATT Breakthrough for Most Developing Countries

As a second note of caution, even in the unlikely event that a GATT breakthrough does lead to significant rich-country farm policy reforms, it is important to note that the impact of those reforms on poor countries might be surprisingly small.

A rich-country farm policy reform would affect developing countries only indirectly, through changes that might take place in the price, volume, and direction of international commodity trade. Numerous efforts have been made to estimate both the direction and magnitude of these changes. Because of widely differing starting assumptions, these results are not always easy to compare (Valdés 1987). What emerges, however, is a picture of price, trade volume, and trade direction change that is hardly revolutionary from the vantage point of the developing world.

One well-known set of estimates is contained in a study by Rodney Tyers and Kym Anderson in 1986 and published by the World Bank (1986). This study takes as its point of reference the farm support levels that prevailed among the OECD (rich) countries in 1980-82. It then simulates the impact on prices, trade, and welfare of a complete elimination of these supports. Not surprisingly, the impact of reform on the rich countries is estimated to be quite large. The impact on the developing world, however, is surprisingly small.

According to this study, OECD reform would increase international prices for wheat, coarse grains, rice, and sugar by less than 5 percent. This is not much, considering that one year of bad weather in North America (as in 1988) can produce international price increases five times as large. Trade volume would be expected to increase more substantially following liberalization, especially in meat and dairy markets. But only a part of this increase would be captured by the developing countries. A summary of estimated price and trade volume changes from this World Bank study is presented in Table 4.1.

One reason these anticipated price and trade volume changes are rather small, according to the World Bank, is the tendency of some highly interventionist developed country support policies (at least in 1980-82) to offset one another. Removing such policies in unison would substantially increase the efficiency of resource use in the developed world, but it would have a relatively neutral impact on international markets. International price levels, as it turns out, have not been so badly distorted by rich-country farm policies as most developing-country officials believe. In fact, the World Bank study finds that international grain prices in 1980-82 were more heavily distorted by poor-country policies than by rich-country policies (World Bank 1986, 131).

In terms of overall welfare gains, the 1986 World Bank study goes on to estimate that OECD farm policy liberalization would produce effects in the industrial world almost five times as large as those felt in the developing world. The industrial market economies overall would enjoy a $48.5 billion gain from increased efficiency. This is exactly why most industrial-country economists are so enthusiastic about the reform endeavor. The developing countries, however, might experience an $11.8 billion welfare loss (World Bank 1986, 131). This projection of a net loss for the developing world has received quite a bit of critical attention, and we will say more about it later. For the moment, however, consider that it is a relatively small loss (less than $3 per capita, for the heavily populated developing countries as a whole).

How could rich-country reforms produce such relatively small effects in the developing world? Perhaps the 1986 World Bank study understates (or even misstates) these effects because of its incomplete commodity coverage. Products grown in the tropics exclusively by developing countries (green coffee, cocoa beans) are not covered in the study, a fault that the bank itself is quick to concede. Valdés and Zietz (1980) have shown that especially in some semiprocessed tropical product markets (for example, roasted coffee, cocoa derivatives, tobacco products, wine, oils, and seeds), the lowering of rich-country trade barriers would produce considerable gains for the developing world as a whole, offsetting the losses that might accompany a temperate zone product liberalization alone. In agriculture, no less than in industry, the tendency of rich countries to place heavier import duties on higher-value processed and semiprocessed goods ("tariff escalation") works significantly to the disadvantage of the developing world.

An independent multilateral negotiation on tropical products is under way in the Uruguay Round, and this negotiation has actually produced—at the December 1988 Mid-Term Review Conference—what would seem to be a significant package of rich-country tariff concessions. The United States offered 25 percent tariff reductions on a total of 43 (mostly unprocessed) tropical products. The EC offered tariff cuts of 20 to100 percent on 78 products, three-quarters of which already had duty-free access to the U.S. market (USDA 1989). These offered tariff cuts are useful but less significant than they seem. U.S. and EC tariffs on most unprocessed tropical products are low to begin with, especially for developing countries with preferential access through agreements such as the Lomé Convention and the Caribbean Basin Initiative. Because the new cuts address mostly these unprocessed tropical products, they add little to the liberalization that has already been achieved. They may even have the perverse effect of increasing relative discrimination against higher value-added tropical country processing industries. Moreover, because these cuts fail to address significant nontariff barriers (mostly health and food safety regulations, such as pesticide tolerances on fruits and vegetables) they leave unaffected some of the most potent means of discriminating against poor-country tropical products. Small wonder that the Latin American developing countries, at the Mid-Term Review Conference, refused to jump at these small concessions on tropical products as an adequate substitute for more substantial rich-country concessions on temperate zone farm policy reform.

The 1986 World Bank study may also underestimate the effects of rich-country farm reform because of its 1980-82 starting point. Much higher levels of industrial-country farm support were introduced several years later in the decade of the 1980s. Between 1980 and 1986, producer subsidy equivalents for the OECD area as a whole soared from 28 percent to 47 percent, and to some extent these higher support levels are still in place. Accordingly, if we select a middecade reference period, then the estimated effects of liberalization, for both the developed and the developing countries, grow somewhat larger.

A 1989 study by Roningen and Dixit, at the Economic Research Service (ERS) of the U.S. Department of Agriculture, produces more dramatic results by measuring rich-country farm support from 1986-87, a year of unusually depressed world market conditions and hence a year of unusually intrusive and distorting industrial country policies. According to this study, full liberalization by all "industrial market economies" (IMEs) in 1986-87, would have boosted the extremely low international price levels of that day by a more substantial margin. The somewhat larger world market price changes simulated in this ERS study were above 50 percent for dairy and sugar, between 25 and 40 percent for cereals, and 10 to 20 percent for meat.

This ERS study also foresees a larger expansion of trade volume following liberalization for some commodities, especially sugar and rice. For wheat and coarse grains, however, it expects global trade volume actually to contract, by 20 percent and 5 percent, respectively (Roningen and Dixit 1989, 19). This expected trade contraction is attributed to a drop in exportable supplies of grains in the industrial countries, following a removal of production supports.

How would the developing world, specifically, be affected by these somewhat more significant price and trade volume changes? Here once more, the significance is less than expected. The net trade balance and net welfare implications for the developing world remain surprisingly small. Only in terms of an internal shift in welfare that might take place between producers and consumers would significant developing-country results be felt.

In terms of farm trade balances, the ERS study shows that gains and losses to developing world exporters and importers would be minimized due to the sizeable production and consumption adjustments that would follow from higher international prices. The conventional assumption that today's net exporting LDCs have a great deal to gain from liberalization is somewhat confounded in the process. The value of total world farm trade does increase significantly under the assumptions of this ERS study, but net exporters in the industrial world are projected to capture most of the gain. The United States, Canada, Australia, and New Zealand are projected to gain more than twice as much in farm export earnings from rich-country liberalization as the developing-country exporters.

Moreover, the largest gains that do come to the developing-country exporters, under the assumptions of this ERS study, are in highly suspect product markets. The largest gains, as shown in Table 4.2, are forecast to come through expanded exports of ruminant meats and sugar (mostly from Latin America), and rice (mostly from Asia).

These larger exports of rice will be possible only after a full liberalization of rice imports into Japan, which is the one reform that now seems least likely to be included in any final Uruguay Round agricultural reform agreement. Japan has consistently demanded that its highly protectionist rice policies be given separate and privileged treatment in the GATT talks. Developing-country trade gains in sugar are also substantially overstated in the ERS study (perhaps by as much as 500 percent), because it does not take into account the important "quota rents" that would be lost to some LDC exporters if U.S. sugar import policies were fully liberalized. The loss of quota rents might also be an offsetting factor for some Latin American ruminant meat exporters to the U.S. market (Williams 1986). The importance of such considerations must be underscored because a more recent study by Zietz and Valdes (1986) agrees that most developing-country export gains from liberalization will have to come, if they come at all, in problematic quota-protected markets, such as sugar and beef.

Just as the net exporters in the developing world do not gain as much as expected from rich-country reform, neither do the net importers lose as much. According to the supply, demand, and price transmission elasticity assumptions contained in the ERS study, higher world prices would trigger enough new LDC production, and would discourage enough consumption, to wipe out for most net importers the adverse trade effects that otherwise might occur. In fact, the "developing importers" overall could experience a surprising net trade gain of $2.8 billion, as internal production and consumption adjusted to world price changes. Small trade losses in dairy and oilseed markets for these countries might be more than offset by gains in rice and sugar. The newly industrializing Asian countries, which currently import wheat and coarse grains in large volume, would experience a small net trade loss as world prices increased, but for these newly industrialized countries (NICs) an easily affordable trade loss of just $500 million.

Overall, then, the trade balance impact of rich-country farm policy reform would be surprisingly small for the developing world. The conventional view that LDC net exporters stand a great deal to gain from liberalization, and the related view that net importers stand a great deal to lose, is largely erroneous. This is true even if the effects of liberalization are simulated, as in the ERS study, from the most extreme middecade reference point.

When we come to the estimated internal welfare effects of rich-country farm policy reform, the ERS study first of all confirms a conclusion reached earlier, that the net impact on the developing world will be quite small. While the 1986 World Bank study projected a modest (on a per capita basis) net loss of $11.8 billion for the developing world as a whole, the 1989 ERS study, as shown in Table 4.3, projects an even smaller net loss of just $4.5 billion. This is the equivalent of less than $2 per capita.

Alongside these small, almost negligible net welfare losses for the developing world, the ERS study projects large net welfare gains ($33.3 billion, or $44 per capita) for industrial market economies, following a rich-country reform. Again, the largest net welfare effects are felt within the rich countries actually undertaking the reform. By implication, if the developing countries want to realize large net welfare effects of their own, they will have to do more than wait for policy changes in the developed world. They will have to undertake reforms of their own.

The various studies being reviewed here all confirm that reforms in the developing world are the only sure path to large developing country net welfare gains. The same 1986 World Bank study that projected $11.8 billion net welfare loss for the developing world from unilateral OECD reform projects that a unilateral developing world reform of food and farm policies would produce a net welfare gain more than twice as large—$28.2 billion. As this study emphasizes, "the main [net] beneficiaries of unilateral liberalization are the liberalizers themselves" (World Bank 1986, 131).

A parallel study by the Australian Bureau of Agricultural and Resource Economics comes to the same conclusion. Especially for developing countries that are net importers, it says, the policy choice is clear: "on economic grounds they do best as a group from liberalizing their own agricultural policies. They attain the largest benefits from liberalizing unilaterally" (Kirby et al. 1988, 36). The ERS study, which projects a small $4.5 billion net welfare loss for the developing world following rich-country reform, projects a small net welfare gain of $2.6 billion for the developing world if the reform process is extended to correct current distortions in the policies of developing countries.

Nor is the gain from LDC policy reform limited to actions that might be taken in the narrow food and farm sector. Developing countries might gain even larger net welfare benefits from a reform of their larger industrial and macroeconomic policies. Agriculture in the developing world is more often harmed by exchange rate and trade regime distortions than by direct price interventions on farm inputs and outputs. In yet another ERS simulation experiment, net welfare consequences were estimated assuming that the developing countries realign (in most instances, lower) their exchange rates according to "free market" rates. When this important macroeconomic reform measure is added to a prior global reform of all agricultural policies, estimated net welfare gains for the developing countries as a whole increase from $2.6 billion up to $9.6 billion (Krissoff, Sullivan, and Wainio 1989).

Certainly, such agricultural and macroeconomic policy reforms will not be easy for the developing countries to take. The anticipated net welfare gains can mask some politically difficult gross welfare shifts, and predictable resistance from the internal constituent groups disadvantaged by such shifts. Despite this resistance, a number of developing countries, in the 1980s, have initiated wide-ranging internal reforms (World Bank 1989). This record of unilateral food and farm policy reform by poor countries may still be woefully inadequate, but it is at least more impressive than the record of multilateral food and farm policy reforms implemented by rich countries so far through GATT.

Here, then, is a second reason for developing-country officials to discount somewhat the significance of the rich-country farm policy reform efforts that are under way in GATT. Not only are the GATT negotiations unlikely to succeed, they are unlikely, if they do succeed, to produce a decisive net trade or net welfare impact on the developing world. For developing countries seeking net welfare gains, unilateral reform efforts at home are probably a more promising strategy than waiting for a significant farm policy reform agreement among rich countries in Geneva.

The Exaggerated Danger of a GATT Agreement to Developing-Country Consumers

We can minimize the net trade and net welfare effects of rich-country farm policy reform on most developing countries, but it is more difficult to dismiss the divergent welfare effects of reform on individual producers and consumers within those countries. As revealed in Table 4.3, producers might be helped and consumers hurt. Recall that the trade balance effects of reform are small, mostly because of the large producer and consumer adjustments expected to take place inside poor countries in response to the higher world market prices that would follow reform. The net welfare effect is also relatively small, but only because these rather large adjustments (producer gains and consumer losses) roughly offset one another. It is fair enough for economists to concentrate on "net" welfare, but developing-country officials—and certainly developing-country consumers—are entitled to take a more selective, disaggregate approach to the problem.

The estimated impact on individual producers and consumers depends, largely, on the willingness of developing-country governments to permit the higher international prices that result from rich-country reform to cross their borders. Even if just a part of that price increase is transmitted into the poor country's economy (the ERS study cautiously assumed a price transmission elasticity of just 0.5 for all developing countries, as opposed to 1.0 for the developed world), the result as shown in Table 4.4, could be a measurable shift in welfare away from consumers of agricultural products and toward producers. The anticipated $17 billion gain in producer welfare throughout the developing world is noteworthy. It is equal in magnitude to roughly four times the total annual agricultural lending of the World Bank. Among reform enthusiasts, quite naturally, this anticipated gain for LDC farmers has been an important selling point. Unfortunately, the even larger projected loss in LDC consumer welfare—$20.2 billion total—has become a considerable sticking point.

Note from Table 4.3 that these significant internal shifts in welfare away from consumers and toward producers do not depend on a

nation's agricultural trade balance. They can take place among the
net exporters as well as among the net importers. In fact, on a per
capita basis, Table 4.4 suggests that the adverse effect on individual
consumers will actually be greater among developing exporters than
among developing importers. This is because the absolute losses
anticipated in these exporting countries are large in proportion to
the smaller number of consumers who actually live there.

We can react in several ways to this discovery that IME
liberalization implies a significant consumer-to-producer welfare shift
throughout the developing world. It is possible, on the one hand,
to react with alarm. The authors of an ambitious trade liberalization
study conducted at the International Institute for Applied Systems
Analysis (IIASA) concluded from similar findings that "[t]he average
per capita calorie intake in the developing countries decreases under
agricultural trade liberalization by OECD countries, and consequently
the incidence of hunger increases." With exaggerated precision, a
3.6 percent increase in "hunger" is projected by the year 2000,
compared to the no reform reference scenario (Parikh et al. 1988).

This IIASA study concludes that "compensation schemes" to
offset such adverse impacts should accompany any OECD
liberalization agreement. The 1989 ERS study, from similar findings,
concludes that "industrial market economy liberalization might be
more acceptable [to the developing world] if accompanied by
increased development assistance or trade concessions in other
areas" (Roningen and Dixit 1989, 36). The Uruguay Round
negotiators have already given some verbal recognition to these
concerns by inserting into their April 1989 framework agreement
an assertion that "ways should be developed to take into account
the possible negative effects of the reform process on net food
importing developing countries" (GATT 1989).

An OECD pledge of increased "food aid" to the developing world
is often suggested as one appropriate compensatory scheme. It is
significant that the original U.S. zero option negotiating proposal
to the Uruguay Round specifically exempted legitimate food aid
shipments from the production and trade distorting practices to be
eliminated under reform. Developing countries, however, would
have reason to suspect that in an OECD world of fewer production

distortions, and hence fewer surpluses, generous food aid shipments would become less likely.

Would it be appropriate, at this point, for concerned developing-country officials to mount a political effort either to block or to redirect the GATT negotiations, in hope of protecting their domestic consumers from the possibly adverse welfare effects of a rich-country reform? Here we shall argue that such an effort would be at best unnecessary, and at worst counterproductive, to the developing world.

Developing-country efforts to redirect or obstruct the GATT negotiations are in the first instance unnecessary, because of the high probability discussed earlier that these negotiations will fail on their own. But even if those negotiations do not fail altogether, their most likely outcome will probably stop far short of full liberalization. Developing world consumers may be marginally vulnerable in the short run to a full liberalization of rich-country farm policies, but we can show that they would have little to fear from a partial liberalization.

One estimate of what a partial liberalization might do is provided in a 1988 Australian study of "early action" on trade reform (Kirby et al. 1988). Using an aggregated version of the same commodity trade model employed in the ERS study but with 1984 rather than 1986 as a starting point, the Australian study estimates the impact on several different categories of developing countries of a 10 percent reduction in "output assistance" to farmers in the EC, Japan, and United States. The impact is estimated to be hardly noticeable. International price levels and trade volume in wheat and corn markets would change by less than 1 percent. Internal producer gains and consumer losses in the developing exporter (Cairns group) countries would be negligible, at slightly more than $200 million in each case.

For African and Latin American importers, these divergent internal gains and losses would be less than $200 million each. For East Asian importers as a group, this partial liberalization by the industrial countries would yield even smaller producer gains and consumer losses of less than $50 million each. A partial 10 percent liberalization might be of significant value to the rich countries undertaking the reform (transfers of welfare between producers, consumers, and taxpayers would be roughly 10 times as large in the developed countries as in the developing countries), but the impact on the developing world would be, especially on a per capita basis, almost nonexistent (Kirby et al. 1988, 32).

A second reason for developing country consumers not to worry too much about rich-country farm policy reform is the possibility, if we consider resource use across sectors, that such a reform would lead to such large net welfare gains that consumers as well as producers would be able to benefit. Loo and Tower have used a four-sector general equilibrium model that captures cross-sector effects (both the ERS and World Bank studies use partial equilibrium models) to argue that real income in the developing countries as a whole might rise by $26 billion following a 10 percent increase in world agricultural prices, such as might accompany IME liberalization. (A part of this more optimistic result may reflect an assumed 10 percent increase in tropical as well as temperate zone product prices. If so, this would not match the assumptions made in the ERS and World Bank studies, and in any case would not be an accurate depiction of IME liberalization.) This sort of rapid growth would be expected, following a price increase, because resources would move out of the inefficient industrial sector and into the more highly responsive farming sector. In India alone the real income gain from such a movement might be over $2 billion (Centre for International Economics 1988).

A third reason for developing countries not to panic about consumer vulnerability to rich-country reform is the fact that, in most developing countries, a large number of all consumers of farm products are also producers. In their capacity as consumers they might be hurt by higher prices, but in their capacity as producers they will be helped. This does not eliminate the problem altogether, because many of the most vocal consumers, living in urban areas, will not be producers, and because even some rural producers are still net purchasers of farm products (Seckler 1988).

In the end, it might be unwise as well as unnecessary for developing-country officials to oppose current efforts at rich-country farm policy reform, consumer welfare concerns notwithstanding.

Opposition would be unwise most of all because these reform efforts, if successful, could produce a considerable hidden benefit for the developing world not yet mentioned in any of the foregoing analyses. The developing countries as a whole may have little to gain from reforms that reduce the level of support for rich-country farmers, hence boosting the level of world prices. But they would all stand to gain a great deal from any reform that reduced the variability of rich-country support, and hence the variability of those prices. If the GATT negotiations can produce a reduction in the procyclical variability of rich-country farm support—especially as practiced in the EC—then all developing countries, including consumers as well as producers within those countries, would gain a great deal.

Potential Gains to the Developing World
from Less World Price Variability

In most of the developing world, agriculture remains the dominant sector of the economy, and consumer spending on food is still by far the dominant use of personal income. This renders the developing world, both citizens and governments, highly vulnerable to fluctuations in agricultural commodity prices.

Regrettably, much of the fluctuation that we see in world farm commodity prices is directly attributable to rich-country farm policies. By embracing trade adjustment policies that stabilize price levels within their own borders, these rich countries destabilize prices in the world marketplace. They damage their own welfare at the same time, because it is costly to import more from a rising world market or to dump more onto a slumping world market. But the welfare losses to the rich that come from such procyclical trade adjustment policies are for them relatively affordable, compared to the losses imposed on outsiders, and especially on the developing world. Poor countries, because they often cannot afford the foreign exchange costs of an offsetting procyclical trade adjustment, and because of their acute vulnerability to the food and farm price fluctuations that accompany countercyclical adjustment, usually are left with a disproportionate burden of pain from world market fluctuations (Nogues 1985).

This burden of price instability caused by rich-country policies can be estimated by comparing the observed coefficient of variation in today's world farm prices to the smaller coefficient that would be expected if one or more rich nations were to liberalize their policies to allow international price signal to cross their borders. Using this technique in a study of world wheat markets, Maurice Schiff (1985) has estimated that global liberalization could reduce the variability of world wheat prices by 48 percent.

For present purposes, however, it is more important to know what a liberalization of rich-country policies alone would do international price stability. The 1986 World Bank study by Tyers and Anderson provides one indicative estimate. According to this study, liberalization in the industrial market economies (from a 1980-82 starting point) would have reduced international price variability in wheat markets by 33 percent, coarse grains by 10 percent, rice by 19 percent, sugar by 15 percent, and dairy products by as much as 56 percent.

Among the rich countries, which ones have been responsible for the worst international price destabilizing effects? In wheat and coarse grain markets, this dubious distinction clearly falls upon the European Community. Through its variable import levies and variable export restitutions, the EC has consistently stressed procyclical trade adjustments at the border over countercyclical internal production and consumption adjustments. Anderson and Tyers estimated in 1984 that if the EC alone were to liberalize these policies, coefficients of international price variation would fall almost as far (93 percent as far for wheat, and 100 percent as far for coarse grains) as if all the industrial market economies, including the United States, Canada, and Japan, were to liberalize together.

In the years since this 1984 estimate, unfortunately, the United States has to some extent joined the EC in destabilizing world prices through an expanded use of procyclical trade adjustments. Under the terms of the 1985 U.S. Farm Bill, it became policy to offer explicit export subsidies, in a slack market, for products such as wheat, wheat flour, barley, soybean oil, and poultry. Marketing loans, which are in part the equivalent of an export subsidy, were introduced for cotton and rice.

Still, U.S. policy does not destabilize world market prices nearly as much as EC policy. The U.S. export subsidy budget, first of all, is only a fraction of the EC budget for export restitutions. Second, by not imposing variable import levies, the United States does not shield its domestic consumers (or its domestic producers of nonprogram commodities, such as beef) from the internal adjustments that accompany price variability. Through large countercyclical adjustments in the feeding of grain to domestic livestock, the United States continues to absorb—not without pain to its producers and consumers—a significant share of the world price instability created by the procyclical policies of others, such as the EC. Third, the United States has usually offset its few procyclicial border measures (such as its export subsidies) with highly countercyclical stock-building and internal supply control measures. U.S. government-held stocks and acreage reductions became so large in the 1980s, in response to the cyclical depression in world market conditions, that world prices for everyone—unfortunately, including the EC—were on balance stabilized rather than destabilized.

For policy officials in both the United States and the developing world, this discussion suggests an important shared political interest, in using the ongoing GATT negotiations in Geneva less as a vehicle for reducing the level of rich-country farm support (the gains for the developing world are ambiguous at best, and U.S. farmers will object), and more as a vehicle for attacking the variability of such support (the gains for the developing world would be significant, and most U.S. farmers would gain rather than lose). So long as support levels are the center of discussion in Geneva, protected farmers throughout the industrial world will find it easy, as they have so far, to maneuver in order to deadlock the negotiation. If negotiations could be shifted to the procyclical variability of support, then most U.S. farmers could support the Uruguay Round with more enthusiasm. Variable levy-protected European farmers would find themselves far more isolated in their objections.

The recent U.S. proposal to GATT to convert support measures to tariffs ("tariffication") has important advantages in this regard. Until now, the proposal has been billed as a first step toward support level reductions. This scares farmers, including U.S. farmers, and brings instant rejection from the EC and Japan. It also somewhat erroneously scares LDC importers. Why not present this tariffication idea, at least initially, more as a means to reduce the variability of support? Japanese and EC farmers might still object, but they would have fewer grounds and they would be more isolated in doing so. Most U.S. farmers (all but those with quota protection) would benefit considerably from a reduction of support variability in the EC and Japan, as would all U.S. consumers and taxpayers. Producers, consumers, and taxpayers in the developing world, in relative terms, would be the biggest winners of all.

The objections of the EC to a negotiated reduction in support variability could be handled gently, by proposing at first not a complete elimination of variable levies, but merely a capping of the variability permitted. The cap could initially be quite loose, so as not to disrupt overnight the workings of EC policy. It could then be progressively tightened, as the community—and its internal stock management capacity—gradually adjusted to the reality of internal price fluctuation (Tangermann 1989).

Perhaps it is too late to shift the focus of the Uruguay Round away from reductions in support levels, and somewhat more toward a reduction in support variability. But barring such a shift, the discussions are likely to produce only a small reduction in support levels, if any, and perhaps no reduction at all in support variability. This would be, especially for the developing world, an unsatisfying result. For the United States and the developing world together, it would represent a missed opportunity to pursue a significant joint gain.

Table 4.1. International price and trade effects of OECD liberalization of selected
commodity markets, 1985

Percent change	Wheat	Coarse grains	Rice	Beef & lamb	Pork & poultry	Dairy	Sugar
World price level	2.00	1.00	5.00	16.00	2.00	27.00	5.00
World trade volume	-1.00	19.00	32.00	195.00	18.00	95.00	2.00

SOURCE: World Bank 1986, Table 6.7.

Table 4.2. Trade balance changes from IME liberalization, 1986/87
($ US billions)

	Developing Exporters	Asian NICs	Developing Importers	Total
Ruminant meats	1.00	0.00	0.60	1.60
Nonruminant meats	0.40	0.10	0.40	0.90
Dairy	0.10	0.00	-0.90	-0.80
Wheat	0.10	-0.20	0.00	-0.10
Coarse grains	0.50	-0.20	0.30	0.60
Rice	0.80	0.00	1.40	2.20
Oilseeds and products	0.30	0.00	-0.20	0.10
Sugar	0.70	0.00	1.00	1.70
Other crops	0.00	-0.10	0.40	0.30
Total	3.90	-0.50	2.80	6.20

SOURCE: Roningen and Dixit 1989, Table 6.

Table 4.3. Welfare implications of IME liberalization, 1986/87 (a) ($ US billions)

	Producer welfare	Consumer welfare	Taxpayers costs	Net benefits	Per capita
Developing Exporters	5.10	-4.80	-0.30	0.70	2.00
Asian NICs	0.50	-0.90	0.10	-0.90	-13.00
Developing Importers	11.80	-14.50	-0.10	-4.40	-2.00
Developing Countries	17.40	-20.50	-0.30	-4.50	-2.00

SOURCE: Roningen and Dixit 1989, Table 10.

(a) Estimated change in producer surplus, consumer surplus, net government
    expenditures, and the sum of all three. Net benefits include losses by other groups,
    e.g., quota holders.

References

Anderson, K., and R. Tyers. 1984. "European Community Grain and Meat Policies: Effects on International Prices, Trade, and Welfare." *European Review of Agricultural Economics* 11(4):366-94.

Centre for International Economics. 1988. *Macroeconomic Consequences of Farm-support Policies*. Overview of an International Program of Studies. Canberra: Centre for International Economics.

Field, Heather, Simon Hearn, and Michael G. Kirby. 1989. "The 1988 EC Budget and Production Stabilizers: A Means of Containing the Common Agricultural Policy?" Discussion Paper 89.3, Australian Bureau of Agricultural and Resource Economics. Canberra: Australian Government Publishing Service.

GATT Negotiating Group on Agriculture. 1989. "Agriculture: Chairman's Text." April 7. Geneva: GATT.

Kirby, Michael G., Henry C. Haszler, David T. Parsons, and Michael G. Adams. 1988. *Early Action on Agricultural Trade Reform*. Discussion Paper 88.3, Australian Bureau of Agricultural and Resource Economics. Canberra: Australian Government Publishing Service.

Krissoff, Barry, John Sullivan, and John Wainio. 1989. "Opening Agricultural Markets: Trade and Welfare Implications for Developing Countries." Mimeo. Washington, D.C.: ERS, U.S. Department of Agriculture.

Loo, Tom, and Edward Tower. 1988. "Agricultural Protectionism in the Less-Developed Countries." Global Agriculture Trade Study Technical Paper. Canberra: Center for International Economics.

Nogues, Julio J. 1985. "Agriculture and Developing Countries in the GATT," *World Economy* (June), 119-33.

Paarlberg, Robert L. 1988. *Fixing Farm Trade: Policy Options for the United States*. Cambridge: Ballinger.

_____. 1989. "International Agricultural Policy Coordination: An Aid to Liberal Reform?" In *Policy Coordination in World Agriculture.* C. Ford Runge, Brian Job, and Harald von Witzke, eds. Kiel: Wissenschaftsverlag Vauk.

Parikh, Kirit S., Gunther Fischer, Klaus Frohberg, and Odd Gulbrandsen. 1988. *Towards Free Trade in Agriculture.* Laxenburg, Austria: Martins Nijhoff.

Roningen, Vernon O., and Praveen M. Dixit. 1989. "Economic Implications of Agricultural Policy Reform in Industrial Market Economies." Mimeo. Washington, D.C.: USDA.

Schiff, Maurice W. 1985. "An Econometric Analysis of the World Wheat Market and Simulation of Alternative Policies, 1960-1980." USDA/ERS Staff Report No. AGES 850827. Washington, D.C.: U.S. Government Printing Office.

Seckler, David. 1988. "Economic Policy Adjustments in Developing Countries: Discussion." *American Journal of Agricultural Economics* 70 (5):1055-56.

Tangermann, Stefan. 1989. "Progress and Issues in the GATT Negotiations: An EC Perspective." Paper prepared for the Annual Conference of the Agricultural Institute of Canada. Montreal, July 9-13.

U.S. Department of Agriculture. 1989. "GATT Negotiations and Trade in Tropical Products." *Agricultural Outlook* (March): 17-20.

Valdés, Alberto. 1987. "Agriculture in the Uruguay Round: Interests of Developing Countries." *The World Bank Economic Review* 1 (4):571-93.

Valdés, Alberto, and J. Zietz. 1980. *Agricultural Protection in OECD Countries: Its Cost to Less Developed Countries.* Research Report 21. Washington, D.C.: International Food Policy Research Institute.

Warley, T. K. 1989. "Agriculture in the GATT: A Historical Perspective." Department of Agricultural Economics and Business, AEB 89/6, July. Guelph, Ontario.

Williams, Robert. 1986. *Export Agriculture and the Crisis in Central America.* Chapel Hill: University of North Carolina Press.

World Bank. 1986. *World Development Report 1986.* New York: Oxford University Press.

World Bank. 1989. *Report on Adjustment Lending.* Washington, D.C.: World Bank.

Zietz, Joachim, and Alberto Valdés. 1986. *The Costs of Protectionism to Developing Countries: An Analysis for Selected Agricultural Products.* World Bank Staff Working Paper 769. Washington, D.C.: World Bank.

DISCUSSION OF CHAPTER 4
Alex F. McCalla

I will begin by summarizing what I see as Paarlberg's major points. His basic argument is that trade liberalization would not have much effect on developing countries for three reasons. First, reforms are not likely to happen given the political interests of the developed countries. Second, even if liberalization does occur, the impact on developing countries would be minimal, at least in the sense of the change of prices of liberalized commodities. He does agree that liberalization would have significant redistribution effects from consumers to producers within countries as prices rise. But he argues that even that is not bad for consumers because the overall economywide growth effect on incomes would be sufficiently positive that consumers also could gain. (One might note that it is this broader effect that appears to be a benefit from liberalization, therefore suggesting that developing countries in fact do have a stake in General Agreement on Tariffs and Trade (GATT) negotiations. I will return to this point later.) Third, price instability caused by domestic intervention in developed countries is more deleterious to the developing countries than is the absolute level of price support. Therefore, altering the means of support to farmers in developed countries while leaving the level of the support the same would have greater benefits than reducing levels of support while leaving the instruments the same. This argument is more complex and I will comment on it in more detail at a later point.

In general, I accept Paarlberg's basic points. As usual there is little doubt where Paarlberg comes from in terms of his views. So, how much do we agree with the weaving together of the partial evidence he presents in his paper? Basically it is a debate between those I call "GATT optimists," those who believe in the GATT process, and those I call "GATT pessimists." It appears now that GATT optimists are in retreat and GATT pessimists, such as Paarlberg, are on the offensive.

The basic question is, will the fourth major attempt to reform agricultural trade fail again? Who can know? I have heard equally plausible assertions that it cannot fail because if GATT does not succeed in agriculture, the whole process will unravel. Or another argument is that because domestic policies are finally on the table, progress will necessarily follow. I do agree with Paarlberg that the inclinations for policy reform in the developed countries are heavily influenced by short-term events, that is, changes in world prices. The argument made by Paarlberg that the 1988 drought has doomed the GATT process, because of the increase in prices and reduction in the pressure for domestic reform, is a point that has to be taken seriously.

But, says Paarlberg, even if we are successful in the GATT negotiations, it will have limited consequences for the developing countries. On this point I think we had better be very careful how we draw our conclusions. In my judgment, his point rests on a very narrow interpretation of the process of liberalization because he limits his attention to liberalization of temperate zone products. He bases his conclusions on a selected set of analyses (models), all of which are very sensitive to base year, commodity coverage, and method of estimation. In general, developed countries subsidize producers and tax consumers. Therefore, the removal of barriers and subsidies reduces supplies and raises world prices. The Paarlberg argument is that the rise in world prices negatively impacts developing-country consumers while benefiting developing-country producers, but the net effect is likely to be small even though negative.

But reality is that developing countries also distort their agriculture and food sectors, generally in the opposite direction: they tax producers and subsidize consumers by fixing domestic consumer prices well below world prices. Therefore, when we discuss liberalization we have to be very careful regarding what kind of liberalization we are talking about. If only developed countries liberalize then increasing prices will increase either the budgetary costs and/or consumer priecs in the developing countries, depending on the extent to which they are passed through to internal markets.

But if you talk about liberalization in both the developed countries and the developing countries, there are broader implications. First, world prices may not rise as much because the effect of developing-country liberalization is to reduce import demand and put downward pressure on world prices. The second implication is that the removal of distortions in developing countries will have substantially greater welfare impacts on the developing countries themselves. Why is this the case? Because if we accept neoclassical analysis then those who distort the most have the most to gain from the removal of those distortions. Under this scenario— that is, both developed and developing countries liberalizing—the impacts are not necessarily marginal.

But there are more basic reasons why the developing countries have substantial interests in the success of GATT in agricultural trade negotiations. The first was hinted at in Paarlberg's paper. Reform in international markets accompanied by domestic reform stimulates broader-based economic growth in developing countries. Similarly, policies that stimulate the demand for LDC exports in the developed countries have a significant positive effect on growth and welfare in the developing countries. Thus, the broader case is that if agricultural protectionism is an increasingly major obstacle to a freer working international economy, then developing countries clearly have an interest in the removal of that agricultural protectionism even though the impacts may not occur in the agricultural sector. It is this broader question, namely, what are the ramifications of a failure in agriculture in GATT, that is of crucial interest. Will it lead to a further balkanization of international markets? Will it lead to the separation of additional sectors outside of the GATT process, as has occurred in textiles, automobiles, steel, semiconductors, and so on? Clearly, in my judgment, the developing countries have a substantial interest in more liberal trading rules for developed countries and the world in general.

The second point, also indirectly mentioned in Chapter 4, is that liberalization in the developed countries, which causes rising commodity prices, could force much needed domestic policy reform in the developing countries themselves. It could allow them to break out of increasingly expensive food subsidy programs. Multilateral reform in a trading system offers an external rationale for what ought to be done anyway at home. Major distortions removed in developing countries (such as food subsidies) would have major benefits. In general, my argument is that a bitter pill is easier to take if it is forced on us by someone else.

The third point I would make is simply to agree with the author that domestic policy reform that increases the interface of developed-country domestic agricultural economies with world markets would lessen international market instability. Instability in food prices is greater because of this intervention and it may be that this instability has a greater impact on the developing countries over time than the level of prices themselves. This is Paarlberg's basic point. But I see a couple of problems here. If you focus only on the instruments, you may not get the double benefit that would occur if you address both the instrument and the level issue simultaneously. For example, if you eliminate instruments such as export subsidies or production control you accomplish both. You accomplish the possibility of increased stability and also different price levels in international markets. So I think that the point to be made here is that if you engage in trade negotiations that remove distorting instruments, you will simultaneously address the question of the level of supports. Both of these changes would then have significant benefits for developing countries.

Overall, it is a provocative discussion, which should cause readers to think carefully about the implications of trade liberalization for the developing countries.

5

Economic Policies of Developing Countries: Consequences for Food Production, Trade, and Food Security

INTRODUCTION
Lehman B. Fletcher

This topic was discussed at the conference by Alberto Valdés, of the International Food Policy Research Institute. Valdés based his presentation on preliminary results of a comparative research project on the political economy of agricultural pricing policies, which was funded by the World Bank and directed by him in collaboration with Anne O. Krueger and Maurice Schiff. Since the results of this research will be published separately, only the measurement of economywide and sector-specific interventions on prices of selected agricultural products in the study countries is included in this chapter, which is reprinted from an earlier publication.[1]

Valdés pointed out the need to use a general equilibrium approach that distinguishes importables and exportables from nontradables in an economy. Most agricultural products are tradable or close substitutes for other tradables. Thus, their relative prices will be affected not only by sector-specific pricing interventions but also by economywide policies. An example is the real exchange rate that determines relative prices of tradables and nontradables in an economy.

While agricultural imports of developing countries are mostly food products, their agricultural exports are dominated by raw materials, beverages, and tropical products. Generally, exportables are taxed; Krueger, Schiff, and Valdés report an overall average rate of taxation of 34 percent on export products included in their study. Importables are also taxed in relation to production incentives; that is to say, imported food products are subsidized. The rate of taxation on importables, however, is much lower than on exportables, and emanates mainly from overvalued exchange rates and high border protection of industry rather than tariffs or other border measures.

Valdés indicated that, to some extent, developing countries try to stabilize their internal prices relative to world prices. Indeed, research has shown that variability of their domestic prices is lower than that of international prices.

This conclusion is related to the earlier discussion of the magnitudes of price transmission elasticities in developing countries. It is also a useful reminder that rates of protection/taxation of tradables are not independent of the level and variability of border prices. If a country maintains a low but relatively stable price for an export crop, its rate of taxation on the crop's producers will rise and fall inversely with the international price. Similarly, if a country maintains a low, stable price for a staple food in which it is deficit, its implicit taxation of domestic producers will be higher or lower as the world price rises or falls.

Valdés reviewed the effects of government pricing interventions on output, consumption, trade, government revenue and expenditure, and net economic welfare. He contrasted the differences in sector-specific price policies, which can be large items in government budgets, with the indirect macroeconomic and exchange-rate policies that yield no revenue and require no budgetary outlays. He reported that comparative analysis had revealed net revenue gains to governments on average, but that these gains fell over the period studied in which world prices of export crops declined. In the countries with high food subsidies and low prices to producers, often offset, in part, by input subsidies, net budgetary costs can be high and unsustainable in the face of government deficit-reduction policies.

By design or default, government direct and indirect market intervention policies serve to transfer income from agriculture to other sectors of the economy and influence income distribution both between the urban and rural sectors and within the rural sector itself. Valdés suggested that the transfer of resources out of agriculture should be compared to offsetting government investments in agricultural technology, resources, and support services. This nonprice approach to generating an agricultural surplus is examined more thoroughly in Roe's discussion of the Valdés presentation.

Notes

1. See Anne O. Krueger, Maurice Schiff, and Alberto Valdés. *The Political Economy of Agricultural Pricing Policies.* 3 volumes. New York: Oxford University Press. (forthcoming)

AGRICULTURAL INCENTIVES IN DEVELOPING COUNTRIES: MEASURING THE EFFECT OF SECTORAL AND ECONOMYWIDE POLICIES*

Anne O. Krueger, Maurice Schiff, and Alberto Valdés

There are four well-known stylized facts about the agricultural policies of developing countries, the interactions among which have not been fully appreciated. First, most developing countries have attempted to encourage the growth of industry through policies of import substitution and protection against imports competing with domestic production. Second, overvalued exchange rates have often been maintained through exchange-control regimes and import licensing mechanisms even more restrictive than those that would have been adopted in connection with import substitution. Third, many developing countries have attempted to suppress producer prices of agricultural commodities through government procurement policies (especially agricultural marketing boards), export taxation, and/or export quotas. Fourth, some governments have attempted to offset part or all of the disincentive effect on producers by subsidizing input prices and investing in irrigation and other capital inputs.

Suppression of producer prices has been extensively studied but there have been few attempts to estimate the combined impact of those direct policies and the three other sets of government policies. While international trade theorists have long known that protection of some activities discriminates against the remainder, that knowledge has not been transformed into usable estimates of the extent of total discrimination against agriculture.

Those few studies that have attempted to measure indirect effects on agricultural prices and incentives have used widely varying methodologies (for example, on Chile, Valdés 1973; on the United States, Schuh 1979; on Brazil, Oliveira 1981; on Colombia, Garcia 1981; on Argentina, Cavallo and Mundalak 1982; on Nigeria, Oyejide 1986; and on the Philippines, Bautista 1987). This has precluded systematic comparative analysis of the effects of differing degrees of discrimination against agriculture.

* *Reprinted by permission.* The World Bank Economic Review. *2,3:255-71. 1988.*

In this article we provide such estimates for 18 developing countries derived as the initial results of the World Bank's research project on the political economy of agricultural pricing policies. The first section gives information about the project and the way the estimates were made. In the second section we estimate the direct, indirect, and total intervention-affecting incentives for agricultural output and the impact of intervention on price variability. We also present some preliminary analyses of the findings. The third section then draws some conclusions.

The Project on the Political Economy of Agricultural Pricing Policies

Although systematic quantification of the extent of discrimination against agriculture has been lacking, observers of the development process have long been aware that developing countries directly intervene systematically and extensively in pricing of agricultural commodities. Newspaper readers will recall riots in the Arab Republic of Egypt after President Sadat attempted to raise the prices of some key foods, riots in Zambia after prices of maize meal—a commodity consumed primarily by the urban middle and upper income groups—were increased to reduce budgetary losses, and other failed attempts at consumer price policy reform, including those in Morocco, Poland, and Tunisia. While headlines have directed attention to increased urban food prices, their counterpart is almost always suppressed producer prices, as government fiscal constraints usually preclude budgetary financing of these subsidies.

The comparative project on the political economy of agricultural pricing policies was undertaken to provide a detailed history of pricing policies, to measure the degree of intervention affecting agriculture, and to analyze the reasons for these and their effects on output, consumption, trade, the budget, intersectoral transfers, and income distribution. Comparability across countries was achieved by applying a common methodology in all the country studies and by bringing together researchers for the individual studies to compare and assess their results during the course of the project.[1]

We focus here on the magnitude of the impact of direct and indirect policies on agricultural prices and outline below the process by which these estimates were derived. For each country, major export- and import-competing agricultural commodities, including both food and nonfood products, were selected on the basis of their importance and the representativeness of the policies adopted toward them relative to agriculture as a whole. In most countries, concentration was on four to six commodities, and that coverage typically represented about one-half to three-quarters of net agricultural product.

Country researchers then obtained estimates of the commodities' domestic producer, consumer, and border prices, adjusted for transport costs to or from producer and consumer locations, storage costs, quality differences, and other elements of the marketing margins. In the case of wheat in Chile, for instance, adjustments were made for customs duties and customs agent fees, transportation costs from the main port of entry to the mills, unloading costs and losses in transit, the annual average quality difference between domestic and imported wheat, and for seasonality (storage). The annual average producer price at the mill is the price received by farmers at harvest time (January). Imports take place six to nine months later, so that the price of imported wheat at the mill was adjusted for storage costs to ensure comparability over time as well as across locations. This adjustment for storage costs reduced the price differential between the import price at the mill (after adjusting for other marketing margin factors) and the domestic price from about 20 percent to about 4 percent on average.

There were few countries in which complexities did not arise in obtaining reliable price estimates, and painstaking research was required to develop those that were used. In Ghana, for instance, in some years use of border prices adjusted for transport costs yielded negative estimates of producer prices for some commodities. In many of the countries studied, governments had a monopsony on purchase and/or distribution of some or all agricultural commodities through state marketing boards, making it difficult to estimate "normal" marketing margins. Marketing boards' costs constituted 50 percent or more of the border price of exportables in some countries, and producer prices represented an even smaller fraction of the border price. Some marketing boards lost money despite low producer prices because their sales to consumers were at or below purchase prices. In some instances, it was also important to account for the extent to which official prices were those that actually prevailed in the majority of transactions. Time series of producer prices were often developed from government files and previously inaccessible sources, and estimates of black market prices had to be weighted by their probable share of the total crop to yield accurate overall price assessments in those cases where parallel markets exist. The resulting time series of actual consumer and producer prices and costs of purchased inputs represent a major contribution of the project in its own right.

For all countries, the impact is measured relative to what prices would have been had there been no interventions and a free trade regime. For all tradable commodities, the reference prices used were the border prices that would have prevailed under an intervention-free regime.

Authors were also requested to estimate effective rates of protection (ERPs). Due mainly to data inadequacy, however, the country and commodity coverage of the ERP estimates turned out to be considerably more limited and less comparable across countries than for nominal rate estimates. For this reason ERPs are not reported in this article. Future work (in Krueger, Schiff, and Valdés [hereafter KSV], forthcoming, vol. 3) will provide further analyses of ERPs, although initial inspection suggests that most input subsidies were inframarginal and that the ratios of value added to output did not vary widely across crops within countries. The implications of the removal of price interventions for the allocation of resources among goods and sectors are also beyond the scope of this article but are examined in KSV.[2]

Estimation of the effects of interventions aimed directly at agricultural inputs or outputs was relatively simple contrasted with the procedures needed to estimate indirect effects. Our analysis focuses on the real exchange rate and on the tax on agricultural production implicit in protection to industry. The economic rationale behind the estimates is discussed below; an abbreviated description of the procedures used to obtain these estimates is given in the appendix.

First, the authors had to estimate the real exchange rate that would have kept the current account at a sustainable level—taking into account normal capital flows—if all quantitative and tariff protection against imports and interventions affecting exports had been removed. This involved estimation of the equivalent tariff of import protection and of foreign exchange demand and supply elasticities and comparison with the actual real exchange rate to estimate the amount of real exchange rate change needed to yield the sustainable current account level.[3]

Taking the border price for each commodity at the equilibrium exchange rate gave an estimate of the border price that would have prevailed in the absence of interventions. Doing the same for purchased inputs, given their shares in domestic prices, yielded estimates of what value-added would have been in the absence of these same policies. Finally, measuring the nonagricultural price index at the equilibrium exchange rate and in the absence of trade interventions (by adjusting the tradable part of the price index) gave an estimate of the value of that price index in the absence of interventions.[4]

Using these estimates, we obtained the indirect effect of the interventions on the price (and value added) of agricultural products (relative to the nonagricultural price index).

There are three major elements in our calculations of the indirect effects: first, the depreciation of the real exchange rate required for the elimination of the nonsustainable part of the current account deficit; second, the depreciation of the real exchange rate due to the removal of trade interventions; and third, the increase in the price of agricultural tradable products relative to nonagricultural tradables due to the removal of trade policy interventions, which mainly protect industry. The first two are changes of the price of tradables relative to nontradables; the third is a change of prices within the tradables category.

Identification of a "sustainable" current account balance is necessarily judgmental. Country authors used their knowledge of normal flows of aid and private investment to estimate what a "normal" current account balance would be, and they used the difference between that and the actual imbalance to estimate the nonsustainable portion of the current account deficit. Calculations of the indirect effects of policies on incentives are less sensitive to the choice of elasticity values for supply and demand for foreign exchange and to the choice of the sustainable level of current account deficit than they might at first appear.

Empirically, industrial protection has a greater impact on incentives for agriculture than does the current account imbalance. In many cases, industrial protection is so high that it is the last effect, the decline in prices of nonagricultural tradables relative to agricultural prices, that dominates the indirect effects. However, industrial protection acts both through the real exchange rate and through relative prices of industrial tradables to agricultural products, so that when the real exchange rate effect of protection is taken into account, the total negative impact of industrial protection on agriculture is even larger. Thus neither the level of the sustainable current account deficit nor the foreign exchange elasticities, which both act only through the real exchange rate, are as critical in the calculations of indirect effects as would otherwise be the case. Moreover, the indirect effect turned out to be less sensitive to the selected value of the elasticities than expected. This is due to the fact that a proportional change in the elasticities of demand and supply for foreign exchange only affects the first component of the indirect effect but has no effect on the second or third component, as reflected in Equations 7 and 8 in Appendix 5.A.

For those countries for which reliable estimates of supply and demand elasticities for foreign exchange were not available, we suggested that the authors use elasticity values of one for supply and two (in absolute value) for demand on the basis of estimated elasticities from other studies. Authors who had evidence to the contrary used it, and also examined the sensitivity of their estimates to the trade elasticities.

It is well known that the "elasticities" approach to analysis of exchange rate changes was fundamentally modified by the recognition that a change in expenditure relative to income would be required for any change in the current account. Our use of elasticities here is justified by two considerations: (1) the counterfactual "experiment" of an altered real exchange rate is undertaken to investigate relative price changes and responses to them; and (2) although underlying macroeconomic policies would clearly have to be altered in order for the real exchange rate to change, it is unlikely that the particular choice of macro policies would significantly affect the equilibrium real exchange rate solution.[5]

In the case of Ghana, calculation of the equilibrium real exchange rate involved an additional complication. The deprecia-tion of the real exchange rate to its equilibrium value, for a given world price of cocoa, would lead to an increase in Ghana's cocoa output. Ghana's output is such a large part of world cocoa trade, however, that this supply rise would result in a reduction in cocoa's world price. The equilibrium real exchange rate was therefore determined in a simultaneous system where the world price of cocoa is determined endogenously as a function of Ghana's real exchange rate. This methodology resulted in a higher equilibrium real exchange rate than the one based on calculations that ignore the impact of Ghana's real exchange rate on the world price of cocoa.

The total effect of the interventions was taken to be simply the sum of the direct and indirect effects (with some adjustment described in Appendix 5.A). As an example, in Argentina agriculture is taxed first through export taxes (a direct effect), which reduce agricultural prices, and second through import protection (an indirect effect), which raises the prices of import substitutes. The net impact of Argentina's trade policies on the real exchange rate was found to be small because while export taxes lead to a depreciation of the real exchange rate, import protection leads to real exchange rate appreciation. However, the degree of real exchange rate overvaluation due to Argentina's monetary and fiscal policies was at times extremely high and provided an additional burden on the agricultural sector. The sum of the (indirect) impact of industrial protection and real exchange rate overvaluation, and of (direct) export taxation, on agricultural incentives in Argentina, for example, has been substantial during the period examined.

Degrees of Intervention

Table 5.1 presents estimates of the degree of nominal direct, indirect, and total intervention in representative export crops for the 18 countries. The numbers on direct intervention provide an estimate of the percentage by which domestic producer prices diverged from those that would have prevailed in a well-functioning market at free trade (given the actual exchange rate and degree of industrial protection). The measure is equivalent to the rate of nominal protection.[6]

Although government policies differ significantly among individual agricultural commodities, the authors of each country study analyzed between three and nine commodities. We selected one that was deemed fairly representative of government policy toward agricultural exportables for reporting in Table 5.1. As can be seen, most countries adopted direct policies that resulted in the equivalent of export taxes. Exceptions were Ghana (where a highly overvalued exchange rate resulted in such strong disincentives that some compensatory action was politically essential), Portugal, Zambia, Chile, and Turkey in 1975-79. For the latter two countries, the nominal protection accorded grapes and tobacco was less than 2 percent—very small indeed—and for Turkey direct protection turned negative in 1980-84. The suppression of producer prices in 1975-79 equaled or exceeded 25 percent in Argentina, Cote d'Ivoire, Egypt, Malaysia, Sri Lanka, and Thailand, and for the years 1980-84, all countries except Ghana and Portugal had negative direct protection of agricultural products.

The indirect effects measured include both the effect of trade and macroeconomic policies on the real exchange rate and the extent of protection afforded to nonagricultural commodities. The impact of indirect interventions on producer incentives was even stronger than the direct ones for Argentina, Brazil, Chile, Colombia, Cote d'Ivoire, the Dominican Republic, Ghana, Pakistan, the Philippines, Sri Lanka, Thailand, Turkey, and Zambia for 1975-79, 1980-84, or both periods. As already noted, indirect negative protection in Ghana was so large that direct agricultural policy provided something of an offset. On average, the indirect effects on incentives to

Table 5.1. Direct, indirect, and total nominal protection rates for exported products (percent)

Country	Product	1975-79			1980-84		
		Direct	Indirect	Total	Direct	Indirect	Total
Argentina	Wheat	-25.00	-16.00	-41.00	-13.00	-37.00	-50.00
Brazil	Soybeans	-8.00	-32.00	-40.00	-10.00	-14.00	-33.00
Chile	Grapes	1.00	22.00	23.00	0.00	-7.00	-7.00
Colombia	Coffee	-7.00	-25.00	-32.00	-5.00	-34.00	-39.00
Cote d'Ivoire	Cocoa	-31.00	-33.00	-64.00	-21.00	-26.00	-47.00
Dominican Rep.	Coffee	-15.00	-18.00	-33.00	-32.00	-19.00	-51.00
Egypt	Cotton	-36.00	-18.00	-54.00	-22.00	-14.00	-36.00
Ghana	Cocoa	26.00	-66.00	-40.00	34.00	-89.00	-55.00
Malaysia	Rubber	-25.00	-4.00	-29.00	-18.00	-10.00	-28.00
Pakistan	Cotton	-12.00	-48.00	-60.00	-7.00	-35.00	-42.00
Philippines	Copra	-11.00	-27.00	-38.00	-26.00	-28.00	-54.00
Portugal	Tomatoes	17.00	-5.00	12.00	17.00	-13.00	4.00
Sri Lanka	Rubber	-29.00	-35.00	-64.00	-31.00	-31.00	-62.00
Thailand	Rice	-28.00	-15.00	-43.00	-15.00	-19.00	-34.00
Turkey	Tobacco	2.00	-40.00	-38.00	-28.00	-35.00	-63.00
Zambia	Tobacco	1.00	-42.00	-41.00	7.00	-57.00	-50.00
Average		-11.00	25.00	-36.00	-11.00	29.00	-40.00

SOURCE: Krueger, Schiff, and Valdés, *The World Bank Economic Review,* 2,3:255-71. 1988.

Note: Korea and Morocco are not included because all main agricultural products are imported.

The direct nominal protection rate is defined as the difference between the total and the indirect nominal protection rates, or equivalently, as the ratio of (1) the difference between the relative producer price and the relative border price, and (2) relative border price measured at the adjusted border price measured at the equilibrium exchange rate and in the absence of all trade policies.

agricultural producers were two-and-one-half times as large as the direct effects.

For most countries, the effective taxation by indirect policies exacerbated the negative direct protection, often resulting in extremely large total negative protection equivalents. As can be seen, in many cases the magnitude of negative protection or effective taxation was quite large. In the Cote d'Ivoire, for example, it is estimated that for 1975-79 cocoa producers received about one-third the price they would have received under a free-trade regime at realistic exchange rates with no direct intervention, and about one-half in 1980-84. Sri Lankan rubber producers fared as poorly in 1975-79 and worse in 1980-84. Producer prices were one-half or less of the nonintervention price in Cote d'Ivoire, Egypt, Pakistan, and Sri Lanka in 1975-79 and in Argentina, the Dominican Republic, Ghana, the Philippines, Sri Lanka, Turkey, and Zambia in 1980-84.

Overall, a simple unweighted average rate of total nominal protection for the 16 countries covered in Table 5.1 was a −36 percent in 1975-79 and a −40 percent in 1980-84. Although the average rose somewhat, the more notable finding is the degree to which total discrimination against agriculture remained essentially constant over the two periods. Although there were sizable variations for individual countries, there is some suggestion that unfavorable indirect changes are to some extent compensated by favorable direct changes (that is, as Argentina's exchange rate became less realistic the extent of direct discrimination against wheat producers fell).

It has long been recognized that there was discrimination against agriculture. What Table 5.1 shows is the degree. The negative protection accorded to producers of agricultural export commodities was a significant factor in depressing export earnings in many countries. Even those countries regarded as successful exporters of agricultural commodities such as Thailand and Malaysia adhered to this pattern. Of the 18 countries covered in the project, only Chile in 1975-79 and Portugal over both periods maintained regimes providing positive total protection to producers. The dominant pattern has been one of systematic and sizable discrimination.

Although developing countries have more agricultural export- than import-competing products, there are a significant number of the latter. Table 5.2 presents data, comparable to those in Table 5.1, for representative import-competing crops.

Several findings are noteworthy. First and foremost, in contrast with the negative direct protection accorded to exportable products, the countries covered here, with few exceptions, provided positive direct protection to import-competing crops. Indeed, the degree of discrimination against exportables and in favor of import-competing crops is remarkable: contrast Malaysian rice, receiving the equivalent of 38 and 68 percent nominal protection over the two time periods, with Malaysian rubber, taxed at the equivalent of 25 and 18 percent. Direct pricing policy led to an increase in the relative price of rice of 84 percent in 1975-79 and 105 percent in 1980-84 (relative to rubber).

However, by definition, those policies that indirectly affect agriculture have the same net impact on import-competing as on exportable commodities, and the listing of indirect protection in Table 5.2 is therefore identical to that in the equivalent columns of Table 5.1. Taking the effects of both direct and indirect policies into account, the effects of direct price policy were in many cases reversed. In Colombia, Cote d'Ivoire, the Philippines, Sri Lanka, and Turkey (in 1975-79), positive direct effects were more than offset by negative indirect effects.

In this regard, one remarkable developing country is Korea, where direct protection of agricultural commodities (there are no exportables) is very high and the impact of indirect policies is not large by comparison. There, total protection for domestic rice production has remained quite stable at about 73 percent over the periods covered here, despite the strong Korean protection, and sizable total protection to rice in Malaysia, the average level of total protection for all the import-competing commodities covered here was negative, although not large, about −5 percent in both periods. If the numbers for Korea and Malaysia are excluded, the average negative total protection for import-competing crops changes to −15 and −18 percent in the two time periods.

These data, and others in the country studies, raise a large number of questions, one of which concerns the reasons for the policies pursued. This becomes an even more pressing question

Table 5.2. Direct, indirect, and total nominal protection rates for imported food products (percent)

Country	Product	1975-79			1980-84		
		Direct	Indirect	Total	Direct	Indirect	Total
Brazil	Wheat	35.00	-32.00	3.00	-7.00	-14.00	-21.00
Chile	Wheat	11.00	22.00	33.00	9.00	-7.00	2.00
Colombia	Wheat	5.00	-25.00	-20.00	9.00	-34.00	-25.00
Cote d'Ivoire	Rice	8.00	-33.00	-25.00	16.00	-26.00	-10.00
Dominican Rep.	Rice	20.00	-18.00	2.00	26.00	-19.00	7.00
Egypt	Wheat	-19.00	-18.00	-37.00	-21.00	-14.00	-35.00
Ghana	Rice	79.00	-66.00	13.00	118.00	-89.00	29.00
Korea	Rice	91.00	-18.00	73.00	86.00	-12.00	74.00
Malaysia	Rice	38.00	-4.00	34.00	68.00	-10.00	58.00
Morocco	Wheat	-7.00	-12.00	-19.00	-	-8.00	-8.00
Pakistan	Wheat	-13.00	-48.00	-61.00	-21.00	-35.00	-56.00
Philippines	Corn	18.00	-27.00	-9.00	26.00	-28.00	-2.00
Portugal	Wheat	15.00	-5.00	10.00	26.00	-13.00	13.00
Sri Lanka	Rice	18.00	-35.00	-17.00	11.00	-31.00	-20.00
Turkey	Wheat	28.00	-40.00	-12.00	-3.00	-35.00	-38.00
Zambia	Corn	-13.00	-42.00	-55.00	-9.00	-57.00	-66.00
Average		20.00	-25.00	-5.00	21.00	-27.00	-6.00

SOURCE: Krueger, Schiff, and Valdés, *The World Bank Economic Review*, 2,3:255-71. 1988.

Note: Argentina and Thailand are not included because their main food products are exported.

The direct nominal protection rate is defined as the difference between the total and the indirect nominal protection rates, or equivalently, as the ratio of (l) the difference between the relative producer price and the relative border price, and (2) relative the adjusted border price measured at the equilibrium exchange rate and in the absence of all trade policies.

when it can be readily demonstrated (as in Table 5.2) that agricultural producers often have larger interests in macroeconomic policies than they do in agricultural pricing policies, yet their representatives usually concentrate on the latter.

A preliminary and partial answer can be given here. In almost all countries, one of the stated reasons for intervention in agricultural markets has been the perceived instability of the international market for agricultural commodities. To test the accuracy of this rationale, authors calculated the ratio of the standard deviation of the real producer price (deflated by the price index of the nonagricultural sector) to that of the real border price (at the official exchange rates) for a variety of crops. The results, for the same commodities as were represented in Tables 5.1 and 5.2, are presented in Table 5.3. A number less than one indicates that real domestic producer price fluctuations (taking into account only direct intervention) were smaller than real border price fluctuations. As can be seen, there are only two importable and three exportable commodities for which internal prices were more volatile than border prices, and on average direct price policies reduced producer price variability by 27 percent for exports and 31 percent for imports.[7]

The standard deviation of the producer price of wheat in Egypt, for example, was only 30 percent of what it would have been had the border price been passed on to producers, while that in Pakistan was 17 percent. Even for export crops, such as Thai rice, producers experienced considerably less fluctuation in real prices than they might have, given the prevailing exchange rates and protection to domestic industry.

On average, the price stabilization as measured by standard deviation is slightly larger for importables than for exportables. However, exportables generally are taxed while importables are protected, so that the producer price is lower than the border price for exportables and higher for importables. Thus it follows that when measured by the coefficient of variation, which divides the standard deviation by the mean, the reduction in price variability is significantly larger for importables (42 percent) than for exportables (18 percent). This should not come as a surprise because all importables considered are staples so that there is pressure for price

Table 5.3. Ratio of standard deviations of deflated producer and
deflated border prices, 1960-84

Country	Exports Crop	Ratio	Imports Crop	Ratio
Argentina	Wheat	0.37	None	-
Brazil	Soybeans	0.80	Wheat	0.41
Chile	Grapes	0.94	Wheat	0.73
Colombia	Coffee	0.87	Wheat	0.93
Cote d'Ivoire	Cocoa	0.42	Rice	1.20
Dominican Republic	Coffee	0.84	Rice	0.66
Egypt	Cotton	0.42	Wheat	0.30
Korea	None	-	Rice	1.58
Malaysia	Rubber	1.02	Rice	0.47
Morocco	None	-	Wheat	0.63
Pakistan	Cotton	0.62	Wheat	0.17
Philippines	Copra	0.94	Corn	0.27
Portugal	Tomato	1.13	Wheat	1.00
Sri Lanka	Rubber	0.44	Rice	0.65
Thailand	Rice	0.26	None	-
Turkey	Tobacco	1.16	Wheat	0.56
Zambia	Tobacco	0.83	Corn	0.75
Average		0.73		0.69

SOURCE: Krueger, Schiff, and Valdés, *The World Bank Economic Review*, 2,3:255-71. 1988.

Note: The border price is measured at the official exchange rate. The deflator is the price index of the nonagricultural sector.

stability not only from producers (as in the case of the exportables), but also from consumers because of the impact of food price variability on real wages.

In the face of uncertain and volatile international markets for agricultural commodities, governments typically have several policy options to deal with the price risk that consumers and farmers may face. Price schemes can be coordinated with supplementary payments (or supplementary taxes) and other risk-diffusing institutions. However, such institutions do not exist or are not easily accessible to producers in most developing countries, and their development is a slow process. Governments therefore typically resort to border-type interventions. The fact that some price stabilization was achieved in the individual countries studied does not prove that the interventions as under-taken were a first-best way of doing it. That is a topic beyond the scope of this article.

Summary and Conclusions

The above discussion, which deals only with the measurement of price intervention, has nonetheless generated some striking insights about the impact of economywide and direct agricultural policies on agricultural prices. Perhaps the most important result that emerges clearly from our findings is the fact that the impact of the indirect, economywide interventions generally dominates the direct effect, whether the direct effect is positive or negative. If the indirect effects of economywide policies on agricultural prices are ignored, on average imported food products were protected (at a rate of approximately 20 percent) and exports were taxed (at close to 11 percent). The results for total price interventions, however, show that both activities were taxed, at a rate of approximately 7 percent for imported and 35 to 40 percent for exported agricultural products.

Furthermore, although direct policies protected imported food at the official exchange rate, protection was significantly less than for nonagricultural tradables. Rates of protection to industry of substantially more than 20 percent have been found, both in past studies and in our calculations. Reinforcing the taxation of agricultural importables is the overvaluation of the currency, which lowers the price of tradables relative to nontradable goods.

On the basis of the data presented, two findings about sector-specific agricultural interventions seem most significant. First, a particularly marked contrast emerges between the direct policies adopted toward imported food products and exported crops: food imports are subsidized on average while exports are taxed. Second, contrary to expectations and to the treatment of exportables products, direct policies have provided protection to the production of food in about 70 percent of the countries studied.

Why does the difference in treatment of exports and imports occur? The individual country studies suggest several reasons. If a country desires self-sufficiency in the production of staples, it may adopt tariffs to promote domestic production, eliminating that protection once self-sufficiency is attained and even taxing the product when it is exported. A dearth of easily administered and enforced taxes in a developing country may also focus government attention on exports as a relatively feasible source of revenue. The taxation of food exports, such as wheat and beef in Argentina and rice in Thailand, not only generates revenues but also encourages domestic sales at lower prices, reducing the cost of food and subsidizing consumers. Direct subsidy of the production of an imported food, however, requires fiscal expenditures, while tariffs provide revenue and promote domestic production. This may also help explain why importable food products tend to be protected rather than taxed.

Because direct policies protect food crops, maintenance of low food prices to keep money wages low does not seem to operate through direct pricing policies. Rather, it results mainly from overvaluation of the exchange rate, one of the indirect policies explored comprehensively in the study.

Our studies also indicate that the operation of direct food pricing policies has resulted in greater price stability, with a larger reduction in price variation for importables than exportables. The relative cost of that stability is another important question suggested for future research.

This article has reported results for only a subset of the products and periods included in the country studies. Future analysis will delve into additional aspects of price policies and the impact of interventions on producer and consumer prices, the effects of those price changes, and the political economy of agricultural price policy.

Many issues of political economy emerge from the analysis and have a bearing on the formulation of direct agricultural policies that are not explored here: the political strength of urban workers and industry, the political imperatives of agricultural marketing boards, fiscal pressures and the fact that price policies, once in place, have tended to have a life of their own with results often quite different from those intended. In addition, given that the impact of exchange rate and industrial protection policies was greater than that of agricultural price policies, why did agricultural producers' groups continue to focus their political attentions on issues pertaining to agricultural pricing, with little or no attention to exchange rate policies and other issues of greater importance?

Hypotheses about these and other phenomena will be set forth and examined in KSV. At this stage, it is evident that one contributing factor has been a failure to comprehend the implications of macroeconomic policy for agriculture. Whereas vested interests, pressures on fiscal and external accounts, and other factors all influence agricultural pricing policies, knowledge is also a contributing factor. As such, further analysis at the country and comparative level, by improving knowledge, may benefit the future development of the political economy of agricultural pricing.

Notes

1.   Subject countries are Argentina (A. Sturzenegger and W. Otrera), Brazil (J. L. Carvahlho and A. Brandao), Chile (H. Hurtado, E. Muchnik, and A. Valdés), Colombia (J. Garcia and G. Montes), Cote d'Ivoire, (A. Arsain, A. M'Bet, and S. Ehouman), Dominican Republic (T. Roe and D. Greene), Egypt (J. J. Dethier), Ghana (D. Stryker), Republic of Korea (P. Y. Moon and B. S. Kang), Malaysia (G. Jenkins), Morocco (H. Tuluy and L. Salinger), Pakistan (N. Hamid and I. Nabi), the Philippines (P. Intal and J. Power), Portugal (F. Avillez, T. Finan, and T. Josling), Sri Lanka (S. Bhalla), Thailand (A. Siamwalla and S. Setboonsarn), Turkey (H. Olgun and H. Kasnakoglu), and Zambia (D. Jansen). Summaries of country studies are forthcoming in two volumes of Krueger, Schiff, and Valdés; Chapter 1 and the appendixes of volumes 1 and 2 will provide information on the concepts and methods used to ensure comparability across countries, and a third (synthesis) volume will cover quantification of the effects on incentives, analysis of the influence of the altered incentives on sectoral and intersectoral performance and characteristics, and a review of the political economy of agricultural price policy and its evolution over time.

2. Several authors also calculated the deviations from the domestic price that would have prevailed if optimal export taxes were applied. These results are not presented here, and are forthcoming in KSV.

3. In three of the 18 countries, the authors used alternative procedures due to data limitations or other circumstance particular to their country.

4. For the estimation of the indirect effect on the price of agricultural products relative to a price index of the nonagricultural sector, there is no need to know whether the change in the real exchange rate occurs through the nominal exchange rate or through the price of nontradeables. Estimation of the change in the real exchange rate is sufficient (see Appendix 5.A).

5. For an analysis of the conditions under which the elasticity approach holds, see Dornbusch (1975).

6. The direct nominal protection rate measures the proportional difference between the domestic producer price (relative to nonagricultural prices) and the border price (after adjustment for transport, storage, and other costs and quality differentials) measured at the official exchange rate. See Appendix 5.A for further details.

7. For Korean rice, prices were much more stable than world prices, but the large standard deviation is due to a few large price changes over the period analyzed.

APPENDIX 5.A:
MEASURES OF INTERVENTION AND
EQUILIBRIUM REAL EXCHANGE RATE

We first present the various measures of intervention, and then derive the equilibrium real exchange rate.

Measures of Intervention

Let P_i be the domestic producer price of a tradable agricultural product i, let $P_i' = P_i^B E_o$ be the border price P_i^B of product i evaluated at the official nominal exchange rate E_o (and adjusted for transport, storage, and other costs, and quality difference), let $P_i^* = P_i^B E^* = P_i' E^* / E_o$ be the border price P_i^B evaluated at the equilibrium nominal exchange rate E^* (and adjusted for transport, storage, and other costs), let $P_{NA} = \alpha P_{NAT} + (1 - \alpha) P_{NAH}$ be the nonagricultural sector price index which consists of a tradable share, α, with price P_{NAT} and of a nontradable home share, $1 - \alpha$, with price P_{NAH}, and let $P_{NA}^* = \alpha P_{NAT} E^* / (1 + t_{NA}) E_o + (1 - \alpha) P_{NAH}$. P_{NA} is the nonagricultural price index where the price index of the tradable part is evaluated at E^* and in the absence of trade policy, t_{NA}, affecting nonagricultural tradables.

Then the direct normal protection rate, which measures the proportional differences between the relative domestic price and the relative border price of agricultural tradables, is

(1) $$NPR_D \equiv \frac{P_i / P_{NA}}{P_i' / P_{NA}} - 1 = P_i / P_i' - 1,$$

and measures the effect of price controls, export taxes or quotas, and the other policies affecting P_i. The indirect nominal protection rate which measures the effect of the exchange rate E_o differing from E^*, and the effect of trade policy on P_{NAT}, is

(2) $$NPR_I \equiv \frac{P_i' / P_{NA}}{P_i^* / P_{NA}^*} - 1 = \frac{P' / P_{NA}}{(E^* / E_o) P_i' / P_{NA}^*} - 1 = P_{NA}^* E_o / P_{NA} E^* - 1.$$

NPR_I is the same for all tradable products since P_i does not appear in equation 2. Finally, the total nominal protection rate is

(3)
$$NPR_T \equiv \frac{P_i / P_{NA}}{P_i^* / P_{NA}^*} - 1.$$

$NPR_D + NPR_I \neq NPR_T$ because the denominator of NPR_D differs from that of NPR_I and NPR_T. To make the three measurements comparable, we define another direct protection rate

(4)
$$npr_D = \frac{P_i / P_{NA} - P_i' / P_{NA}}{P_i^* / P_{NA}^*}$$

which measures the impact $(P_i / P_{NA} - P_i' P_{NA})$ of the direct policies as a percent of P_i^*/P_{NA}^*, the relative price which would prevail in the absence of all interventions and with $E = E^*$. Then $npr_D + NPR_I = NPR_T$. These measures are the basis of the levels of nominal protection presented in tables 1 and 2.

The calculations of NPR_I and NPR_T include adjustments in the nominal exchange rate. As is shown below, these adjustments are also relevant when the real exchange rate is used.

The Equilibrium Exchange Rate

We assume an economy with three goods: an exportable, X, an importable, M, and a nontradable, H, with prices P_X, P_M, and P_H, respectively.[1] We also assume a domestic and a foreign currency with relative price E, the nominal exchange rate, defined as the domestic currency price of foreign currency. We define the real exchange rate, e, as the ratio of the nominal exchange rate and the price of the nontradable H, that is,

(5)
$$e \equiv E/P_H.$$

We do not consider the foreign prices of X and M in the definition of e because in the case of a small country in the world market, these prices are given and are not affected by policy changes.

---

[1] *Our model of real exchange rate determination is based on a variant of the "elasticity approach." That approach (as described in, say, Magee 1973) provides a framework for examining the impact of changes in the* nominal *exchange rate.*

We are interested in the change in e which would result from the elimination of interventions and of the unsustainable part of the current account deficit. For those countries where removal of policy interventions affects world prices (for example, Ghana), that effect was taken into account.

We assume that both the demand for and supply of foreign exchange, Q_D and Q_S, are functions of the real exchange rate, with elasticities $-\varepsilon_D$ and ε_S, respectively.

Assume that the unsustainable part of the deficit in the current account is ΔQ_o. Then it can be shown that the real exchange rate needed to eliminate ΔQ_o is

$$(6) \qquad e_i = \left[\frac{\Delta Q_o}{\epsilon_s Q_s + \epsilon_D Q_D} + 1 \right] e_o$$

where e_o is the prevailing real exchange rate and $\varepsilon_S Q_S + \varepsilon_D Q_D$ measures the reduction in excess demand for foreign exchange (the deficit) due to a one unit increase in the real exchange rate.

Assume now that the tariff equivalent of protection on the importable good is t_M and the export tax on the exportable good is t_X. Eliminating both measures was found to lead to an increase, ΔQ_1, in excess demand for foreign exchange in the eighteen countries, where

$$(7) \qquad \Delta Q_1 = \frac{t_m}{1 + t_M} Q_D \epsilon_D - \frac{t_x}{1 - t_x} Q_s \epsilon_s.$$

Define the real exchange rate where $\Delta Q_o = t_X = t_M = 0$ as the equilibrium real exchange rate e^*. Then

$$(8) \qquad e^* = \left[\frac{\Delta Q_o + \Delta Q_1}{\epsilon_S Q_S + \epsilon_D Q_D} + 1 \right] e_o.$$

The solution of the model of exchange rate determination is the equilibrium real exchange rate e^* rather than the nominal rate E^* used in NPR_I and NPR_T above, where $e \equiv E/P_H$. The nontradable sector, *H,* is assumed to consist (almost) entirely of nonagricultural goods and services, *NAH,* and therefore $e = E/P_{NAH}$. Assume t_x measures the impact on p_i of a price control, an export tax, or an import subsidy, and $t_x \lesseqgtr 0$.

Then:

$$\frac{P_i}{P_{NA}} = \frac{P_i^B E_o (1 - t_x)}{\alpha P_{NAT} + (1 - \alpha) P_{NAH}} = \frac{P_i^B E_o (1 - t_x)}{\alpha P_{NAT}^B E_o (1 + t_{NA}) + (1 - \alpha) P_{NAH}}$$

$$= \frac{P_i^B (E_o / P_{NAH}) (1 - t_x)}{\alpha P_{NAH}^B (E_o / P_{NAH}) (1 + t_{NA}) + (1 - \alpha)},$$

or

$$(9) \qquad \frac{P_i}{P_{NA}} = \frac{P_i^B e_o (1 - t_x)}{\alpha P_{NAT}^B (1 + t_{NA}) e_o + (1 - \alpha)}.$$

Then,

$$(10) \qquad \frac{P_i^I}{P_{NA}} = \frac{P_i^B e_o}{\alpha P_{NAT}^B (1 + t_{NA}) e_o + (1 - \alpha)},$$

and

$$(11) \qquad \frac{P_i^*}{P_{NA}^*} = \frac{P_i^B e^*}{\alpha P_{NAT}^B e^* + (1 - \alpha)}.$$

As can be seen from equations 9, 10, and 11, to derive NPR_I and NPR_T it is sufficient to know e_0 and obtain e^*, and information on E^* and P^*_{NAH} is not needed.

References

Bautista, Romeo M. 1987. "Production Incentives in Philippine Agriculture: Effects of Trade and Exchange Rate Policies." International Food Policy Research Institute Research Report 59 (May).

Cavallo, D., and Y. Mundlak. 1982. "Agriculture and Economic Growth in an Open Economy: The Case of Argentina." International Food Policy Research Institute Research Report 36 (December).

Dornbusch, Rudiger. 1975. "Exchange Rates and Fiscal Policy in a Popular Model of International Trade." *American Economic Review* 65, no. 5 (December): 859-71.

Garcia Garcia, Jorge. 1981. "The Effects of Exchange Rates and Commercial Policy on Agricultural Incentives in Colombia: 1953-1978." International Food Policy Research Institute Research Report 24 (June).

Krueger, Anne O., Maurice Schiff, and Alberto Valdés. Forthcoming. 3 vols. *The Political Economy of Agricultural Pricing Policies: Country Studies*. Oxford University Press.

Magee, Stephen. 1973. "Currency Contracts, Pass-Through and Devaluation." *Brookings Papers* 3:303-23.

Oliveira, J. do C. 1981. "An Analysis of Transfers from the Agricultural Sector and Brazilian Development, 1950-1974." Ph.D. dissertation, University of Cambridge.

Oyejide, T. Ademola. 1986. "The Effects of Trade and Exchange Rate Policies on Agriculture in Nigeria." International Food Policy Research Institute Research Report 55 (October).

Schuh, G. Edward. 1979. "Floating Exchange Rates, International Interdependence, and Agricultural Policy." Paper presented at Meetings of the International Association of Agricultural Economics. Banff, Alberta, Canada (September).

Valdés, Alberto. 1973. "Trade Policy and Its Effect on the External Agricultural Trade of Chile, 1945-1965." *American Journal of Agricultural Economics* 55, no. 2 (May): 154-64.

DISCUSSION OF CHAPTER 5
Terry L. Roe

These comments will begin with the conceptual and methodological issues underlying the country studies reported in. Krueger, Schiff, and Valdés (1988). My key point is that results of the country studies need to be interpreted within the context of numerous qualifications. Then, I will focus in a qualitative way on some of the economic impacts on agriculture of policies pursued by countries that tend to follow what might be described as import-substitution industrialization policies. The surprising implication is that policies of this type often serve to transfer resources from agriculture and to decrease agriculture's contribution to the growth process in subtle but important ways. I will conclude by briefly focusing on the question of why countries may persist in their pursuit of interventions that yield an inefficient allocation of resources and exacerbate adjustments to external shocks.

Conceptual and Methodological Issues

Essentially, the framework of the country studies presupposes that market and institutional failures are not present so that optimality conditions of neoclassical theory are used to measure price distortions.[1] The framework also presupposes that other distortions present in the economy are either accounted for or that they have negligible effects on the sector studied so that "getting relative prices right" will lead to a Pareto superior outcome.[1]

Hence, the approach is generally consistent with the view that free markets alone give rise to an allocation of resources that enables an economy to attain an equilibrium growth path along which patterns of production, investment, and capacity creation follow static and dynamic comparative advantage, thereby minimizing the time-discounted present value of resource costs needed to meet final demands. And, any undesirable impact on the distribution of income can be simply solved by lump-sum transfers. In this context, the role of government is limited. According to Buchanan (1980, 14), "as long as governmental action is restricted largely, if not entirely, to the protection of individual rights, personal and property, and enforcing voluntarily negotiated private contracts, the market process dominates economic behavior and ensures that any economic rents that appear will be dissipated by the force for competitive entry."

As is well known, market failures abound (and hence the possibility of high returns to collective action) while at the same time institutional structures in most countries preclude the implementation of first best instruments. Consequently, public revenues are typically generated by interventions in the traded goods sectors and income transfers are induced through implicit taxes and subsidies that appear as a departure of domestic price relative to their border market counterparts.[2] Thus, in this environment although contrary to the framework of the studies, some departure from the first best rules may lead to Pareto superior outcomes.

For some countries in selected years, there was evidence to suggest that price policy was used to transfer resources back to agriculture. Some country authors found that transfers back to agriculture actually exceeded the transfers out of agriculture due to the effects of price policy. If the discounted net social product of the transfers back to agriculture exceeded their opportunity cost, then the implication that price distortions led to a misallocation of resources would be misleading; the focus instead could be more appropriately placed on questions of institutional structures for collecting public revenues, identification of the social costs of market failures, and the political economy of choosing policy instruments that were less wasteful of resources.[3] Hence, care needs to be exercised so that the results of the studies are not interpreted to imply, without considerable qualification, that countries should get their prices right.

Of the numerous methodological issues that analyses of this type typically confront, I will briefly comment on four. These are (1) whether a single annual measure of nominal or effective protection can reasonably reflect the opportunity cost of resources allocated to the production of traded goods; (2) whether the computation of the price index on nonagricultural goods that would prevail in the absence of price distortions led to an underestimate of the degree to which the domestic industrial sector was protected in many countries; (3) whether the selection of a small number of commodities and the exclusion of home goods from the analysis may have led to underestimates of the resource transfers induced by price distortions; and (4) aside from conceptual questions, whether estimates of the exchange rate that would prevail in the absence of trade distortions provides any real measure of the opportunity cost of resources allocated to the production of traded as opposed to home goods.

Agriculture in developing countries is obviously characterized by substantial heterogeneity in the use of purchased inputs, the mix of traditional and modern technology, and the diversity in spatial and temporal costs that alter farm-level prices for both inputs and outputs. While country authors attempted to make adjustments to account for many of these differences, it is not likely that an annual measure of nominal or effective protection can provide reliable insights on the direct effects of price policy. In my view, an important strength of these studies is that consideration can and should be given to the entire 1966-84 period. Even then, these measures provide insights into direction and general tendency to distort relative prices, as opposed to magnitude. Measures of the direct effects of price distortions on the order of, say 10 percent, should be interpreted with caution, in my opinion.

The procedures used to estimate the price of traded non-agricultural goods that might prevail in the absence of trade distortions generally yielded values of protection that, when compared to industry specific estimates, appeared low. An International Monetary Fund study (Anjaria et al. 1985) reports estimates of the average effective rate of protection for 35 developing countries of about 50 percent during 1962-72 and about 60 percent in the late 1970s. The estimates from many of the 18 countries in the World Bank study averaged less than 10 percent. If the price of the traded nonagricultural goods is underestimated, then, all else constant, the estimates of the indirect rates of protection are also underestimated.

The exclusion of home goods from the analyses largely precludes the drawing of insights into how price policy for traded goods impacts on the markets for home goods, and in turn, the extent to which these markets compete for resources allocated to the production of traded goods.[4] To see the nature of these interactions, consider the reasoning that typically flows from models of the current account in which home goods play an important role (see, for example, Krueger 1985).

In these models, households respond to policy or economic shocks that impact on income streams by changing consumption expenditures. If a country cannot alter its terms of trade, the prices of traded goods in the economy remain unchanged. But the effect of changes in expenditure on nontraded goods gives rise to a change in their price.

A change in these prices can lead to an allocation of resources out of the production of traded goods and into the production of home goods, a decrease in the supply of export goods, an increase in the demand for import competing goods, an increase in a country's external imbalances, and an appreciation of the real value of its currency. Since, as mentioned, many countries' source of tax revenue is derived from the traded goods sector, price policy, through its impact on home goods, can lead to a decrease in revenues and hence fiscal deficits. If these deficits are monetized, or if they lead to an increase in external debt, then another round of distortions can be induced. Thus, by limiting the analysis to traded goods alone, insights into many of the other effects of price policy, for the most part, cannot be obtained.

Literature on the economics of exchange rate determination is not only vast, but it is also diverse. For the most part, a consensus has not emerged as to the factors or methods that would permit a reliable estimate of an "equilibrium" exchange rate, or to an estimate of an exchange rate that might prevail in the absence of trade distortions. Nevertheless, these facts—that many of the countries in the study experienced large changes in official rates of exchange prior to debt restructuring and that currency exchange rates can be used, in conjunction with other instruments, to protect producers in import competing sectors, to implicitly tax producers of exportable goods, and to implicitly subsidize the consumers of traded goods— are ample evidence that the value of a country's currency is a key determinant of price policy. Hence, measures of the extent to which the value of a country's currency overvalues or undervalues real incomes and departs from the true opportunity cost of allocating resources between traded and nontraded goods are almost surely essential to obtaining insights into the effects of price policy.

Furthermore, there is ample evidence for most of the countries to suggest that their currencies were overvalued. Many of the countries experienced trade deficits that could not be accounted for by inflows of foreign investment capital, many employed regimes to ration foreign exchange, and as mentioned, many devalued in the face of a liquidity crisis in foreign exchange. Moreover, if the methodology resulted in a tendency to underestimate the value of a country's currency that might prevail in the absence of trade distortions, the impact of this on the measures of the direct effects may be small when account is taken of the tendency, mentioned above, to underestimate the level of trade protection afforded nonagricultural goods.

While studies of this sort raise numerous conceptual and methodological questions, the results are nevertheless in general agreement with studies of trade protection in other countries (Ray 1989), and evidence of discrimination against agriculture (Bale and Lutz 1981; Scobie 1983). For example, Ray's review of trade protection literature for the case of industrial goods finds that countries import substitutes in sectors where they have a long-standing comparative disadvantage. Recall that many of the country studies also found that the effect of price policy was to protect the import-competing agricultural sectors relative to the exporting sectors.

Furthermore, the results fit the general pattern of findings from studies of country adjustment to economic shocks. For example, studies by Balassa (1986) and Mitra (1986) found that countries that followed policies to maintain internal market distortions in spite of changes in world market conditions experienced slower rates of growth than countries that followed more outward-oriented policies. The countries attempting to maintain internal market distortions can be characterized as having pursued policies of import-substitution industrialization while attempting to maintain abundant supplies of low-cost staple foods to urban centers. The majority of the countries included in the country studies tend to fall into the category of countries pursuing these types of policies.

Some Implications of the Results
for Agriculture in Developing Countries

It is clear that agriculture is an integral part of the import-substitution industrialization policies that many developing countries pursue. Since food is a wage good in many of these countries (that is, food expenditures are a proportionally large component of the consumer price index in most low-income countries), policies to lower food prices amount to an increase in real wages and, hence, an important benefit to food-deficit households. The benefit to industrial enterprises is the maintenance of lower nominal wages. Thus, import-substitution industrialization policies are often concomitant with policies to provide urban markets with supplies of food staples that support low and stable food prices.

The effect of these policies on agriculture include the following six points:

1. Protection of the industrial sector tends to induce a structure that is capital intensive, with small, relatively high-cost plants that are not able to compete in world markets.[5]

    Scale economies are limited to the domestic market. As the industrial structure becomes more concentrated and less competitive, agriculture tends to suffer another source of taxation. The intermediate industrial goods it obtains from protected industries (fertilizers, machinery) tend to be of inferior quality relative to those available in world markets, and to rise in price while the price of goods sold to domestically protected industries (such as cotton) tends to fall.[6]

    In the case of Brazil, for example, Brandao and Carvalho (forthcoming) report that the farm gate prices of soybeans were lowered by export taxes placed on soybeans to encourage the domestic milling of oil; Intal and Power (forthcoming) report that the Philippines banned the export of copra to encourage the domestic processing of oil. If inputs are subsidized, then part of the burden is passed to the government, although poor quality and problems of timely delivery can be viewed as an increase in the real prices of inputs to producers.

2. Prospects of relatively high real wages in urban areas tend to induce a rural-to-urban migration. Migration is further induced as these policies tend to draw more resources into the production of nontraded goods produced in urban areas. In spite of the migration into urban areas, the absorptive capacity of urban labor markets tends to be limited because of the industrial structure that import-substitution policies tend to induce. Labor, which for numerous reasons finds it difficult to migrate, seems to get "locked" in agriculture. In the presence of high population growth rates, the absence of technological change and increased capital inputs, land-labor ratios can decline leading to a decrease in the real wage in agriculture (see Hayami and Ruttan 1985, Table 13-1). These outcomes often create the *illusion* of economic problems in agriculture when the actual problem lies with the industrial sector of the economy.

     The narrowing of the marketing margins, which intervention in agricultural input and output marketing systems commonly implies, often leads to an exodus of the private sector from these activities.[7]

     Effectively, the public sector assumes many of the functions of resource allocation over time (storage), space (transportation), and form (processing). While these interventions tend to lower temporal variation in prices (Krueger, Schiff, and Valdés 1988), the result is inefficiencies in both public and private sector resource allocations and the emergence of fiscal deficits in parastatel enterprises that are eventually funded through domestic resource transfers, money creation, or foreign borrowing.

3. Since protection makes the industrial sector appear profitable relative to agriculture, agriculture is forced to compete for

resources that are artificially made more expensive. This includes peak seasonal demand for labor and credit. Agriculture must also compete for public investments. If the analysis of the net social value of public investments by authorities does not adequately take into consideration the artificially induced profitability of returns to investments in the protected sectors, then public investments in the rural economy, and agricultural technology in particular, are likely to be less than they would be in the absence of protection.

4. The returns to the fixed factors of production in agriculture (such as land, land improvements, fixed structures, agricultural technology) and the wealth embodied in these factors are also influenced by policies that discriminate against agriculture. The importance of wealth embodied in these factors is frequently overlooked. The value of fixed factors affects farmers' incentives to invest in their maintenance (such as land improvements). The value of fixed factors also largely determines the capacity of the sector to obtain credit. Hence, distortions that undervalue these factors also tend to decrease the level of private investment in the sector.

5. The fiscal deficits invariably associated with the policies of this sort often give rise to a tendency to underinvest in areas where markets fail. Underinvestment in these areas is particularly deleterious to agriculture since, as is well known, the efficiency with which labor and purchased input and output markets function in rural areas is particularly dependent on access to educational opportunities, market and technological information, spatial costs, production technology, capital markets, and so on.

Furthermore, evidence suggests (see Elias 1985; Binswanger et al. 1987) that public sector investments in these areas induce private sector investments as well, so that supply becomes more elastic to output price changes and less elastic with respect to changes in the price of an input, that is the brunt of adjustment tends to be spread over more inputs.[8]

Herein lies an important source of economic growth for agriculture.

6. Through a combination of price distortions and macroeconomic imbalances, both the demand and supply of agricultural technology can be altered. Not unlike the industrial sector, the agricultural sector can be launched on a growth path that cannot be sustained when policies are liberalized, nor is the sector likely to attain its potential level of economic efficiency so that it can be competitive in world markets.

Hence, these policies tend to decrease agriculture's contribution to the growth process. Following Kuznets (1964), this includes (1) the low-cost supply of food and raw materials for processing, (2) a market for producer and consumer goods produced by domestic industry, (3) a source of factor contributions (labor, capital) to the industrial sector, and (4) a source of foreign exchange earnings. These policies tend to retard this entire process with strong implications for the types of technological packages that are optimal for households in an environment of distorted markets and macroeconomic imbalances compared to more open economies (Roe 1987).

Some Political Economy Issues

An interesting question is, why have countries persisted in their pursuit of interventions that yield an inefficient allocation of resources and exacerbate adjustments to external shocks? Is a possible answer that interventions are the outcome of political pressure exerted by domestic interest groups seeking to achieve outcomes that provide them with some advantage, but that are socially wasteful. Or, are interventions the result of policy mistakes? But, if this were the case, why have countries failed to learn from their mistakes?

Evidence suggests that economic policy pursued by governments is at least in part explained by political pressure exerted by domestic interest groups seeking to achieve outcomes that, while socially wasteful, provide them with a differential economic advantage. The key strands of literature that support and contribute to this perspective include Bhagwati and Srinivasan (1980), Olson (1982), Bates (1983), Becker (1983), Colader (1984), Anderson and Hayami (1986), Roe and Shane (1986, 1988), and Roe and Yeldan (1988).[9]

Essentially, since economic policy has an impact on real incomes, these theories suggest that it is rational for households to form coalitions and to expend resources to influence policy. This process can be costly to an economy because resources are withdrawn from the production of goods and services and allocated to rent-seeking activities. Also, as governments increase interventions in the form of trade restrictions, the incentives to allocate more resources to seek trade restrictions that are beneficial to members of the coalition, or to allocate more resources to countervail the lobbying of others, tend to increase.

In the face of policies to liberalize an economy or to adjust policy as a consequence of market shocks, new coalitions may form to lobby against liberalization because the value of sector-specific assets may decline. Moreover, theory suggests that it is quite possible for a solution to the "rent-seeking game" to come about where any small movement from "political equilibrium" will yield lower returns to groups supporting the equilibrium, but that large changes may yield higher returns to all. Presumably, large changes are not sought for reasons of knowledge, uncertainty, and institutional rigidities.

In the presence of market failure, however, the expenditure of resources to influence policy can lead to Pareto superior outcomes because lobbying can substitute for the failure of prices to reflect the true opportunity cost of resources. Roe and Yeldan (1988) showed that it was indeed likely for a cost-reducing production technology to increase the willingness to pay to influence policy choices because of the potential increase in quasi-rents from a policy change.

While balanced growth strategies, as advocated by Srinivasan and others, and the need to invest in public goods may be necessary to attain growth, the political economy of special interest groups combined with institutional structures may make governments unwilling to liberalize and pursue these types of interventions. Instead, methods need to be found that enlighten special interest groups about the long-run costs of economic distortions and institutional innovations that lower market transaction costs while providing less-powerful interest groups with access to the political process that influences policy choices.

Notes

1. Market failure is typically described as a situation in which market forces alone will not lead to a Pareto efficient allocation of society's resources. The treatment of institutional failure in the literature is more illusive. For purposes here, it is useful to view this as a situation in which collective action, either by government or some group of economic agents, involves policy instruments that do not lead to a Pareto superior outcome.

2. Tanzi (1987) finds from a cross-section of developing countries that about 50 percent of their total tax revenue was generated from the traded good sector. This is in contrast to an average of about 12 percent in the case of the industrial market economies.

3. For an enlightening discussion of questions on tax policy, see Peter Diamond, Chapter 24 in Newberry and Stern (1987).

4. In Appendix 5.A, the authors show that the procedure used to compute the real exchange rate does not require knowledge of the price of home/industrial goods. This is only the case, however, if equations for the demand and supply of foreign exchange are derived from a general equilibrium framework where changes in the prices of home goods as functions of world prices and policy instruments are taken into account. The equations used in the studies were based on partial equilibrium assumptions.

5. See Krueger (1978) and Bhagwati, Becker, and Srinivasan (1984) for an insightful discussion of import-substitution indus-trialization policies.

6. Technological advances embodied in imported capital and intermediate goods also tend to become less available to agriculture

as the domestic industrial sector attempts to supply these needs.

7. For specific examples, see Von Braun and de Haen (1983) and Greene and Roe (1989) for the cases of Egypt and the Dominican Republic, respectively.

8. This is the point of Mundlak (1985) that agricultural supply response to price occurs through capital accumulation in the rural sector and that technological change is central to that process. Since price distortions, macroeconomic imbalances, and fiscal deficits are symptoms of the same policy, the debate between "getting prices right" as opposed to investments in rural education and infrastructure (see for example, Delgado and Mellor's reply [1987] to Schiff) seems somewhat misdirected.

9. As part of the country studies, empirical evidence was found to support the view that agricultural price policy in the Dominican Republic was the outcome of the political pressure of special interest groups. In spite of three changes in political leadership, interest groups were successful in maintaining essentially the same agricultural price policy "rules." External debt negotiations under World Bank and IMF auspices eventually led to a change in these rules.

References

Anderson, K., and Y. Hayami, eds. 1986. *The Political Economy of Agricultural Protection*. Sydney: Allen and Unwin.

Anjaria, S., N. Kirmari, and A. Petersen. 1985. "Trade Policy Issues and Development." Occasional Paper No. 38. Washington, D.C.: International Monetary Fund.

Balassa, Bel. 1986. "Policy Responses to Exogenous Shocks in Developing Countries." *American Economic Review* 76:244-48.

Bale, Malcolm D., and Ernst Lutz. 1981. "Price Distortions in Agriculture and Their Effects: An International Comparison." *American Journal of Agricultural Economics* 63:8-22.

Bates, Robert. 1983. "Governments and Agricultural Markets in Africa." In *The Role of Markets in the World Food Economy*. D.G. Johnson and E. Schuh, eds. Boulder, Colorado: Westview Press.

Becker, Gary. 1983. "The Theory of Competition among Pressure Groups for Political Influence." *The Quarterly Journal of Economics* 93(Aug.):372-400.

Bhagwati, J. N. and T. N. Srinivasan. 1980. "Revenue Seeking: A Generalization of the Theory of Tariffs." *Journal of Political Economics* 88:1069-1087.

Bhagwati, J. N., Richard Becker, and T. N. Srinivasan. 1984. "DUP Activities and Economic Theory" In *Neoclassical Political Economy*. D. Colsander, ed. Cambridge, Mass.: Ballinger Publishing Co.

Binswanger, Hans, Maw-Cheng Yang, Alan Bowers, and Yair Mundlak. 1987. "On the Determinants of Cross-Country Aggregate Supply." *Journal of Econometrics* 38:111-31.

Brandao, A. S. P., and Jose L. Carvalho. Forthcoming. "A Comparative Study of Agricultural Pricing Policies: The Case of Brazil." In *The Political Economy of Agricultural Price Policy in Selected Latin American Countries.* Anne Krueger, ed. Baltimore: Johns Hopkins University Press.

Buchanan, J. M. 1980. "Rent Seeking and Profit Seeking." In *Toward a Theory of Rent-seeking Society*. J. M. Buchanan, R. D. Tollison, and G.Tullock, eds. College Station: Texas A&M University Press.

Colander, D. C., ed. 1984. *Neoclassical Political Economy: The Analysis of Rent-Seeking and DUP Activities*. Cambridge, Mass.: Ballinger.

Delgado, Christopher, and John Mellor. 1987. "A Structural View of Policy Issues in African Agricultural Development: Reply." *American Journal of Agricultural Economics* 69 (2):389-91.

Diamond, Peter. 1987. "Optimal Tax Theory and Development Policy." In *The Theory of Taxation for Developing Countries*. D. Newberry and N. Stern, eds. New York: Oxford University Press.

Elias, Victor. 1985. *Government Expenditures on Agriculture and Agricultural Growth in Latin America*. Research Report 50. Washington, D.C.: International Food Policy Research Institute.

Greene, Duty, and Terry Roe. 1989. "Trade, Exchange Rate, and Agricultural Pricing Policies in the Dominican Republic." *The Political Economy of Agricultural Pricing Policy*. Vol. 1. World Bank Comparative Studies Series. Washington, D.C.: World Bank.

Hayami, Yujiro, and Vernon Ruttan. 1985. *Agricultural Development: An International Perspective*. 2nd edition. Baltimore: Johns Hopkins University Press.

Intal, Ponciano, and John Power. Forthcoming. "Government Intervention and Philippine Agriculture." In *The Political Economy of Agricultural Price Policy in Selected Latin American Countries*. Anne Krueger and others, ed. Baltimore: Johns Hopkins University Press.

IMF. April 1989. *World Economic Outlook*. Washington, D.C.: International Monetary Fund.

Krueger, A. 1978. *Foreign Trade Regimes and Economic Development: Liberalization Attempts and Consequences*. Cambridge, Mass.: Ballinger.

_____. 1985. *Exchange Rate Determination*. New York: Cambridge University Press.

Krueger, A., M. Schiff, and A. Valdés. 1988. "Agricultural Incentives in Developing Countries: Measuring the Effect of Sectoral and Economy Wide Policies." *The World Bank Economic Review* 3:255-71.

Kuznets, Simon. 1964. "Economic Growth and the Contribution of Agriculture." In *Agriculture in Economic Development*. C. K. Eicher and L. Witt, ed. New York: McGraw-Hill.

Mitra, P. 1986. "A Description of Adjustment to External Shocks: Country Groups." In *Stagflation, Savings, and the State of Perspectives on the Global Economy*. D. Lal, and M. Wolf, ed. New York: Oxford University Press.

Mundlak, Yair. 1985. "The Aggregate Agricultural Supply." Center for Agricultural Economic Research Working Papers No. 8511. Rehovot, Israel.

Olson, Mancur. 1982. *The Rise and Decline of Nations*. New Haven: Yale University Press.

Ray, Edward. 1989. "Empirical Research on the Political Economy of Trade." Paper presented to the International Agricultural Trade Research Consortium Meetings, Montreal, Canada, July 7 and 8.

Roe, Terry L. 1987. *Agricultural Policy in Developing Countries: The Transfer of Resources from Agriculture.* Economic Development Center Bulletin #87-4. Minneapolis: University of Minnesota.

Roe, Terry L. and M. Shane. 1986. "Government in the Process of Trade and Development." *Trade and Development: Proceedings of the Winter 1986 Meeting of the International Agricultural Trade Research Consortium.* ERS Agricultural Trade Analysis Division. Washington, D.C.: USDA.

_____. 1988. "A Political Economy Approach to Agricultural Trade and Development." Paper presented at the American Agricultural Economics Association Meetings, Knoxville, Tennessee.

Schiff, Maurice. 1987. "A Structural View of Policy Issues in African Agricultural Development: Comment." *American Journal of Agricultural Economics* 69 (2): 389-91.

Scobie, Grant. 1983. *Food Subsidies in Egypt: Their Impact on Foreign Exchange and Trade.* Research Report 40. Washington, D.C.: Institute for Policy Reform Institute.

Tanzi, Vito. 1987. "Quantitative Characteristics of the Tax Systems of Developing Countries." In *The Theory of Taxation for Developing Countries.* D. Newberry and N. Stern, ed. Washington, D.C.: World Bank.

Von Braun, Joachim, and Hartwig de Haen. 1983. *The Effects of Food Price and Subsidy Policies on Egyptian Agriculture.* Research Report 42. Washington, D.C.: International Food Policy Research Institute.

PART III

U.S. Agricultural Assistance and Food Aid in the 1990s: Directions and Priorities

Japan has surpassed the United States as the world's largest aid donor. Moreover, the United States now ranks at the bottom of country members of the Development Assistance Committee in aid as a percentage of GNP. Overall U.S. foreign aid rose somewhat in real terms in the early 1980s but more recently has fallen back to the level of the late 1970s (see table below). Prospects for future levels of foreign assistance are poor given continuing pressures to reduce federal budget deficits and lack of a strong political constituency supporting the aid effort.

U.S. foreign aid, 1977-1990, by major programs ($US billions, 1989 constant)

Year	Development assistance	Food aid	Other economic	Multi-lateral assistance	Economic support fund	Military aid	Total
1977	2.20	2.30	0.50	2.30	3.30	4.10	14.70
1978	2.90	2.20	0.40	2.40	3.90	4.20	16.00
1979	2.60	2.10	0.60	3.10	3.20	11.00	22.60
1980	2.40	2.20	0.90	2.60	3.30	3.20	14.60
1981	2.30	2.10	0.80	1.70	3.00	4.60	14.50
1982	2.30	2.70	0.70	1.90	3.50	5.50	15.60
1983	2.40	1.70	0.60	2.10	3.60	6.90	17.30
1984	2.50	1.80	0.60	2.00	3.70	7.70	18.30
1985	2.80	2.30	0.70	2.20	6.00	6.60	20.60
1986	2.60	1.80	0.60	1.60	5.40	6.40	18.40
1987	2.40	1.60	0.70	1.60	4.20	5.50	16.00
1988	2.50	1.50	0.60	1.50	3.20	5.50	14.80
1989 (est)	2.40	1.50	0.70	1.50	3.60	5.40	15.10
1990 (req)	2.30	1.40	0.90	1.80	3.20	5.70	15.30

SOURCE: Committee on Foreign Affairs, U.S. House of Representatives, 1989.
Report of the Task Force on Foreign Assistance, p. 7.

The table shows the sharp fluctuations in U.S. military aid and recent levels of economic support funds (ESF) compared to relatively stable levels of the other major foreign aid programs (measured in constant 1989 dollars). ESF is now no larger than in 1977-79, having declined from its high levels reached in 1985-86. Funding for bilateral development assistance has remained relatively stable in real terms since 1977, showing only a slight decline since 1985-86. Both food aid and multilateral assistance have declined in real terms since 1977. The decline in food aid has been slow but steady except for the mid-1980s when the United States responded to the famines and food emergencies in Africa with larger shipments of food supplies. In real terms, funding for food aid in 1987-89 will average one-third less than in 1977-79. At the present time, food aid constitutes about 10 percent of total U.S. foreign aid and some 16 percent of total economic assistance. Nevertheless, it is substantially more than one-third as large in monetary terms as total U.S. development (excluding ESF) assistance provided bilaterally and multilaterally.

This recent erosion of U.S. foreign aid in real terms has not stilled the growing volume of criticism voiced against aid programs. Complex, cumbersome procedures try the patience of aid officials, nongovernmental participants, and recipients alike. Money is said to be spread thinly across countries, problems, and projects. Critics cite the growing proportions of total funds earmarked for foreign policy and military purposes, charge that assistance activities harm U.S. export opportunities, claim that aid promotes extensive and inefficient interventions by recipient governments, and point to growing poverty and environmental degradation in aid-assisted countries. Reviews and recipes for reform of foreign aid are rife.

Vernon Ruttan summarizes the self-interest and ethical arguments for foreign economic assistance in Chapter 6. Finding neither compelling, he presents several important questions that the philosophical arguments for foreign aid leave unanswered. He points out that any case for foreign aid is based on the premise that the transfers have desired developmental impacts, or at least do no harm. Thus, the consequences of development assistance must be evaluated and related to the design and implementation of the aid programs themselves. He draws historical lessons about this relationship from agricultural and rural development experience.

Ruttan uses food aid as an example of the difficulty of answering the question, "Why foreign assistance?" Discussion of food aid is continued in Chapter 7, which first places it in a factual context in relation to overall foreign assistance. Next, the analytics of food aid are reviewed to show its inherent nature and limitations as a development resource. Its multiple objectives and patterns of allocations to recipient countries are then analyzed. Finally, specific recommendations to reform food aid and integrate it more completely with other development assistance are given.

In the final chapter of Part III, Raymond Hopkins assesses the political possibilities for renewal of food aid legislation due in the early 1990s. He skillfully sketches the conflicting interests in and out of the federal government that must be balanced and reconciled to settle the scope and direction of food aid for the final decade of this century.

Lehman B. Fletcher

6

Foreign Economic Assistance and Agricultural Development

Vernon W. Ruttan

When the Bush administration assumed office in 1989, the development assistance program was in disarray. Bilateral assistance had declined from $3.5 billion (in 1989 dollars) in the last Carter budget to $2.8 billion in the last Reagan budget—a decline of 20 percent. Security supporting assistance, which experienced rapid growth during the first Reagan administration, declined continuously during the second Reagan administration. Contributions to multilateral assistance programs remained stable in nominal terms but were lower in real terms than a decade earlier. Storage reserves, from which the commodities used in food assistance programs are drawn, declined as a result of the 1988 drought.

The decline in economic assistance during the second Reagan administration was a response to both internal and external pressures. During the first Reagan administration the efforts of the State Department, particularly during the tenure of Alexander Haig, to expand the assistance budget and link it more closely to U.S. security interests, "rolled over" Budget Director David Stockman. Stockman had criticized the aid program for "turning Third World countries into quagmires of self-imposed inefficiency and burdening them beneath mountainous external debts they would never be able to pay" and had reportedly characterized the multilateral banks as "the leading edge of socialist penetration into the Third World."

During the second Reagan administration, the issue of debt relief and economic reform in debtor countries replaced security concerns as the central focus of the Reagan administration's interest in the Third World. But the easing of political tensions between the United States and the Soviet Union contributed to a decline in the willingness of Congress to sustain foreign assistance at the level achieved in the mid-1980s. Congressional reluctance to fund administration requests for greater foreign assistance was reinforced by the budget stringency imposed by efforts to reduce the federal deficit by the Balanced Budget and Emergency Deficit Control Act of 1985 (the Gramm-Rudman-Hollings Act). As the resources available to the United States's bilateral assistance program declined, the Reagan administration adopted a much more positive view toward the multilateral institutions, such as the International Monetary Fund and the World Bank.

Anticipation of continued budget stringency and the prospect of further decline in the real resources that would become available to support the U.S. assistance program gave rise during the last two years of the second Reagan administration to a number of official and unofficial efforts to specify the reforms that could lead to more effective use of assistance resources in the 1990s. In February the House Committee on Foreign Affairs, under the leadership of Congressman Lee Hamilton (D-New York), issued a report calling for the enactment of new legislation that would create a restructured foreign aid agency to replace the Agency for International Development (AID). The agency itself issued, under the imprimatur of then-administrator Alan Woods, an exceedingly frank review of its deficiencies and accomplishments. On June 29, the House passed the 1989 International Cooperation Act that, while embodying several of the Hamilton Committee proposals, negated its general intent. The Senate has held hearings on a proposed International Security and Development Cooperation Act. Memoranda are being furiously circulated among the relevant offices in AID, U.S. Department of Agriculture (USDA), Office of Management and Budget (OMB), and other relevant agencies in preparation for revisions of the Food for Peace provisions of the 1990 Farm Bill.

These were not the first efforts to reform or reorganize the U.S. economic assistance effort. During the 1950s, U.S. economic assistance programs went through a series of reorganizations. Between 1950 and 1959 there were eight major official program and policy reviews of U.S. assistance programs. It was not until 1961, however, that the several U.S. bilateral assistance programs were merged into a single organization—the Agency for International Development—established as the lead agency for assistance policy and programs. During the 1960s and 1970s, reports of study commissions continued to proliferate. In the late 1970s, Senator Hubert H. Humphrey prodded the administration into proposing a coordinating body, the International Development Cooperation Administration (IDCA), which would provide policy guidance for the entire U.S. economic assistance effort. The effort had little impact other than to demonstrate that USAID no longer had sufficient political clout to be the lead agency.

Why Foreign Economic Assistance?

Before entering into the debate about contemporary foreign aid policy, I want to discuss the philosophical bases for foreign economic assistance—why we should or should not be in this business at all.[1] Two arguments have typically been used in support of foreign economic assistance. One set of arguments is based on the economic and strategic self-interest of the donor country, while the second is based on the ethical responsibility of the donor to the recipient. I would like to explore these two arguments since they both are factors, often both simultaneously and inconsistently, in discussions of foreign aid.

The Self-interest Argument

The donor self-interest arguments generally rest on an assertion that development assistance promotes the economic or strategic interests of the donor country. It should be technically possible to specify the conditions under which government-to-government aid transfers could improve welfare in both donor and recipient countries. The empirical analyses needed to support the economic self-interest argument are, however, surprisingly limited. It is not sufficient simply to assert that the transfer of assistance resources may be followed by the growth of exports from the donor to the recipient country. The welfare gains and losses to donors and recipients must be calculated. As yet these calculations have not been made.

The strategic self-interest argument rests on even more fragile grounds. It has been subject to even less rigorous theoretical or empirical analysis than the economic self-interest argument. The single background paper on the effectiveness of military assistance prepared for the Commission on Security and Economic Assistance (the Carlucci Commission), while asserting a positive linkage between U.S. security assistance expenditures and security assistance, noted that the evidence to support the assertion was "elusive."

There is an inherent contradiction in both the economic and strategic or security self-interest arguments. There is danger that a donor country may be compelled to pursue its self-interest under the rubric of aid even if it harms the recipient country. If the donor self-interest argument is used as a primary rationale for development assistance, it imposes on donors some obligation to demonstrate that its assistance does no harm to the recipient. It is hard to avoid a conclusion that the self-interest arguments have been used more as a cynical effort to develop a constituency for foreign assistance than a serious economic or political rationale.

The Ethical Argument

Both the popular and official sponsors of foreign economic assistance have typically treated the ethical bases for foreign assistance as intuitively obvious. Most economists have generally felt fairly comfortable—probably too comfortable—with a straightforward utilitarian rationale for foreign assistance. If private rates of return to capital investment are higher in developing countries than in developed countries, investment should flow from developed to less-developed countries. If, because markets are imperfect, social rates of return exceed private rates of return, then developed country governments should transfer resources to developing countries to assist in physical and institutional infrastructure development. But few economists would be willing to embrace the full implications of the utilitarian income distribution argument—that rich countries ought to give until the point at which, by giving more, the loss in utility in the donor country would exceed the gain in utility in the recipient country or countries.

In contrast, most political philosophers, and those economists who adhere to a Hobbesian contractarian view of the role of government, have found it difficult to discover any intellectual foundation for development assistance based on considerations of distributive justice. At the most extreme there is the libertarian argument that in a society of free people the concept of social or distributive justice has no meaning. This argument, in effect, says that justice is a function of the rules or processes that govern individual and group behavior and not of the outcome generated by the rules. It follows that the appropriate role of public policy is rule reform. The Hobbesian contractarian argument with respect to foreign aid has been forcefully articulated by Bansfield (1963): "Our political philosophy does not give our government any right to do good for foreigners." This argument has been forcefully restated by Mozick (1974), and it has recently reemerged with renewed force in the debate over foreign assistance in the late 1970s and early 1980s. The emergence of social justice as a basis for political action, both within nations and in international relations, is due to lack of confidence that the actual behavior of economic markets and political institutions adequately approaches the conditions specified by libertarian political philosophers.

Attempts have been made to develop a contractarian argument drawing on the Rawlsian "difference principle" to establish a moral obligation for foreign assistance. The central part of Rawls's theory is that in a just society departures from an equalitarian income distribution would be permitted only when differential rewards contribute to the welfare of the least advantaged members of society. Rawls argues that this difference principle would be agreed to by rational individuals attempting to design a constitution—given full general knowledge of the political and economic nature of society, except the positions that they would occupy by virtue of social class, individual talent, or political persuasion. The Rawlsian constitution does not imply perfect equalization of incomes. If, for example, inequality calls forth economic activity that benefits the least as well as the more advantaged members of society, it would be permitted.

Both Beitz (1979) and Runge (1977) have argued that an intuitively obvious extension of the difference principle to the international economic order is that justice would imply equal access by citizens of all countries to global resources, except in those cases where departure from inequality could be justified on the basis of benefits to citizens of the least advantaged countries. To the extent that this argument draws on the Rawls framework, however, it remains vulnerable to the weakness of attempting to derive rules of justice from an "imagined social contract." I would personally prefer a stronger behavioral foundation on which to rest convictions about moral responsibility for assistance to poor countries.

An Implicit Global Contract

A contractarian argument that limits the responsibility of the rich toward the poor to national populations has great difficulty in confronting a world where citizens hold multiple loyalties, where national identity may be wider or narrower than state boundaries, where policy interventions as well as market forces guide the flow of labor and capital and the trade in commodities and intellectual property across state boundaries. The ethical foundation for a system of development assistance rests on the premise that the emergence of international economic and political interdependence has extended the moral basis for social or distributive justice from the national to the international sphere.

International interdependence has resulted in an implicit extension of the philosopher's argument for redistribution to include the international sphere:

> There are significant gains to social interaction above and beyond what individuals can achieve on their own. The owners of scarce personal assets do not have substantial private use f these assets; it is only their value in a large system which makes these assets valuable. Hence, there is a surplus created by the existence of society which is available for redistribution.

This argument can be extended to countries as well as individuals—there are significant gains from economic relations among states that go beyond those that can be obtained by individual countries in a state of autarchy. The growth of global and political interdependence implies a decline in the significance of national boundaries. Since boundaries are not coextensive with the scope of economic and political interdependence, they do not mark the limits of social obligation in the sharing of the benefits and burdens associated with interdependence. A functioning international economy increases the value of the natural, human, and institutional resources of the developed countries and makes part of this surplus available for redistribution.

Some Questions

Acceptance of an ethical responsibility by the citizens and governments of rich countries for assistance to poor countries still leaves unanswered a number of important questions.

Acceptance of an ethical responsibility for development assistance by the rich countries does not resolve the question of what level of assistance is appropriate. It was noted earlier that the utilitarian, or consequentialist, argument seems to be based on equating marginal utilities—the rich countries ought to give until the point is reached at which by giving more, the loss in utility in the donor country would exceed the gain in utility in the recipient country or countries. However, the actual level of aid allocations by donor countries seems to reflect the much weaker moral premise that if it is possible to contribute to welfare in poor countries without sacrificing anything of moral or economic significance in the donor country, it should be done. There seems to be an implicit moral judgment among the citizens and governments of rich countries that the moral obligation to feed the poor in Ethiopia is stronger than a moral obligation to raise the annual growth rate of Ethiopia's GNP from 5 to 6 percent.

Neither the commitment to development assistance nor the commitment to a particular level of development assistance provides guidance as to who should receive aid. The acceptable ethical considerations that support the distributive justice argument imply that assistance should be directed to improving the welfare of the poorest individuals in the poorest countries. But there is also an ethical argument that aid should be directed into uses that produce the largest increments of income from each dollar of assistance— the argument that assistance resources are limited and should not be wasted.

The empirical evidence does not permit any clear inferences concerning aid impact on savings, investment, and rate of growth. There is, however, evidence that assistance resources have generated relatively high marginal rates of return—rates of return that are high relative to what the same resources would have earned in the donor countries. What little empirical evidence we do have also suggests that donor governments are willing to trade off some efficiency for equity in their aid allocations—that recipient income levels do carry modest weight in the allocation of aid resources. But we have little more than anecdotal evidence on the distributive impacts of development assistance in recipient countries.

Acceptance of responsibility for assistance does not resolve the question of what form of assistance to offer. The goals of assistance range from attempting to ensure immediate "subsistence rights" through food aid or other basic needs programs, to assistance designed to strengthen the capacity of a nation to meet the subsistence requirements of its own people, or to modifying the institutions that influence the resource flows among nations. On some grounds it would seem obligatory to secure some minimum level of subsistence before allocating resources to the other two objectives. But this conclusion is not at all obvious if the effect is to preclude either expansion of the capacity needed to assure future subsistence or reform of the rules of conduct that govern economic and political relationships among nations, such as reforming the GATT rules on agricultural trade.

A fourth issue is the extent to which development assistance policy and administration should be directed to bringing about institutional reform in the recipient country. The extent to which development assistance directed either toward meeting basic needs or to strengthening the recipient countries' capacity for economic growth will depend on the institutions that influence relations among individual citizens, economic and social organizations, and the government.

If a donor government's ethical concern extends to an obligation to assure the citizens of the donor country that the resources devoted to assistance are used effectively, either for immediate relief of subsistence needs or to generate longer term economic growth, it can hardly avoid also entering into a dialogue with the recipient country about institutional reform when it enters into negotiations with a recipient country about resource transfers. The rationale for focusing on institutional reform is the hope that any moral concern that provided a rationale for assistance will contribute to capacity in the recipient country to more effectively provide for basic needs and generate the growth necessary to improve the quality of life. The obligation to enter into a dialogue on issues of institutional reform imposes on the donor country the requirement to build in its own cultural and social science disciplines the capacity necessary to enter into the dialogue. These capacities should be guided more by pragmatic consideration about the potential impact of policy reform in the recipient country than either ideological considerations based on the donor's internal political processes or its own economic or political self-interest.

Some Inferences

The first conclusion that emerges from this review is the weakness of the self-interest argument for foreign assistance which, when examined carefully, often turns out to represent a hidden agenda for domestic rather than international resource transfers from taxpayers. The political "realists" have not been able, or have not thought it worthwhile, to demonstrate the presumed political and security benefits from the strategic assistance component of the aid budget. Rawlsian contractarian theory does provide a basis for ethical responsibility toward the poor in poor countries that goes beyond traditional religious and moral obligations of charity. It also provides a basis for making judgments about the degree of inequality that is ethically acceptable.

But the contractarian argument cannot stand by itself. The credibility of the contractarian argument is weakened if, in fact, the transfers do not achieve the desired consequences. Failures of analysis or design can produce worse consequences than if no assistance were undertaken. There is no obligation to transfer resources that do not generate either immediate welfare gains or growth in the capacity of poor states to meet the needs of their citizens. It becomes important, therefore, to evaluate the consequences of development assistance and to consider the policy interventions that can lead to more effective development assistance programs.

Why Food Aid?

Support for food aid has moved through three phases.[2] In the 1950s and into the mid-1960s, major support came from agricultural constituencies and their congressional patrons. During the 1960s and into the 1970s when food aid was being heavily oriented toward political and security objectives, the administration itself became the major constituency for food aid. By the late 1970s, the humanitarian assistance constituency, operating through private voluntary organizations, had become the dominant constituency for food aid. While the use of food aid as an instrument of development has received, from the beginning, strong rhetorical support, it has never been able to generate substantial constituency support. Since 1980, funding for the promotion of agricultural exports through subsidies has increased substantially, but principally for programs other than PL 480. As a result, those interested in market development and trade expansion have shifted much of their attention from food aid to other programs.

It has been difficult to find a satisfactory answer to the question, "Why food aid?" There has been a continuing effort among some proponents to show that food aid is, at least for some purposes, a more effective instrument of economic assistance than financial aid. This has not been an easy task. This section examines the rationale for the objectives of food aid.

Method for Surplus Disposal

Is food aid an effective method for agricultural surplus disposal? The dominant objective of food aid in the 1950s and early 1960s was to dispose of U.S. agricultural surplus. Yet the program was, even then, unable to move sufficient commodities within the enforced operational constraints to have much more than a marginal impact on U.S. surplus stocks. The program found it difficult to avoid substituting concessional sales for commercial sales. It has been argued that in some sense the program could be viewed as an offset to the increasingly overvalued dollar during the 1950s and 1960s. But an earlier devaluation or more rapid transition to a floating exchange rate would have been more effective. In the absence of devaluation, a straightforward two-price "domestic allotment" program, which held domestic prices above world market levels and permitted exports to move into world markets at border prices, would have been more effective in disposing of surpluses.

Market Development

A second important objective of U.S. food aid, from the very beginning, has been its use as an instrument of market development for U.S. producers. There have been three elements in this effort. The most direct were the "Cooley loan" subsidies, in the late 1950s and 1960s, to agribusiness for facility investments in recipient countries. The second was support for commodity organizations for promotional, technical assistance, and consumer education programs in recipient countries. The third was the more subtle effect of commodity imports in changing the tastes of consumers in favor of wheat, and in some cases rice, and away from "inferior" domestic carbohydrates. The facilities subsidies have, at times, been important in the development of national capacity to produce the inputs needed to sustain agricultural production—fertilizer in India, for example. The latter two programs have been credited with some success in situations where the growth of consumer income was consistent with changes in the consumption patterns being promoted—higher consumption of wheat products in Japan and the use of U.S. feed grains in pork and poultry production in Taiwan and Korea. It seems doubtful that a program justified primarily on market development criteria would have been able to claim more than a small fraction of the resources allotted to PL 480.

Political Leverage

What about food aid as an instrument of political leverage? The history of efforts to employ food aid to induce other governments to initiate economic or political reforms or to support the U.S. global political agenda indicate that it is an exceedingly blunt instrument. The limited successes against India in the mid-1960s and Bangladesh in the early 1970s, for example, suggest that success has been achieved only when there was substantial political support for the reform in the recipient country or the recipient country was in an exceedingly weak bargaining position. As an instrument to create generalized good will toward the United States, food aid has been, when sensitively administered, somewhat more effective. But it would be difficult today to find serious advocates of the "food power" perspective that briefly captured the imagination of populists and politicians in the early and mid-1970s.

Development Resource

If there is any area in which food aid might be expected to have a substantial impact, it is on recipient countries' economic development. A very high share of the commodities transferred under Title I have been used by recipient governments to generate revenues that could be used to support their development budgets. It is generally agreed that the potential release of other resources for development is greatest where food aid replaces commercial imports because it then frees foreign exchange for other purposes. But donors, particularly the United States, have insisted that food aid be additional—that it not displace commercial imports. Substantial quantities of the food transferred under Title II have been used to support "food-for-work" or other local development projects. In spite of efforts to direct the resources generated by food aid into development-related invest-ment, it is generally conceded that there continues to be very substantial leakage into routine budget support, current consumption, and the pockets of public officials and their clients. Almost no one argues that PL 480 commodity transfers are as effective as financial transfers when measured against development objectives. It is somewhat discouraging, after more than 30 years of effort, to find program designers and managers claiming little more than that food aid could become an effective instrument for development—but that radical changes in the way most food aid is programmed and administered will be necessary.

Humanitarian Aid

The strongest support for the view that food aid is a superior instrument of assistance has been put forward by the basic needs or humanitarian aid constituency for food aid. It has been argued that food aid for disaster relief and for meeting the needs of the nutritionally deprived is a superior form of assistance. It can, in principle, be mobilized quickly for disaster relief and it can be targeted to the nutritionally deprived. If targeted to improved nutrition and as an incentive to participation in formal schooling and training programs, food aid could, it is argued, contribute effectively to human capital formation without having significant disincentive effects on agricultural production.

Multiple Objectives

The multiple objectives of food aid continue to serve as a focus for substantial criticism of the PL 480 program. At an April 1988 Congressional Research Service workshop on the effectiveness of food aid, the charge was made by proponents of food aid as an instrument of market development that food aid had been "hijacked" by agricultural development interests. A representative of a private voluntary organization (PVO) countered that the development of U.S. export markets bears no essential or necessary relationship to satisfying human need and creates a dependency on imported foods. Egypt is usually cited as a horror case—food aid has permitted the subsidization of wheat to the extent that bread has sometimes been a cheaper livestock feed than feed grains.

It is quite clear, however, that it has been this diversity of objectives that has accounted for the continuing political viability of food aid as a component of U.S. development assistance. There has been a constituency for food aid in times of food surpluses and in times of food scarcity. The commodity interests and the human needs constituency have not been able to agree on the objectives of food aid but they have been able to cooperate in support of PL480 appropriations. Those in the administration who have been concerned with foreign policy and development assistance have seldom believed that food was as useful as money, but they have welcomed it because it was accessible, fungible, and additional.

The importance of the multiple objectives of the program for its continued political viability was recognized and insisted upon by Senator Humphrey. This point was stressed by a former Senate Committee on Agriculture and Forestry staffer, Thomas R. Saylor, in a discussion of the 1975 revision of the PL 480 legislation when he said,

> The multiple objectives and accompanying multiple constituencies provide a much broader base of support than other foreign assistance programs provide. To undermine this would be to severely weaken PL480 and leave it much more vulnerable to the budget cutting process.

It is hard to disagree that up until at least the late 1960s, the food aid program was larger than it would have been if targeted to more specific, and less inconsistent, objectives. And the total aid effort was also larger than it would otherwise have been in the absence of food aid. But it is doubtful if this argument can be made to carry as much weight in the late 1980s as it did in the past. The coalition of commodity groups, shippers, and PVOs was ineffective in preventing a substantial decline in food aid shipments in the 1970s. During the 1980s, when surpluses reappeared, agricultural interests chose to support other disposal efforts outside the PL 480 framework.

Future of Food Aid

What can be anticipated regarding the orientation and size of any future U.S. food aid program? The next reauthorization of PL 480 is scheduled to occur in 1990. The size of the U.S. carryover stock of wheat in 1990 will certainly represent an important influence on both any revisions of the legislation and on the size of the program. But less transient forces are also at work. During 1988 and 1989, there were signs that the old congressional agency-interest group coalition was continuing to erode. The 1988 drought and the poor wheat crop in 1989 resulted in a drawdown in commodity stocks in government hands to below the level of the mid-1970s. Several USDA studies have found that export subsidy programs, including PL 480, were a less cost-effective method of enhancing exports than either export credits or con-sumption-oriented market development programs. As personnel ceilings continued to erode AID staff capacity, both in Washington and in the field, the agency found that the administrative require-ments necessary to make food aid an effective instrument for development was excessively burdensome. Conflicts were emerging between the PVO community—particularly CARE and Catholic Relief Services—and AID over the use of food aid monetization to support the development of indigenous PVOs in recipient countries. Yet the PVOs themselves were finding it increasingly burdensome to respond to emergency food aid needs, particularly in African countries characterized by weak institutional infrastructure.

Forecasts of program levels in areas as highly politicized as food aid are notoriously hazardous. Yet it seems unlikely that the economic and political forces that have contributed to an increasing separation of supply management and market development objectives from economic development and humanitarian assistance aspects will become weaker in the immediate future. An implication of this conclusion is that agricultural commodities distributed under PL 480 auspices will continue to decline both in volume and relative to commercial exports, to assisted exports, and to other forms of bilateral aid—in spite of projections that point to a need for food aid levels several times as high as in the 1980s.

The positive perspective on PL 480 is that it has generated substantial benefits to each of its domestic clientele groups and some benefits to recipient countries that would not otherwise have been available. It was used not because it is superior to other forms of aid, but because the commodities were available. A minimalist defense might be that it was the least bad use that could be made, given the surpluses that became available. This defense cannot, however, avoid confronting the argument that better use could have been made of the same resources.

Some Lessons from Development Assistance

Before turning to the future of foreign aid, it is worth reviewing some of the historical lessons from development experience.[3] Four lessons are particularly relevant for agricultural and rural development.

Physical Infrastructure Development

During the 1950s and 1960s, large-scale investment in transport facilities (roads, railroads, ports, and airports) and multipurpose resource development projects (power, flood control, irrigation) occupied a very prominent place in both bilateral and multilateral development assistance. In the 1960s and 1970s, disappointment with the flow of benefits, resulting from both bad planning and poor implementation, led to severe criticism of large infrastructure projects. During the 1980s, infrastructure projects have become an important target of the environmental movement. The evidence suggests, however, that we should now be taking a much more positive view of assistance for infrastructure development. Both the technical and economic aspects of project planning and evaluation have become more sophisticated. A number of countries that were formerly recipients of infrastructure assistance have now become major exporters of construction services (Turkey, Korea, India).

Agricultural Research

The capacity to develop and manage agricultural technology is one of the most important variables accounting for differences in agricultural productivity among nations. Returns to investment in land and water resources are usually low and the production response to reform of factor and product markets are typically sluggish unless accompanied by technical innovations that can lead to productivity growth in crop and livestock production. Agricultural research has consistently achieved rates of return that are among the highest available to either national governments or development assistance agencies. These high rates of return reflect substantial underinvestment by national governments and development assistance agencies. Failure of bilateral and multi-lateral assistance agencies to invest in the development of agricultural research capacity (including the human resources necessary to staff agricultural research systems) in Africa during the 1970s represents a major reason for the continuing poor performance of African agriculture. The erosion of research capacity in a number of important developing countries in the 1980s is a serious source of concern. And the decline in commitment by USAID to the Consultative Group on International Agricultural Resource (CGIAR) system will turn out to be an expensive misjudgment of priorities.

Rural Development Programs

Implementation of community and integrated rural develop-ment programs has been a continuing challenge and a source of frustration to development assistance agencies. One major source of disillusionment has been the lack of consistency between the dynamics of community development and the imperatives of donor assistance. A second source of disillusionment has been the difficulty of achieving consistency between the local self-help and resource mobilization philosophy of rural development programs and the need of donors to achieve measurable improvements in basic human needs indicators. Yet mobilization of local physical and institutional resources and the strengthening of local governance remain important resources for development.

Human Resource Development

Both development theorists and development assistance agencies were slow to recognize the importance of investment in human capital—in education and health—for economic growth. It is now abundantly clear that the absence of a high level of literacy and numeracy in rural communities severely depresses the returns that can be realized from investments in rural infrastructure, agricultural technology, and community development. Yet, there is little evidence that the development assistance community has been effective in supporting the development of primary and secondary education.

Some Concerns about the Future

It is quite clear that, except for the very smallest states such as Hong Kong and Singapore, most food that is consumed must be produced in the nation or region in which it is consumed. This is not to deny the gains from food trade or food aid.

There are several reasons for believing that many developing countries' gains in agricultural production and in the well-being of rural people will be more difficult to achieve in the next several decades than in the recent past. These include (1) greater dif-ficulty in removing constraints on yield increases for a number of important crops; (2) the emergence of a series of resource and environmental challenges to the sustainability of growth in agricultural production; (3) a number of indicators that suggest the possibility of an emerging global health crisis; and (4) the limited institutional capacity in many developing countries to mobilize local resources for rural development.

Technical Constraints on Yield Increases

One of the great success stories of development assistance and of natural development efforts has been the rapid growth in crop yields that have been achieved in many developing countries during the past 25 years. This progress has been uneven. The most rapid gains have been achieved in crops such as wheat, rice, and maize, for which substantial research capacity already existed in the developed countries or in crops such as sugar, rubber, and oil palm that have been important in trade between tropical and temperate countries.

It seems apparent that agricultural production gains will be achieved with much greater difficulty in the next quarter century than they were in the past. By the first decade of the next century, there will be few areas where agricultural production can be expanded by increasing area cultivated. There has not yet been a Green Revolution in the countries of Africa south of the Sahara. In most Africa countries, and in some of the poorer countries of Asia and Latin America, the institutional capacity to generate improvements in agricultural technology that will lead to high yields has not yet been established.

The sources of yield gains, even for those countries that have established substantial research and technology delivery capacity, are not as apparent as during the last quarter century. In the mid-1960s it was apparent that large production gains could be achieved from three sources: (1) the development of modern fertilizer-responsive crop varieties; (2) the uses of higher levels of fertilizer; and (3) the expansion of the area irrigated. Difficulty is currently being experienced in raising yield ceilings for cereal crops that have experienced rapid yield gains in the past. The environmental response to increases in fertilizer use has declined. Maintenance research is rising as a share of research effort. Expansion of irrigated area has become more difficult.

It is possible that, within another decade, advances in basic knowledge will create new opportunities for advancing agricultural technology that will reverse the urgency of some of these concerns. Advances in molecular biology and in genetic engineering are occurring rapidly. But the date when those promising advances will be translated into productive technology has receded. And for most developing countries, the problem of establishing the capacity to address the crop- and location-specific technologies needed to sustain advances in crop yields will be even more difficult to attain than past advances that have con-tributed to yield gains.

Resource and Environmental Constraints on Sustainable Growth

In most developing countries, it will be necessary to achieve and sustain growth in agricultural production in the 3 to 5 percent per year range during the next quarter century. This is well above the historical growth rates obtained by developed countries. There is growing concern about the impact of a series of resource and environmental constraints that may seriously impose on the capacity to sustain growth in agricultural production in this range.

One concern is with the impact of agricultural production practices now being employed in those areas that have already made the transition to more intensive systems of agricultural production. These include salinization of soils in irrigated areas, groundwater contamination from plant nutrients and pesticides, and growing resistance of insect pests and pathogens to present methods of control. A second set of concerns relates to the extension of agriculture into more fragile environments. These include soil erosion, desertification, and potential climate changes resulting from deforestation in the humid and subhumid tropics. A third set of concerns stem from the impact of industrialization on climate and other environmental changes. These include the effects of acid rain, destruction of the ozone layer, and global warming.

An Emerging Global Health Crisis

During the 1950s, it became clear that lack of effective and appropriate technology was becoming a major constraint in growth of agricultural production and that capacity to meet food needs were emerging as a major threat to quality of life of both rural and urban people in developing countries. Between the mid-1960s and mid-1970s, the commonly used quantitative health indicators—life expectancy and infant mortality—experienced substantial improvement in almost all developing countries. Although daily calorie supply per capita did decline in a number of the poorest countries, particularly in Africa during this period, concern about nutritional deficiency as a source of poor health has receded in most developing countries over the last several decades.

There are, however, a number of indicators suggesting that other threats to health will become increasingly important by the early decades of the next century. Dramatic progress has been made in the control and reduction of losses due to infectious disease. Advances in the control of diarrheal disease have been impressive. But relatively little progress has been made in the control of parasitic disease. A number of parasitic diseases continue to have serious implications for health and productivity of rural people, particularly in Africa where the coevolution of humans and disease has been the longest (trypanosomiasis, schistosomiasis, onchecerciasis, amebiasis). The sustainability of advances in malaria control is a subject of serious concern. AIDS could emerge as a major threat to economic viability in both developed and developing countries.

A second set of health concerns arises out of the environmental impacts of agricultural and industrial production already iden-tified. Two decades ago, it was not uncommon to view the ability of less-developed countries to absorb the negative residuals from agricultural and industrial production as an economic advantage. As environmental pollution has intensified, particularly in the centrally planned and developing countries, the effects on environmental pollution have become better understood, and complacency has been giving way to concern.

It is not completely unrealistic to anticipate that in many rural villages in the developing world the number of sick people will become a serious burden on productive capacity as we approach the first decade of the next century.

Institutional Capacity to Mobilize Local Resources

One of the major advances in our understanding of the development process over the last several decades has been our recognizing the importance of human capital accumulation and institutional innovation as sources of economic and social development. As this understanding has broadened, it has come to represent an important challenge to the planning ideology that dominated early postwar development doctrine. The more successful developing countries have experienced dramatic growth in schooling and in literacy and numeracy.

It is apparent, however, that relatively few developing countries have been successful in creating an institutional environment capable of mobilizing the resources of rural people for their own development. The political and economic resources accumulated at the center tend to become unavailable for local development. The relationship between growth and distribution of political resources and growth and distribution of economic resources has been neglected since the naive views of political and economic modernization of the 1950s and 1960s.

Attempts have been made to implement rural development programs without giving adequate attention to the institutions of local governance. There is great enthusiasm in some areas about the potential role of nongovernmental voluntary organizations. But this enthusiasm has not been accompanied by careful analysis.

The Future of U.S. Foreign Economic Assistance

Anyone who has attempted to review the history of trends and policies with respect to food security and foreign assistance realizes they should know better than to try to anticipate future trends. Yet, one fact does stand out in the history of U.S. foreign assistance effort: the United States's commitment to foreign economic assistance has largely been a response to times of tension between the United States and the USSR. Major increases in foreign assistance resources were made during such periods—the late 1940s and early 1950s, the late 1950s and early 1960s, and again in the late 1970s and early 1980s. It is hard to believe, if the easing of tension between the United States and the Soviet Union continues, that decline in the resources committed to foreign economic assistance will not continue—as they have since the mid-1980s. Furthermore, development in domestic and international agricultural commodity policies are likely to make food aid less favored by an availability of surplus commodities and hence more expensive. It is possible that a global health crisis, shared by both the undeveloped and developed countries, could provide the motivation for a renewed commitment to foreign assistance, but this is a development we can hardly welcome.

I am not optimistic about the shape of any new legislation from current House and Senate deliberations. But it does seem that we should be making a fairly rapid transition from an "aid" per-spective to a perspective that might be captured by a rubric such as International Scientific, Technical, and Economic Cooperation Agency. The activities of such an agency should not be bound by artificial boundaries. It should be free to work cooperatively on a global basis—with the developed market economies, the centrally planned economies, the newly industrializing economies, the middle-income developing economies, as well as the poorest underdeveloped economies.

Notes

1. The material in this section is discussed more fully in Vernon W. Ruttan, "Why Foreign Economic Assistance?" *Economic Development and Cultural Change* 36 (January 1989): 412-24.

2. The material in this section is from Vernon W. Ruttan, "Food Aid: Surplus Disposal, Strategic Assistance, Development Aid and Basic Needs," mimeo, University of Minnesota, Department of Agricultural and Applied Economics, Saint Paul, Minnesota July 10, 1989.

3. This section draws primarily on Anne O. Krueger, Constantine Michalopoulos, and Vernon W. Ruttan, *Aid and Development* Baltimore: The Johns Hopkins University Press, 1989.

References

Bansfield, E.C. 1963. "American Foreign Aid Doctrine." In *Why Foreign Aid?* Robert A. Baldwin, ed. Chicago: Rand McNally.

Beitz, Charles. 1979. *Political Theory and International Relations.* Cambridge, Mass.: Harvard University Press.

Mozick, Robert. 1974. *Anarchy, State, and Utopia.* Oxford: Blackwell.

Runge, C. Ford. 1977. "American Agricultural Assistance and the New International Economic Order." *World Development* 5(8):225-46.

7

Food Aid as a Development Resource: Performance, Potential, and Prospects

Lehman B. Fletcher

Food aid has been the target of a disproportionate share of criticism concerning its effectiveness as a development resource. Its detractors claim that it can reduce incentives for domestic food production and thus raise the probability that recipients receive short-term benefits at the cost of long-term dependence on food imports. The literature also discusses pernicious policy disincentives through which food aid, by alleviating food shortages, can enable governments to postpone, if not actually avoid, politically difficult policy reforms. While domestic food production and policy reforms can be discouraged, a country's consumers can be encouraged to shift their food preferences to commodities not easily grown there. Feeding and food-for-work programs can be costly to sustain, complex to manage, and poorly targeted to intended recipients. Their benefits can take the form of welfare handouts to the politically powerful with little impact on the long-term income streams of the poor.

Proponents of food aid see its potential. Several possible ways it can further the economic development of poor countries have been propounded in voluminous publications. First, it can add to a country's resources to be used for current consumption or capital accumulation, a contribution dependent on the extent to which the food aid is an addition to, rather than a substitute for, other assistance. It can augment foreign exchange and budgetary resources available to recipient countries. It can increase the income and improve the nutritional and health status and educational levels of the poor, thus directly their alleviating hunger and poverty and adding to their human capital. It can help ameliorate the adverse effects of policy reforms and structural adjustments on a country's lower income population groups.

The most significant word in all of this litany about the costs and benefits of food aid is *can,* which many authors wittingly or unwittingly convert to *will.* Whether food aid's potential for furthering development success or causing development failure dominates in any given situation depends in large measure on donors' objectives and terms for making food aid available, and whether the policy environment and institutional capacities of its recipients are conducive to its effective utilization as a development resource.

The next section reviews some facts about food aid. The following section concentrates on the analytics of food aid. Next, some experience with food aid is assessed to identify success and failure elements. The final section considers recent suggestions for improving food aid and concludes with some recommendations for modifications with primary reference to the U.S. program.

Food Aid Facts

Food aid is now not more than 10 percent by value of total official development assistance given by Development Assistance Committee (DAC) countries (Table 7.1). Yet, as already noted, it is a highly visible component of foreign aid, attracting attention and generating controversy far beyond its relative importance in the aid portfolio. Its high visibility is due partly to its role as a humanitarian response to natural and other disasters and partly to its perceived potential for the direct alleviation of hunger and poverty in the least-developed countries.

In the 1950s and 1960s, the United States was the main donor of food aid. The food aid was directed mainly to Asia and wheat

Table 7.1. Share of net food aid disbursements in the official development assistance of DAC member countries (percent)

Countries	1977	1978	1979	1980	1981	1982	1983	1984	1985	1986
Australia	6.10	6.90	12.80	9.60	15.90	11.50	13.50	15.10	6.80	11.20
Austria	1.80	2.80	2.20	7.30	4.60	3.40	5.70	1.10	3.20	1.50
Belgium	6.30	5.20	5.30	6.60	7.80	7.60	7.60	6.30	10.00	3.60
Canada	18.70	21.20	14.80	15.40	13.50	17.90	14.90	19.20	16.10	15.50
Denmark	11.10	6.30	7.30	9.40	9.40	7.20	7.30	6.70	5.70	3.90
Finland	15.40	2.00	6.20	3.60	5.20	5.60	5.90	6.70	5.70	6.70
France	2.30	2.90	2.40	3.00	4.00	3.50	2.50	3.90	3.20	2.40
Germany, Fed. Rep.	7.70	7.00	5.10	6.00	8.70	7.20	5.30	9.00	6.90	5.70
Italy	23.00	13.20	17.30	11.10	21.60	14.30	13.80	12.30	14.90	10.80
Ireland	-		-	-	-	2.10	3.00	20.00	20.50	3.20
Japan	1.10	1.00	4.20	7.80	10.90	4.60	3.80	1.00	0.70	1.20
Netherlands	7.10	11.10	5.80	6.40	7.10	5.40	7.00	9.10	7.50	6.30
New Zealand	2.50	0.90	0.10	1.40	a	1.50	1.60	1.80	1.90	a
Norway	6.60	5.20	4.30	4.50	4.90	5.00	4.50	4.40	4.70	3.40
Sweden	5.00	6.30	4.60	4.90	4.80	3.60	2.90	4.30	4.50	3.20
Switzerland	13.90	13.40	11.80	11.10	9.70	9.10	7.80	9.40	9.60	7.10
United Kingdom	4.20	5.50	4.00	6.30	8.10	8.20	6.20	9.90	8.90	5.60
United States	25.80	19.70	27.80	18.30	21.80	13.80	16.70	17.70	19.80	15.90
Total DAC countries	12.20	10.20	10.00	9.60	11.50	8.90	9.10	10.40	10.60	7.90

SOURCE: Compiled by FAO from data provided by OECD. Taken from CFA/WFP, *Food Aid Policies and Programs.* Rome, 25/P/5, April 1988.

(a) New Zealand supplied 440 tons of dried skim milk in 1981 and 394 tons in 1986, the value of which is not reflected in the data provided by OECD.

was the major commodity. India, Pakistan, and Sri Lanka, and to a lesser extent Korea and the Philippines, were large recipients. Beginning in the 1970s, other donors have become suppliers—some major—of food aid, notably the EC, Canada, Australia, and Japan (Table 7.2). With the exception of Bangladesh, the earlier main recipient countries in Asia have become largely self-reliant. Egypt and Bangladesh continue as major recipients. Food aid to several Latin American and Caribbean countries has risen signif-icantly in the 1980s. But the bulk of food aid now goes to Africa, especially sub-Saharan Africa (see Statistical Appendix Table A.5). Ethiopia, Sudan, and Mozambique are receiving large shipments after recent crop failures and devastation due to civil wars. Cereals are still the dominant food supplied but the amounts of noncereal food aid have increased, especially vegetable oil and skimmed milk powder (Statistical Appendix Table A.6).

According to the estimates in Table 7.2, cereal aid shipments in 1988-89 fell below the 1974 World Food Conference target of 10 million tons for the first time since the buildup in food aid in 1984-85. Tight aid budgets and continued strong prices for cereals could imply that food aid shipments may decline again in 1989-90. However, most donors continue to meet their minimum commitments under the 1986 Food Aid Convention.

Cereal shipments by the United States in the 1980s have averaged barely more than one-third of the level of cereal aid provided in the 1960s (Table 7.2). Nevertheless, cereal food aid from the United States still constituted one-half to two-thirds of total cereal food aid in the last decade.

The share of cereal aid in the world total provided by the United States shows considerable year-to-year fluctuations. The lowest U.S. shares were recorded in 1974-75, the early 1980s, and 1988-89. Shipments from the United States in 1988-89 declined by more than 25 percent from 1987-88, the sharpest year-to-year drop since 1973-74 when shipments fell by 50 percent. Both of these reductions were associated with high grain prices and tight do-mestic supplies. Since U.S. food aid budgets are fixed in dollars, volumes of shipments tend to fall when grain prices are high, which are also likely to be the years of greatest need in the recipient countries. This pattern

Table 7.2. Cereal food aid by principal donors (million metric tons)

	United States	Canada	Australia	EEC	Japan	Others	Total
1965/66	17.32	NA	NA	NA	NA	NA	17.73
1966/67	NA	NA	NA	NA	NA	NA	NA
1967/68	13.50	0.80	0.19	NA	NA	NA	16.22
1968/69	NA	NA	NA	NA	NA	NA	NA
1969/70	10.01	0.66	0.22	1.36	0.40	0.01	12.66
1970/71	8.93	1.61	0.24	0.98	0.75	0.29	12.80
1971/72	8.99	0.61	0.19	0.91	0.73	0.55	11.98
1972/73	6.95	0.81	0.26	0.99	0.53	0.31	9.85
1973/74	3.19	0.50	0.22	1.22	0.44	0.35	5.92
1974/75	4.72	0.61	0.33	1.41	0.30	0.18	7.55
1975/76	4.28	1.03	0.26	0.92	0.05	0.03	6.57
1976/77	6.15	1.18	0.23	1.13	0.23	0.05	8.97
1977/78	5.90	1.00	0.25	1.45	0.66	0.14	9.40
1978/79	6.24	0.74	0.33	1.16	0.35	0.68	9.50
1979/80	5.34	0.73	0.32	1.21	0.69	0.60	8.89
1980/81	5.21	0.60	0.37	1.29	0.91	0.56	8.94
1981/82	5.34	0.60	0.48	1.60	0.50	0.62	9.14
1982/83	5.37	0.84	0.35	1.60	0.52	0.56	9.24
1983/84	5.66	0.82	0.46	1.92	0.44	0.55	9.85
1984/85	7.54	0.94	0.47	2.50	0.28	0.76	12.49
1985/86	6.68	1.22	0.35	1.56	0.37	0.62	10.80
1986/87	7.86	1.24	0.37	1.74	0.43	0.56	12.20
1987/88	7.50	1.00	0.30	1.60	0.35	0.45	11.20
1988/89	5.49	0.98	0.29	1.96	0.39	0.69	9.80

SOURCE: CFA/WFP, Various publications. Where country data are missing, columns do not add to the total.

Note: NA indicates data not available.

contributes to the view that food aid is erratic, subject to short-term interests of donors, and less likely to be available when needed most.

Overall, within the availabilities of food aid, donors are giving higher priority in allocations to low-income, food-deficit countries that now receive 85 to 90 percent of total cereal food aid. The significance of this food aid to the receiving countries is a good deal higher than suggested by its share in their overall foreign aid. While it constitutes only around 10 percent of all cereal imports by developing countries, its role in cereal imports of low-income food-deficit countries rises to 20 percent or more (see Statistical Appendix Table A.1). In recent years, food aid has contributed more than one-half of all cereal imports by least-developed countries and one-third of those by sub-Saharan countries. Of course, these percentages would be even higher for a few individual countries, reaching as much as 90 percent of cereal imports and half of the total staple food supply available for consumption in the most aid-dependent.

The three main categories of food aid are program, project, and emergency. As compared to the 1975-80 period, the buildup in food aid in the mid-1980s went first for emergency needs and then to project use (Statistical Appendix Table A.7). These types of food aid are discussed in greater detail in a later section dealing with food aid experience.

While the bulk of food aid is provided bilaterally, the emergence of large multilateral programs was a feature of the 1970s (Statistical Appendix Table A.8). The multilateral percentage was 23.3 percent in 1986, near its highest level reached in the early 1980s. The World Food Program is the major multilateral food aid agency, although some food is also distributed by UN relief and refugee agencies. All multilateral food aid is grant assistance but bilateral food aid involves both grants and loans. Bilateral grants are currently about two-thirds of total bilateral food aid. This percentage has increased significantly in the 1980s (Statistical Appendix Table A.8). The U.S. Title I concessional sales program accounts for most of the loan-funded food assistance.

The Analytics of Food Aid

Earlier investigations of the potential effects of food aid on domestic food prices and production were generally carried out in a partial equilibrium framework. The two-commodity general equilibrium international trade model has recently been used to good effect by Bhagwati (1986) and Srinivasan (1989) to provide more rigorous analysis of the issues. I summarize their main results here to identify the key analytical questions involved in food aid.

The model starts with a country producing and consuming two aggregate commodities, food and nonfood, with a production possibilities curve reflecting given resources and technology. Consumer preferences are represented by a set of social indifference curves incorporating lump-sum income transfers between individuals to allow social welfare maximization through decentralized consumption decisions. This specification permits the separation of allocational efficiency from distributional equity. If lump-sum transfers are not feasible then achieving distributional equity may involve use of policy instruments that create efficiency losses, which means unavoidable trade-offs arise between ef-ficiency and equity.

Closed Economy

Assume the country receives a given amount of food aid, which the government sells in the domestic market and returns the sale proceeds to consumers as lump-sum transfers. How will domestic prices, food production, and economic welfare be affected?

In the absence of any further government response and conditions imposed by the donor on the recipient, the relative price of food will fall, leading to a decline in domestic food production. This result is often cited as the basis for production disincentive effects of food aid. Consumer welfare, nevertheless, will rise. Moreover, the government can avoid the fall in domestic production by intervening to keep the relative price of food from falling. This can be achieved by either a consumer food subsidy (nonfood tax) or a food production subsidy (nonfood production tax). Srinivasan (1989, 44) shows that although use of a distorting tax/subsidy intervention to prevent a fall in domestic food prices will reduce the welfare gain from the food aid, the gain nevertheless remains positive.

Open Economy

Now add to the model the assumptions that the country is open to international markets in which it is a price taker, imports food, and follows a free trade policy. If the country receives food aid, other things equal, domestic food prices will not change but food consumption will rise and commercial imports will fall. The food aid will in part replace previous commercial imports.

But food aid donors do not like to see their commercial exports fall as a consequence of their food aid. If the donor applies a "usual marketing requirement" (UMR) such that the recipient country must continue to import commercially at least as much as it did prior to food aid, then the domestic price of food will decline until domestic production is lowered and consumption raised sufficiently to absorb the required level of import. The theory of noneconomic objectives can be used to show that the optimum policy to increase imports of food to the required extent is to apply an import subsidy that lowers the domestic price of food below world prices (Bhagwati and Srinivasan 1969). Such a policy is optimal because it minimizes the welfare loss imposed by the UMR.

While the use of a UMR protects commercial export markets for the food donor, if a recipient country responds optimally by reducing the domestic price of food, then incentives for its domestic food production will be affected adversely. Can the donor insist on both objectives being met, so that its export market is not maintained at the expense of food production by the recipient? Yes, but this conditionality will force the recipient country to use a distorting food consumption subsidy rather than the first-best import subsidy, thereby imposing a further loss in welfare relative to food aid given without the UMR condition.

Of what importance are these theoretical results in a more realistic world of nonoptimal policies and noneconomic objectives? One important difference is that no recipient government actually returns the proceeds from the market sale of food aid to consumers as lump sum transfers. More commonly, the revenue from the sales accrues to the government to be used as part of its budgetary resources. Donors often try to influence or even control the uses of these so-called counterpart funds. To the extent that these funds are used for investments that improve agricultural productivity, and agricultural supply, they can expand food production in the recipient country. These supply-shifting impacts are unlikely to be realized contemporaneously with the delivery of the food aid but rather enhance the domestic production of food only in subsequent years. This lagged impact of food aid on production would shift the production possibilities curve outward on the food axis over time in the simple static model described above.

Targeting the Poor

The rationale for food aid is often based on the idea that it is better to use food surpluses created by domestic policies in donor countries for the poor in recipient countries than storing them or dumping them in world markets. Disincentive effects can be mitigated to the extent the food reaches the poor as a gift, as a wage payment in kind, or at a price sufficiently low so that its positive income effect expands their market demand. Markets can be segmented by regions, commodities, or channels of distribution to implement price discrimination and demand expansion in favor of the poor. In practice, perfect market segmentation is unlikely so that some disincentive effects are to be expected and costs of this form of surplus disposal made correspondingly higher.

Assessing Food Aid Needs

Projecting the future is inherently difficult and the estimation of food aid requirements of recipient countries is no exception. The analyst is confronted with a series of questions, the answers to which largely determine the magnitudes of the estimates that result. These questions involve trends in population, per capita income and its distribution, food production and consumption by households, nutritional requirements and status, and commercial import capacity, among other important factors.

Various approaches have been used to establish criteria and estimate countries' needs for food aid in a given year and in the future. A frequently used approach involves estimates of total import requirements under various growth and consumption scenarios, and then calculation of the portion of import require-ments likely to be met with commercial imports based on the country's ability to pay. The residual between total import requirements and projected commercial imports represents a "cereals gap" that must be covered by food aid if consumption targets are to be met. Evaluation of ability to import commercially usually takes into account a country's export earnings, foreign exchange reserves, and total merchandise imports.

Estimates of food aid requirements reported in Huddleston (1984) are an example of the type of need assessment. This study included 99 middle-income and low-income countries. Only middle-income countries with weak food production and balance of payments positions were assumed to need food aid. However, the amount was limited to an extent by imposing the condition that food aid be given only when the quantity of cereal imports adequate to meet nutritional needs exceeded 5 percent of export earnings.

All low-income countries were assumed to require food aid. In the few cases in which per capita availability was adequate by the specified nutritional norms, food aid was still assumed to be needed for balance of payments support. The amount of the requirement for each country was estimated to fulfill minimum per capita nutritional needs, with an allowance for commercial imports equal to 2 percent of export earnings. The last adjustment forced allocation at least some minimum amount of foreign exchange for cereal imports before the quantities of food aid needed to close the gaps between food requirements and availabilities were calculated.

The 39 low-income countries received 4.3 million metric tons (mmt) of food aid in 1978-79. The study concluded that the amount required was far larger, totaling 27.3 mmt. The principal reason for the large size of the total food aid requirements was the increase to meet nutritional needs. While the estimates would be lower if other data showed lesser nutritional deficiencies, the study's basic conclusion that much larger amounts of food aid are needed to alleviate hunger in the low-income countries would not change.

Projections of this same type, but using a more complex model and including separate estimates for nonproject, project, and emergency food aid, have been presented by FAO (1983). In addition, project food aid for each country was linked to the amount that could be effectively utilized under existing economic conditions and management constraints. To this extent, this study integrated a second approach to food aid requirement (absorptive capacity) with the cereals-gap approach. It concluded that food aid needs exceed 20 mmt per year.

Another example of the gap approach is the Food Aid Needs and Availabilities (FANA) periodic projections made by the Economic Research Service of the USDA. The FANA model contrasts the cereals import requirements to maintain status quo consumption, defined as the average per capita level of the preceding three years in each country, with the nutrition-based requirement of providing 100 percent of the FAO/WHO standards for average per capita intake of calories. Projection of total cereal requirements is made for each of the two succeeding years.

The next step in the FANA approach is to estimate food aid needs within the total cereal import requirements. The FANA procedure incorporates a decision rule reflecting the assessment of a country's ability to finance cereal imports from export earnings: food aid requirements are calculated on the assumption that the percentage of export earnings spent on cereals does not exceed the share during the base period. The FANA procedure also incorporates the best estimates of the production of staple foods in the coming year, using the latest USDA forecasts. In this way, short-term food aid required to avoid a fall in food con-sumption due to production shortfalls is included in aggregate food aid needs. In some countries, logistics and administration are assumed to limit the amount of food aid a country could actually absorb.

Recent FANA results for Nepal are quoted below as an example (ERS 1988).

Total cereal production in 1987-88 is currently estimated at 3.0 million tons, 29 percent less than earlier forecasts and slightly below the drought-reduced harvests of 1986-87. The decline stems largely from rice losses from drought, followed by heavy downpours, in the central and eastern parts of the country. Rice production is now estimated at 1.6 million tons, revised downward 53 percent.

Because of the drop in domestic cereal production, the estimated status quo cereal import requirement has risen from zero to 327,000 tons in 1987-88. Similarly, the nutrition-based estimate has nearly tripled, increasing to 848,000 tons from 300,000.

There have been no revisions in Nepal's financial situation, which remains extremely weak. The commercial import capacity continues to be estimated at $7 million (28,000 tons), leaving 1987-88 status quo and nutrition-based additional cereal needs of 299,000 tons and 821,000 tons, respectively. According to some observers, it is unlikely these needs can be met because logistical and administrative problems would limit imports to about 200,000 tons.

Assuming average weather in 1988-89, a rebound in overall cereal production is projected. Status quo import requirements are forecast to fall to 131,000 tons, with about 697,000 tons needed to raise consumption to the FAO/WHO recommended minimum diet. Compared with 1987-88, additional cereal needs will also drop to 100,000 tons and 667,000 tons, using the status quo and nutrition-based methods, respectively.

Although based at the time on the latest agricultural projections available in Washington, the divergence of the estimates given by FANA for 1987-88 and the actual situation that prevailed in Nepal is striking. A bumper crop was produced in 1987-88, leading to the highest per capita domestic supply in a decade. Assuming the production estimates in the country were closer to reality, the FANA conclusion that 327,000 tons of cereal imports were required just to maintain "status quo" utilization levels was totally un-warranted. Had the situation been as represented by FANA, Nepal's government would have been seeking emergency food aid with the same diligence it demonstrated in earlier years of drought or other natural disaster.

This leaves for discussion the 600,000+ tons FANA concluded was needed in Nepal for nutrition-based requirements. The first point about this figure, as well as the status quo requirements given earlier, is that the FANA analysts recognized that "it is unlikely these needs can be met because logistical and administrative problems would limit imports to about 200,000 tons." How this particular limit on Nepal's absorptive capacity was established is not explained. It far exceeds any historical level of food aid the country has ever received.

But understanding that food aid, even at the level of 200,000 tons, would not necessarily alleviate hunger and reduce malnutrition in Nepal is essential to understanding Nepal's food situation and the role of food aid. If sold into the major domestic market, prices would likely change little and more food grains would flow across the border into India. This would happen because the Nepal price level for food prices is tied to the geographically contiguous and larger Indian market by effective spatial arbitrage. Thus, the effects would depend on how the food aid was used. Only if it were made available to food-deficit households free or through subsidized sales or food-for-work programs would the food-deprived population benefit. Most of these households are located in more remote hill and mountain areas of the country with little or no road access, which makes internal distribution expensive if not impossible. Nepal has neither the financial resources nor management capability to mount a domestic food assistance program of the required magnitude.

The implication is that food aid requirements calculated by a gap approach are likely to be well above the amounts that could be effectively utilized in a given country. Management constraints and costs associated with use of the "free" food almost always restrict the amounts that can be put to effective use. In fact, the other approach that could be used for estimating requirements is based on this concept of a country's absorptive capacity. No standard methodology has been created for this approach so its use remains based on subjective estimates by analysts.

The underlying implication of this second approach is that food aid needs cannot be defined independently of some assessment of financial and programmatic capacity at different levels in the country to handle the food resources. Both local budgetary and institutional capacities need to be included in this assessment. The extent to which binding constraints prevent countries from absorbing the quantities of food aid they appear to need will differ widely from country to country.

The common practice by which gap assessments are made on the basis of average availabilities of calories in a country is also a serious weakness. Enough data have accumulated in many countries to show that poverty limits the access of much of the poor population to food available in the market. This poverty is often concentrated in rural areas and in specific regions of the country. Assessments that recognize the limited access of the low-income population to food will show higher food needs than aggregate analysis based on national averages.

Finally, much of the work that ostensibly deals with food aid needs might better term the results "food gaps." Food aid is one program for possibly addressing those food deficits. It is not the only one, nor is there anything in its historical record to suggest it alone can solve a country's hunger and malnutrition problems and create food security. (A more complete review of the approaches and comparative results of food aid assessments is contained in Appendix 7.A at the end of this chapter.)

Experience with Food Aid

Food aid is fully tied in the sense that it comes embodied in specific commodities. Of course, most foreign aid ultimately results in expanded imports of commodities and services. Only budget support and project aid converted to local currency retain their character as cash inside the receiving country's borders. While commodities rather than their cash equivalent can never be preferred from the perspective of recipients, the more pertinent question relates to the disadvantages of commodity aid.

The answer to that question turns on the effectiveness of food aid in promoting a country's development, and is discussed later in this chapter. Two other important considerations involve the extent to which food aid is additional to other aid and to what extent its use requires the allocation of scarce complementary resources by the recipient government. Food aid is probably, in part, additional, but no one has ever been able to quantify to what extent it results in larger aid flows overall. The complementary resources required may be financial or managerial or both, and either is likely to have high opportunity costs to the country in terms of alternative development programs.

Donors' Objectives and Allocations

In its contemporary incarnation, food aid grew out of com-modity surpluses in the United States in the 1950s and 1960s, and more recent surpluses in the EC. More often than not, it has been offered in the commodities that were in storage, mainly wheat, rice, corn, and dairy products. Donors' and recipients' interests may conflict over the commodity composition of the food aid. Donors are unlikely to allow recipients to trade part or all of the aid given in one commodity for commodities they would prefer. And the donors may apply UMRs. Forced to absorb the food aid in the given commodities while in theory maintaining commercial imports, recipients often find it difficult to avoid production disincentives or distortionary consumption subsidies. Moreover, substitution effects in production and consumption can spread the disincentives and demand distortions widely in their food baskets.

There are two interrelated issues about commodities utilized for food aid. The first is that of acceptability. Are the foods provided included in the normal diet of the population? If not, are the commodities acceptable substitutes or complements to traditional foods in the recipient country? Stories abound about the shipment of socially and culturally unfamiliar or unacceptable foodstuffs. The second is the cash equivalent value of the commodities supplied based on local prices in relation to the costs of the commodities (Reutlinger and Katona-Apte 1987). How do the economic costs of the commodities, including ocean and inland transportation and storage/handling costs, compare to their value to consumers in the recipient countries as indicated by local market prices? Could the cost effectiveness of the aid for donors and recipients be improved by more appropriate choices of commodities? These questions cannot even be posed when the commodity composition of food aid is arbitrarily fixed by its donors.

U.S. food aid clearly reflects multiple legislative objectives. From its inception in 1954 through the mid-1960s, PL 480 stressed surplus disposal and export market development as well as humanitarian goals. Legislative revisions in 1966 deleted the act's objective of surplus disposal and placed emphasis on food aid to promote economic development in recipient countries. This revision also incorporated the concept of self-help, requiring recipients to undertake measures to increase their agricultural production, improve their marketing of agricultural products, and reduce their population growth rates.

Although the argument has been made that the development objective has eclipsed competing goals (Hopkins 1987), actual food aid allocations do not support that optimistic assessment. Major recipients of U.S. food aid are shown in Statistical Appendix Table A.12 for 1975 and 1985.

Egypt currently receives the largest amount of U.S. food aid, both total and per capita. In FY 1987, Egypt was allocated 1.5 mmt of food, which represented about 20 percent of total U.S. food aid. While Egypt does qualify as a low-income country, the amount of food aid it receives reflects U.S. foreign policy interests far more than development objectives. The aid is used by the Egyptian government primarily to help provide massive food subsidies in the form of cheap bread. As a result, its cereal consumption has grown at a phenomenal 15 percent annual average and the country now imports more than half its food. Cereal imports have increased from about 50 percent of domestic production in 1975 to 100 percent in the 1980s. Despite self-help measures and other attempts by donors at policy conditionality, Egyptian policymakers have so far been unwilling to dismantle their heavily subsidized food distribution policies backed by food aid. The political dangers of doing so are well illustrated by the riots that took place in 1977 when reductions in bread and flour subsidies were attempted.

Other country allocations where foreign policy interests loom large are for El Salvador, Guatemala, Indonesia, Morocco, Pak-istan, Bolivia, Peru, and Costa Rica. The relative emphasis given to this objective is a continuing source of controversy and tension in the interagency process through which U.S food aid is administered.

In relation to export market development, the direct contribution of food aid to U.S. agricultural exports has declined from 25 percent in the 1960s to as little as 3 percent in the 1980s (see Statistical Appendix Table A.9). The boom in commercial agricultural exports in the 1970s and early 1980s substantially reduced the proportional importance of shipments under PL 480. Other subsidy programs have also been instituted to address market development and share concerns (Statistical Appendix Table A.15).

Proponents for the market development role of food aid argue that it helps to develop buyers' preferences for U.S. products, build commercial relations, and expand imports based on income growth in receiving countries. Countries that were recipients of food aid and are now important commercial buyers of U.S. agri-cultural exports include Japan, South Korea, and Taiwan. As pointed out in Chapter 1, the weakness of this argument is that even though several former recipients of food aid are now important importers of U.S. farm products, the association does not prove that food aid itself was a unique and effective form of foreign aid in promoting those countries' rapid and sustained economic growth. For several, studies have tried to evaluate the factors responsible for their success and have usually identified foreign aid as one important factor but not specifically food aid. The tendency for higher growth and income-developing countries to become food importers is well established. While that associa-tion may reconcile foreign aid and the long-run interests of U.S. grain producers, it does not itself support use of food as a development resource. Making that connection requires that food aid be shown to be additional to other aid and a cost-effective means to promote a recipient's economic and agricultural development.

In the 1980s, slow growth and large debt service have stalled commercial imports by many developing countries. For these countries program-type food aid can provide balance of payment support to help them maintain import and consumption levels. Since much of this food may not represent additional imports above previous commercial levels, UMRs as usually calculated could be violated, although commercial imports may not in reality be displaced.

Food Emergencies, Famines, and Food Aid

Humanitarian relief for victims of natural disasters, wars, and other food emergencies is the most widely recognized and publicly supported objective of food aid. While few wish to object to food aid used to avert starvation or severe malnutrition, criticisms have been directed at delays in responses, poor plan-ning and execution of shipments and food distribution, and excess deliveries arriving after the emergency is over that then create disincentives for local production.

Another important point, made by Srinivasan (1989), is that emergency food aid may neither prevent starvation nor reduce chances of future famines. Drawing on evidence that shows that famines often are not associated with rapid declines in food availability, he pointed out that crop failures that erode incomes of the rural poor may reduce their access to food and cause starvation regardless of food availability in the aggregate. In these cases, food aid from either internal or external sources can be used for relief and food-for-work programs to avoid mass starvation. To the extent that the food aid is utilized to employ rural labor to build irrigation, transport, and other infrastructure, both in crop-failure years and in slack seasons of normal years, production can be increased and possibly the number and degree of crop failures reduced in the long run (Mellor and Gavian 1987). This means that no sharp division should be drawn between emergency relief and development objectives of food aid.

From Food Aid to Self-Reliance or Dependency?

Several aspects of this crucial question have already been mentioned. A shift in preferences away from locally produced commodities toward commodities supplied as food aid is one possible long-term consequence. Such a shift toward imported wheat and rice and away from domestically produced coarse grains has allegedly been observed in West Africa (Delgado and Miller 1985). Some of this grain was commercially imported (Nigeria) while some was supplied by food aid and commodity import assistance. The domestic prices of the imported grain were often lowered by macroeconomic policies (overvalued exchange rates) and supply expansion from absorbing food aid. These circumstances led Mellor and Ezekiel (1987) to point out that the consumption shifts may actually reflect higher income elasticities for "superior" cereals such as wheat, compared to "inferior" coarse grains like sorghum. Income effects from lower relative prices for the more preferred commodities could have changed the com-modity composition of consumption without a shift in preferences.

Another argument is that food aid reduces pressures on recipient governments to improve the country's own agricultural performance. To change this attitude would require withdrawal of the aid or use of policy dialogue and conditionality. India is often cited as an example where policymakers became convinced of the dangers of food aid dependency and domestic discrimination against agriculture: policies were changed, neglect of agriculture was reversed, the Green Revolution was supported, and con-sequently India became self-sufficient in food grains in the 1980s.

Srinivasan (1989) challenged this cause-and-effect contention. He concluded that India's agricultural sector was not more favored by allocation of investment by planners in the period since the mid-1960s than before. Moreover, he pointed out that the trend rate of growth of food grains was not significantly different between the two periods. The sources of output growth shifted from area expansion to improvements in yields, and production of wheat accelerated because of adoption of biochemical technology, but this technology became available only in the mid-1960s and afterwards.

If the recipient country does not view food aid as permanent (and what foreign aid can rationally be so regarded?) it can (1) consume the food while avoiding negative impacts on prices or incentives, (2) let prices fall and hence incentives to produce food and invest in capacity to produce it, or (3) use the food as a resource to promote long-term agricultural and overall develop-ment. The outcome thus depends on the success donors and recipients have in devising approaches to achieve the last of these three possibilities.

Program Food Aid

This type of food aid, offered through Title I concessional sales under the U.S. program, accounts for 55 to 60 percent of food assistance both by the United States and on a global basis. It provides balance of payments support for countries to import food for which they do not have the necessary foreign exchange.

With program food aid, recipients first receive the commodities themselves, which adds to their food supply. They also receive foreign exchange savings to the extent that the food aid substitutes for commercial imports. When food aid is monetized, that is, sold by the recipient government in the domestic market, local currency is generated. This local currency does not itself supply any real resources to the economy but its use to fund expenditures via the government budget does add to aggregate demand. Thus, it can be inflationary in the absence of further inflows of goods from abroad or compensatory monetary and fiscal policies. Questions about ownership of the local currency and how its use is to be decided have plagued donor-recipient relations.

The use of self-help requirements and the Title III program that converts Title I loans to grants in response to agreed policy changes anticipated the increasing tendency to use food aid as a condition to promote structural adjustments and policy reforms. For example, the United States has provided food aid to Bang-ladesh on grant terms under Title III to encourage reductions in food subsidies and a more open-market food pricing system. Title III has been difficult to implement and involves only a relatively small part of the Title I food aid. While no systematic comparative appraisal of self-help measures under Title I has been undertaken, there is serious doubt as to their effectiveness as a lever on recipient countries. They have tended to include a wide range of activities and policy changes, and have sometimes been undermined when subsequent Title I allocations have been fixed based on other criteria (such as foreign policy interests).

Title I food is not free to recipient countries. Its real cost depends on how hard the loan terms are and to what extent recipients must pay for ocean transportation and handling costs. In contrast, most project food aid is provided free at recipients' borders. Some donors also pay part or all of the internal trans-portation and handling costs for project food.

Project Food Aid

This type of food aid accounts for less than 20 percent of the global total. Its purpose is to use the donated commodities directly in feeding programs or in food-for-work projects. Project food aid is mainly provided bilaterally (under PL 480 Title II) and multilaterally by the World Food Program.

These projects have given rise to a great many questions. To what extent are the feeding programs targeted to the neediest and most vulnerable groups? Do they result in sustainable improve-ments in nutritional status or are they mostly welfare handouts that disappear when the food aid ends? Are they integrated into the recipients' long term plans for human resource development? Are work projects chosen in accordance with development priorities or to benefit particular groups? In addition to the wages in kind, do the poor also receive some of the longer term economic benefits resulting from the projects themselves?

Food-for-work is often advocated as an approach that can both target the poor in the short term and enhance their income earning opportunities and food security in the longer term. India has made the most sustained effort, using rural work programs to gainfully employ rural workers in slack seasons to create productive assets and social infrastructure.

There, as in other countries, these programs have been criticized on the grounds that the works are poorly designed and hence their benefits largely accrue to nontarget groups. Corruption and other management problems can also reduce benefits going to the target groups.

Food-for-work projects require complementary financial resources to make them effective. There are costs for the internal storage and distribution of the food. The projects must be man-aged and monitored. Work projects often require tools and other equipment and at least partial payment of wages in cash is preferred.

Proponents claim that well-targeted and well-executed programs could have large and favorable impacts on the poor, making them the direct beneficiaries of both the expenditures and their outputs. But a sustained effort to develop the managerial capacity and mobilize the complementary resources, as well as a multiyear commitment of the food aid itself, will be required to realize this potential.

The Future of Food Aid

Should food aid be viewed as a unique and necessary element in foreign aid, so that if it did not now exist donors would need to invent it, or as a form of aid that evolved out of historical circumstances that have shifted to the point that it should now be used sparingly, if at all? Several aspects of this intriguing question are considered here.

Agricultural Trade Liberalization

Success in liberalizing agricultural markets and reducing agricultural subsidies that affect both domestic and international markets would have several effects on food aid. It would completely eliminate the surplus disposal element since the domestic policies that give rise to excess domestic stocks would disappear. The real costs of food aid to donors would rise since the commodities utilized would have clear opportunity costs in world markets.

In most developing countries the majority of the poor are net purchasers of food, many being small farmers or landless farm workers. Increases in world prices passed on to food consumers raise the purchase price of food to the poor while income effects from output and employment increases are likely to be inadequate to offset the adverse price changes, at least in the short run. In contrast, agricultural protection in OECD countries and the resulting surplus commodity disposal can actually reduce hunger in poor developing countries by lowering world market prices and raising food aid levels. These considerations suggest that agricultural trade liberalization would intensify the need for food aid while at the same time possibly lowering its availability.

Structural Adjustment: Protecting the Vulnerable with Food Aid

A potentially important role for food aid in support of struc-tural adjustment programs in developing countries has attracted the attention of bilateral and multilateral donors. Eleven food aid donors are providing food aid to Mali to assist in restructuring its food grains marketing system, stabilizing prices, reducing deficits of the marketing boards, and raising producers' incomes. Wide-ranging reforms in the agricultural sector conditional on food aid are being implemented in Madagascar and Senegal. In Ghana, food aid provided by the World Food Program (WFP) and the World Bank is being used to raise real wages of workers engaged in export production and the improvement of infrastructure. In Grenada, local currency resources generated from the sale of food aid are being used for structural adjustment and policy reform. In Morocco, policy reforms aimed at the elimination of food subsidies in 1990 were supported by food aid targeted at the very poor. By expanding supplementary and school feeding programs using additional project food aid provided by the United States and the WFP, the nutritional risk for the very poor, whose real income may fall by one-fifth because of policy reforms, was expected to be reduced.

Since results from most of these programs are not yet available for evaluation, it is too early to judge their effectiveness. However, it seems very likely that food aid will be increasingly utilized to ease the social costs of structural adjustments and policy reforms and to promote other desirable environmental and conservation goals, like the proposed food aid to Poland and the Soviet Union.

Conclusions and Recommendations

For a number of reasons, the present is a propitious time for reformulation and reorientation of food aid. The recom-mendations below are intended to encourage discussion about that process with reference mainly to the U.S. program. Only minor mention is made of other bilateral and multilateral food aid.

Food aid can be useful in furthering development and al-leviating hunger and poverty in situations in which the recipient country is basically following an appropriate overall strategy and the aid is used either for financing high priority and well-implemented investment projects or in support of targeted sup-plementary feeding or food-for-work projects. These uses conform roughly to program and project food aid.

These uses require that a country have both a need for food aid and also a capability to manage and administer it effectively. Many who recommend major expansion of food aid seem either to neglect the problem of absorptive capacity or assume it already exists or can rather easily be created. In reality, strengthening this capacity— if not a precondition—needs to be an early and con-tinuing part of food assistance itself.

Use of food aid to support policy reforms has to be thought through carefully so that inappropriate policies are, in fact, discouraged rather than encouraged (Srinivasan 1989). Tying food aid—or any other aid—to policy reforms raises one troublesome issue: if a country's policies, and not external factors, are at fault, giving additional aid for adjustment costs from a given policy reform may actually discourage additional self-initiated reforms. Policymakers may have motivation to persist in aid-attracting but economically misguided policy choices.

The effectiveness of food aid for the uses mentioned earlier can be enhanced through proper program design, choice of commodities, length of commitment, and flexibility of manage-ment. It appears that many of these success-enhancing features are largely suppressed by numerous legislative provisions and complex administrative procedures that apply to U.S. food aid, which should be modified and simplified.

In light of the potential under GATT to reduce agricultural subsidies and liberalize agricultural trade, the connection of food aid to surplus disposal should be severed. The United States might wish to keep the Section 416 surplus disposal program active but administer it separately from development food aid.

Similarly, the use of food aid as a market development tool should cease. The United States and other donor countries now have a variety of export promotion programs in operation. If concessional loan-funded food sales are useful and cost effective in comparison to alternatives, they can be retained in the market development portfolio. The possibility that export subsidies will be ended by the GATT negotiations is not a good enough reason to continue to confound market promotion and development objectives of food aid.

Next, that part of food aid that is allocated for foreign policy purposes should be separated from development food aid and linked to Economic Support Funds (ESF). Since Congress already mandates that a minimum percentage of all commodity import programs funded by ESF must be used for agricultural products, this part of food aid can be readily administered as program and commodity-import assistance along with other ESF.

Emergency and development food aid together should be given a separate program identity. An emergency reserve could be created for use in bilateral and multilateral responses to food crises. As described earlier, attempts should be made to manage emergency programs in response to crop failures so that they do not create disincentives for subsequent local production but do help to reduce the probabilities and intensities of future food shortages.

Development food aid should be allocated to countries on a cash and multiyear basis, taking into account relative needs and absorptive capacities. If needed food were found to be available in the country or in nearby developing countries, it should be purchased locally or triangularly. If not, it should be purchased and shipped from the United States choosing the most cost-effective commodities and means and methods of shipment. Safeguards are hardly needed for domestic U.S. supplies since overall quantities are not likely to be large, and in periods of high prices and tight supplies the quantities that could be purchased with the given amount of aid would automatically fall. Future food aid will never be large enough to enable low-income countries to outbid consumers in rich countries for scarce supplies.

Using this approach, the need to monetize project food aid would be moot. Well-designed development projects would only import as much food as could be effectively utilized with the complementary financial and managerial resources available.

If development food aid were used in the program mode, that is, sold by the recipient government to generate local currency, the local currency should be owned entirely by the recipient country and its use addressed as a part of overall policy dialogue and program development between the government and its donors. Conditionality would be handled primarily through multiyear commitments: the use of funds generated this year would affect food aid flows next year and thereafter.

PVOs can continue to play a useful operational role in implementation of food aid. In addition, closer coordination of bilateral programs with WFP should be emphasized. WFP frequently has country staff that can effectively assist the govern-ment in logistical and management requirements. Sometimes WFP has food, a part of which may be procured locally, and can even contribute to internal handling costs, but the recipient government lacks the complementary resources needed to effectively implement food-for-work or other projects. In these cases, the flexible approach recommended here would permit use of U.S. bilateral resources in cash as part of a coordinated food-based assistance package. Other donors (like the World Bank) could also participate in these cash-food assistance partnerships.

To implement this vision of more integrated and fungible food aid, several actions are needed:

1. A clear legislative mandate for food aid that removes the ambiguities about its development objectives and modalities.
2. Termination of UMR conditions.
3. A simplified management and decision making structure within the U.S. government.
4. Full integration of development food aid with other assistance by USAID.
5. Appreciation by U.S. commodity producers, processors, and handlers that cost-effective food aid that accelerates economic growth and alleviates hunger and poverty in developing countries is in their own long-term best interests.

Notes

1. Section 416 of the Agricultural Act of 1949 provided for domestic and foreign donations of surplus U.S. commodities. After PL 480 Title II became the chief mechanism for foreign donations, Congress withdrew that authority from Section 416. In 1985, when surpluses were again accumulating, Section 416 was reopened to foreign donations, first of dairy products and later of wheat and other commodities.

APPENDIX 7.A: METHODOLOGIES
USED TO ASSESS FOOD AID NEED
Khalid Riaz

This appendix summarizes methodologies that have been used to assess food aid needs. The approaches employed by the Food and Agriculture Organization of the United States (FAO), International Food Policy Research Institute (IFPRI), U.S. Department of Agriculture (USDA), and International Institute of Applied Systems Analysis (IIASA) are reviewed. These approaches differ primarily because of differences in objectives of these organizations.

FAO addresses the question of global food security over a longer time. Consequently, it is concerned with projections that capture long-term trends rather than fluctuation around the trends, which are a shorter term phenomenon.

The USDA focuses on food aid needs in the very near future—the next six months. Therefore, it emphasizes factors that explain shorter-term variations. This tends to make its models more elaborate. But since the variables, such as exchange rates and debt service obligations, that are exogenous in the USDA model cannot be successfully predicted far into the future and for a large number of countries, this approach is difficult to use for long-term projections.

The IFPRI approach lies between FAO and USDA. For instance, its method used to estimate future import requirements is similar to that of FAO, but a country's capacity to finance commercial imports is also taken into account, using a simpler version of the USDA methodology.

IIASA uses a general equilibrium approach that shows the impacts of policy choices on hunger and malnutrition. It is the only approach reviewed that explicitly links policies to income generation and food consumption.

Despite differences in the emphasis placed on various aspects of the food situation, these approaches have a common framework.

Appendix 7.A was prepared by Khalid Riaz, graduate research assistant in the Department of Economics, Iowa State University.

All of them involve estimating a food gap based on some measure of domestic food demand (or need) and availability. Food aid needs are considered to be those parts of the food gaps that cannot be met through commercial imports. However, the estimates of food aid requirements are sensitive to the definitions of three key variables, namely, domestic demand or consumption requirements, commercial imports, and domestic production. Since different agencies do not use the same definitions of these variables the estimated requirements vary significantly. Tables 7.A.1 and 7.A.2 present a summary of food and needs estimates of various studies. It was found that estimates were most sensitive to definition of *consumption requirements.* The figures for food aid based on market demand were generally lower than those obtained by assuming some kind of minimum nutritional standard. For example, the USDA status quo estimates for food aid needs in year 2000 was 29.4 mmt, while the nutrition-based criteria yielded a food aid needs figure of 56 mmt. The corresponding figures from IIASA were 30 mmt and 50 mmt, respectively (see Table 7.A.2). Similarly, the FAO estimates for food aid needs in 1990, based on alternative market demand scenarios, varied between 15 and 26 mmt, while the nutrition-based estimate was 66 mmt (see Table 7.A.1). In addition to differences in definitions of consumption requirement, differences in underlying assumptions regarding income growth, import trends, and the proportions of commercial food imports also contributed to variation in estimates.

FAO Methodology

Assessing food aid needs requires estimating the food gap as measured by differences in projected effective food demand or food needs and projected domestic production. In the FAO methodology an estimate of the former was made in two stages. First, each country's production, net import requirements, export availabilities, and domestic demand were projected. This was done assuming no changes in national policies affecting these variables and constant (1975) prices. In the second stage, country results were aggregated and suitably adjusted to eliminate imbalances in global supply and demand. These imbalances arose because of the particular assumptions made about prices and policy environments.

Demand for cereals was decomposed into human consumption and feed. Growth in private consumption expenditures and time trend were used as explanatory variables to obtain commodity-specific projections for per capita human consumption. The feed use projections were made using input-output coefficients.

On the supply side, production projections involved projecting the area under annual crops and yields. The econometric model for area had time, deflated prices, and lagged area as explanatory variables. Extrapolations of yields were based on time series analysis. These projections were then adjusted to take into account national commodity policy objectives, expected impact of commodity development projects, and major biological and physical constraints that might limit future supply expansion.

The differences between demand and domestic supply as projected above provided an estimate of total food import requirements. In view of the inability of many countries to meet these requirements through commercial imports, food aid needs were taken to be the residual or unmet portion. Commercial imports were projected using the behavioral relationship

$$\overline{I}_i = a_i \, (\overline{E}_i / \overline{p}_i)^{b_i}$$

where I_i denotes projected commercial imports in 1985, E_i is the projected earnings in 1981, and p_i is the projected unit price of cereal imports in 1985. In addition to filling food gaps, food aid is used for development projects, is provided within the framework of projects that fall into the following three broad categories:

1. Food-for-work projects, for example, those aimed at promoting employment or investment in agriculture. Usually, aid under these projects is provided on the condition that their operation would lead to increased food consumption.
2. Building national food reserves.
3. Nutritional projects.

An estimate of project food aid requirements cannot be made by adopting a general approach for all countries. Recipient countries are too dissimilar in terms of their development possibilities and constraints on the operations of projects. Therefore, a country-by-country approach is needed, which takes into account, among other things, the absorptive capacity of the recipients. This is undertaken by the World Food Program (WFP).

The WFP experience indicates that a number of factors limit recipient countries' absorptive capacity. In particular, logistical constraints inhibit the operations in all three categories of projects and are also considered the most serious in all of them. For food-for-work projects, administrative, organizational, and management constraints ranked second. The lack of continuity and assurance of food aid supplies occupied a similar rank for food reserves. The second most serious bottleneck for nutrition projects was shortage of financial resources and acceptability of commodities provided as food aid.

IFPRI Methodology

The IFPRI methodology, as presented in "Food Needs of Developing Countries' Projections of Production and Consumption to 1990," Research Report 3, IFPRI, is based on four alternative food demand scenarios: (1) per capita staple food consumption constant at a base level, (2) income growth at past trends, (3) income growth at 75 percent of past trends, and (4) meeting minimum nutrition requirements.

Growth of domestic food production is projected at past trends. The import needs for food is given as the difference between projected domestic production and projected consumption in each of the above scenarios. Huddleston (1984) provided two estimates of import demand for food. One was derived assuming that consumption equals 1975 per capita levels, plus the additional amount required to satisfy market demand if per capita GNP continued to grow at rates prevailing between 1960 and 1974. Population was assumed to grow at UN medium variant growth rates for 1960-90. The other estimate of import demand for food was derived by first estimating market demand under high, assumed income growth, and then adding the amount of cereals needed to fill the dietary gap.

The estimates of import demand were converted into value terms using the average of U.S. soft red winter wheat at Atlantic ports for 1960-75 expressed in 1977 dollars.

To estimate food aid requirements, the values of cereal imports, under each scenario, were compared to projected export earnings. Two estimates were provided. One was obtained by considering cereal imports in excess of 5 percent of export earnings as requiring concessional financing. The other used a 2 percent criterion for commercial imports.

Not all the countries with cereal import expenditures exceeding the above threshold levels were considered eligible for food aid. Those with per capita income more than $900 in 1976-78 were assumed to be able to finance their own food import requirements. For countries with per capita incomes between $300 and $900, export strength, measured by export to GNP ratio and per capita staple food production, were considered indicative of need. Export strength, along with the ratio of foreign exchange holdings to the size of merchandise imports, was also assumed to reflect a country's ability to finance commercial food imports. Middle-income countries, which are strong in both exports and foreign currency reserves or which have high per capita crop production but weak balance of payments positions, were assumed not to require food aid.

All low-income countries that needed to import cereals to insure adequate food supplies were assumed to need food aid.

USDA Methodology

The USDA calculates two different measures of food import requirements on a regular basis (USDA 1987). The first is status quo food import needs. This provides an assessment of additional food needs if consumption has to be maintained at levels achieved during recent years. Alternatively, a nutrition-based assessment is also made, which takes into account the nutritional gap that would persist even when effective market demand for food has been met.

The first step in assessing import needs, using either criteria mentioned above, is to calculate import requirements to support consumption. This is done by first obtaining the import requirements in quantity terms and then converting them into value terms using a unit value index for imports. The quantity of imports required to support consumption is the difference between domestic requirements (quantity) and forecasted domestic production. The procedures for making both the status quo and nutrition-based assessments have a common structure up to this point. However, the two methods differ in their calculation of domestic requirements, which go into the estimates of import quantities required to support consumption.

The status quo domestic requirements are the sum of domestic feed and nonfeed requirements, the latter being derived from per capita nonfeed consumption. Subtracting forecasted domestic production from this sum gives status quo import requirements for consumption.

The nutrition-based method requires comparison of a fixed minimum consumption norm against both domestic availabilities and nonfeed requirements. Therefore, both of the latter estimates have to be net of milling, seed, waste, and nonfeed use. Domestic nonfeed requirements (net) are calculated by first determining commodity caloric shares in total diet in a base period and, on the basis of those shares, determining the per capita caloric requirement for achieving the FAO recommended minimum. The per capita daily caloric estimates are then converted to annual country wide requirements.

The difference between domestic requirements for nonfeed use and domestic availability plus feed use gives import requirements.

Since a country's ability to finance imports is limited by foreign exchange availability, an estimate of commercial import capacity is necessary for determining food aid needs. Such estimates are made on the assumption of continuance of recent debt payment performance.

Finally, account is also taken of the capacity of the country's infrastructure to absorb food aid. Often limits on absorption are imposed by capacity of the country's transport, communication, storage, and distribution systems. In addition, financial and management resources at the disposal of national and local agencies often prove to be binding constraints.

To arrive at estimates of maximum absorbable imports, two assumptions are made: (1) carryover stocks are at highest historical levels during the past eight years, and (2) per capita consumption is at highest historical levels.

Total consumption is derived from per capita figures by multiplying by population figures. Adding estimates of carryover stocks calculated in the manner described above to total consumption gives maximum absorbable imports for a particular commodity. The maximum absorbable import levels indicate the highest proportion of estimated nutrition-based food aid needs that could actually be disbursed to a particular country in a given year.

IIASA Methodology

The methodologies described above use a partial approach. According to this approach, food aid estimates are obtained by varying only the factors closely related to food systems. All other variables in the economy are assumed to remain constant. The limitation of this approach is that it does not take into account the indirect or secondary effects. When these are large relative to the direct effects, general equilibrium is the more appropriate framework of analysis.

The Basic Link System (BLS), developed at the International Institute of Applied Systems Analysis (IIASA) is a general equilibrium model covering European Community (EC) countries, Council for Mutual Economic Assistance (CMEA) countries, and 14 other regions including all other countries (Frohberg 1989). The agricultural sector is considered in more detail and has nine subsectors. The primary purpose of the BLS is to analyze agricultural policies rather than make projections. This sets it apart from the forecasting models, such as the one used by FAO. The BLS has two indicators of the nutritional status of population, nutritional intake and number of hungry people. In addition, food requirements as calculated by the World Health Organization and the World Bank are taken as a third indicator. An estimate of nutritional intake is derived from per capita intake of calories and protein, assuming utility maximizing behavior of the consumers. In considering the number of hungry people, only chronic hunger (and not famine) is taken into account. The number of hungry people is determined by using methods developed by FAO.

As mentioned earlier, an important feature of the BLS is its ability to simulate the impacts of alternative policies. Frohberg reports simulated effects on malnutrition and hunger of trade liberalization and increased availability of food aid, considered separately as well as in conjunction with each other. The results indicate that increasing food aid is a more effective strategy in reducing malnutrition than trade liberalization. This is because the latter policy leads to increases in food prices, which neutralize some of the income gains to the poor. Another factor in favor of direct food aid is the possibility of targeting the poorest nations, which was one of the assumptions underlying the IIASA analysis.

Limitations of the Methodologies

In each of these methodologies, food aid is considered to be the excess of food import requirements over what the country can afford to acquire commercially. But what proportion of its food import requirements should a country be reasonably expected to meet commercially? Most approaches to assessment of food aid needs either fix commercial imports as a percentage of import gap (same percentage is applicable to all countries) or they specify functional relationships for determining this proportion on the basis of certain key economic variables such as export earnings, foreign exchange reserves, or debt service ratio. As practical as this may be, there is no sound economic rationale underlying it. As Ezekiel wrote, "Without any statement of the policy objectives underlying the provision of food aid for sale in the market, earlier studies were not able to provide a rationale for determining the extent to which commercial imports of food should fill the food import gap in order to determine the residual requirement for food aid" (1989, 51).

In Ezekiel's view, the ad hoc approach has difficulties at two levels. On one level, there are methodological difficulties of obtaining good statistical estimates of functional relationships, and using these for predictive purposes and difficulties pertaining to misspecifiction of the relationship itself. Frequently, the explanatory power of these functions is inadequate, and many variables have signs contrary to a priori expectations. Furthermore, explanatory variables are almost impossible to predict accurately, especially far into the future. This leaves the models with little predictive usefulness. Finally, misspecification occurs "because the availability of food aid itself affects these proportions and relationships so that it must also be used to explore commercial food imports" (Ezekiel 1989, 51).

However, on a more fundamental level, Ezekiel considers the ad hoc approach to be inappropriate because it encourages persistence in policies even when changes may be desirable. For example, countries are not alike in allocating scarce foreign exchange resources between commercial food aid and financing development needs. This allocation, although resulting from a complex interplay of economic as well as noneconomic forces, need not be optimum. A country leaning too heavily in one direction or the other may stand to gain by changing its policy. The food aid criterion, however, based on countries' historical allocations, provides no incentives for the country to do so. The countries that have traditionally ignored development needs and imported more food, get less food aid, thereby not freeing foreign exchange to finance development. Of course, the opposite is true for countries that have tolerated a higher degree of malnutrition of their populations than was warranted by scarcity of resources at their disposal. Such countries would get more food aid despite their capacity (as opposed to willingness) to purchase food in the international market.

Once food aid is recognized as a development tool, the next question is where to look for criteria for allocating food aid. In this regard, the links between volume of a country's future commercial food imports and its growth are of crucial importance. Commercial food imports are a function of the economy's growth and export performance. At the same time, the chosen level of such imports would affect its growth prospects. This latter impact should be taken into consideration at least in a qualitative way. The ad hoc determination of the proportion of food imports that needs to be self-financed by the country is difficult to justify on economic grounds. There is need for a clear statement of economic objectives to be achieved by food aid. These in turn should provide explicit criteria for allocation applicable to all countries.

Another issue is the difficulty in arriving at a satisfactory definition of food requirements. Effective demand is one criterion used to estimate these requirements. But market prices may be so high that some consumers constrained by low incomes are not able to buy enough food to meet nutritional requirements. On the other hand, the nutrition-based method has its own difficulties. Huddleston points out that "the total calorie requirement for nutritional adequacy may be overestimated, and requirements of malnourished groups cannot be divined from aggregate estimates" (1984, 52-53). Overestimation may occur because there are differences in requirements among individuals of the same body weight and energy expenditure. Further, individuals may vary their intake from day to day or season to season without adversely affecting their health. Finally, average figures do not reveal how food is distributed. In Huddleston's view, poor distribution of food is a more important cause of malnutrition in most countries than is its scarcity.

Table 7.A.1. Projections of gross cereal imports and food aid requirements of developing countries

	Period	Total Imports	Food aid
WFP (1979): All LDCs	1985	-	17.00 - 18.50
FAO (1981)			
Scenario 'A', all LDCs	1990	110	15.00
Scenario 'B', all LDCs	1990	121	24.00
[most vulnerable]		[38]	[20]
Trends and nutrition-based, all LDC's	1990	175	66.00
WFP/FAO (1983): All LDCs	1985	-	20.20
Huddleston (1983): 90 LDCs			
Import trends (1961-63 —1976-78)	1990	175	18.00
Income based	1990	92	17.00
Consumption based	1990	109	20.00
Nutrition based	1976-78	-	27.00
	1990	84	35.00
USDA (1982): 69 LDCs			
"Status quo" (1978-1981)	1982-83	32	12.00
Nutrition based	1982-83	52	34.00

SOURCE: Edward Clay, "Food Aid Forecasting: The Literature on Needs and Requirements."
Food Policy, Vol. 11, No. 1, p. 44. © Butterworth-Heinemann Ltd. Oxford. 1966.

Table 7.A.2. Estimates of food aid requirements for LDCs

Projection	Status quo mmt	Australia mmt	Japan mmt CE/yr
USDA	29.40	56.00	-
World Bank	23.00	-	-
IIASA/BLS	30.00	50.00	165 + 11
IFPRI	-	-	74.00
All countries w/ < $800 GNP/head	-	-	39.00
FAPRI (1995)	-	-	117.00

SOURCE: "Food Aid Projections for the Decade of the
1990s (1989)." Report of Ad Hoc Panel. Board of Science and
Technology for International Development. Washington, D.C.:
National Research Council.

Note: The abbreviation *mmt* is defined as million metric tons.

References

Bhagwati, J. 1986. "Food Aid, Agricultural Production and Welfare." In Essays on Economic Progress and Welfare in Honor of I. G. Patel. S. Gahan and M. R. Schroff, ed. New Delhi: Oxford University Press.

Bhagwati, J., and T. N. Srinivasan. 1969. "Optimum Policy Intervention to Achieve Non-Economic Objectives." Review of Economic Studies 36(1):27-38.

Clay, E. 1986. "Food Aid Forecasting: The Literature on Needs and Requirements." *Food Policy,* 11, 1:44.

Delgado, C., and C. P. J. Miller. 1985. "Changing Food Patterns in West Africa." Food Policy 10(1): 55-62.

Ezekiel, Hanan. 1989. "Mid-term estimates of Demand-based Food Aid Requirements and their Variability (Appendix A)." In *Food Aid and Projection for the Decade of the 1990s.* Report of Ad Hoc Panel. Board of Science and Technology for International Development. National Research Council.

Economic Research Service, U.S. Department of Agriculture. 1988. World Food Needs and Availabilities, 1987/88: Winter Update. Washington, D.C.: USDA.

FAO. 1983. Assessing Food Aid Requirements: A Revised Approach. Economic and Social Development Paper No. 39. Rome: Food and Agriculture Organization.

Frohberg, K. 1989. "Food Aid Requirements of Developing Countries." In *Food Aid Proceedings for the Decade of the 1990s.* Washington, D.C.: Office of International Affairs.

Hopkins, Raymond F. 1987. "The Evolution of Food Aid: Towards a Development First Regime." In Food Policy: Integrating Supply, Distribution, and Consumption. J. P. Gittinger, and others, ed. Baltimore: John Hopkins University Press.

Huddleston, B. 1984. Closing the Cereals Crop with Trade and Food Aid. Research Report No. 43. Washington, D.C.: IFPRI.

Mellor, J., and H. Ezekiel. 1987. Food Aid in Sub-Saharan Africa. MADIA Report 16. Washington, D.C: World Bank Country Economic Department.

Mellor, J., and S. Gavian. 1987. "Famine: Causes, Prevention, and Review." Science (January):539-45.

Reutlinger, Shlomo, and J. Katona-Apte. 1987. "The Nutritional Impact of Food Aid: Criteria for the Selection of Cost-Effective Foods." In Food Policy: Integrating Supply, Distribution, and Consumption. J. P. Gittinger, and others, ed. Baltimore: Johns Hopkins University Press.

Srinivasan, T. N. 1989. "Food Aid: A Cause of Development Failure or an Instrument of Success?" The World Bank Economic Review 3(1):39-65.

U.S. Department of Agriculture. 1987. *World Food Needs and Availabilities*. Washington, D.C.: U.S. Department of Agriculture.

DISCUSSION OF CHAPTER 7
Gerald Trant

There is a great deal to agree with in Fletcher's thoughtful, well-balanced chapter and if one is to differ with him it must be primarily in terms of point of view and emphasis.

On humanitarian grounds the need for food aid as an emergency response to natural or other disasters is clear. The effectiveness of prepositioning is also clear, that is to say, establishing fast-track decision making procedures in donor and recipient countries to provide rapid response in such emergencies. International agreement to allow passage of humanitarian food aid at all times would also assist in its effective delivery.

The humanitarian basis for food aid to meet the needs of refugees is also clear and there is a compelling humanitarian logic that justifies the need for food aid in those instances in which developing countries are simply unable, through their own production and commercial imports, to meet the minimum daily caloric requirements of their people and time is needed to increase food production to adequate levels from domestic sources. As is often the case, time and circumstances blur the borders between humanitarian food aid, development food aid, and what can only be regarded as inefficiency-engendering food transfers.

Some of the difficulties associated with achieving effective food aid use will be discussed later. However, there is one common shortage that links serious attempts to analyze many food aid issues and that is the shortage of adequate examples of successful food aid development programs or projects, which, on analysis, could yield the practical paradigm of the successful use of food aid for development.

One of the ways in which food aid security dialogue can be rendered less complicated is to develop a common definition or concept of food aid. In this presentation it is proposed that food security should mean that people have access to enough food at all times that they can lead active, healthy lives. For most countries, food security implies attaining desirable levels of food production, increasing the stability of food supplies, and ensuring access to food supplies on the part of those in need.

The 550 million hungry people who have the greatest need for improved food security live primarily in rural areas. Fifty-seven percent live in Asia, 27 percent in Africa, 11 percent in Latin America, and 5 percent in the Near East. The majority of these people live existences of chronic undernourishment.

Famines, which, of all the manifestations of hunger, have received the greatest media coverage in recent years, have shifted their incidence from Asia to Africa.

Three-quarters of the 79 emergency actions by the World Food Program in 1987 were prompted by human actions like civil strife or war and the remaining one-quarter were caused by drought, crop failures, and sudden natural disasters. Even in these cases human causes were often present.

The impact of food insecurity can engender different forms of hunger and malnutrition. For example, undernutrition and starvation result when people simply do not have enough to eat; malnutrition results when the nutritional quality of diets does not meet requirements. This is often the case among young children, women, and the elderly. Nutritional deficiency diseases such as xerophthalmia and mykedema, are the result of the lack of specific nutrients in the diet. In the case of famine, whole populations are affected by food insecurity. Chronic and/or seasonal undernutrition affects more selectively those households that are too poor to grow or acquire a large enough stock of food. Malnutrition and nutritional diseases affect some individuals within the household more than others. The different forms of hunger have different causes and require appropriate responses.

With few exceptions, however, responses are rooted in problems of poverty and underdevelopment. Successful efforts to combat hunger and malnutrition more effectively must begin with an assessment of how many people are affected by the various kinds of hunger, where they live, and what the specific conditions are that cause each type. In this connection, it is sad commentary on our neglect of the human condition in development efforts that we know more about economic growth, balance of payments, inflation, and money supply than we know about poor and hungry people, their living conditions, and their aspirations. The statistics and information available on poverty, hunger, and malnutrition are both scarce and inadequate. There is a desperate need for better information.

There can be little doubt that a major reason for the world's failure to halt the growth of hunger and malnutrition has been the lack in many countries of effective policies to ensure food security for all their people. Even where such policies appear to be in place, their effectiveness has been inhibited by a concern for economic indicators at the expense of human needs. Although the statistics may be imperfect, some countries provide us with useful examples. In general, those countries that have truly made the elimination of hunger and malnutrition a key objective of their development have generally made significant progress toward it through effective programs. In countries where the elimination of hunger and malnutrition did not rank high on the development or economic policy agenda, even high and growing levels of economic activity did not result in tangible progress towards the goal of reducing hunger.

Possibly the most important fact about hunger and development is simply this: economic development measured by gross national product per person cannot be taken as a reliable proxy for the incidence of malnutrition and hunger in a country. High GNP levels tell us nothing about the way income is distributed among the members of the population, how many children went to bed hungry, or how many died from diseases that were related to nutritional deficiencies. What the level of GNP per capita does indicate is the ease with which effective antihunger programs could be paid for in aggregate. It does not say that they will be put in place.

It follows that all those things often thought to be stimulants to growth in an economy level of activity, such as an effective price mechanism, a liberalized trading environment, and a net inflow of capital with more productive technology, whether taken individually or together will not in and of themselves result in increased food security for a country. It is difficult to avoid concluding that effective government programs biased in favor of the poor and hungry are a necessary condition for the conquest and eradication of hunger in any part of the globe.

While developing countries have taken varying approaches to the solution of the hunger problem, those that have made significant progress have adopted a tripartite overall strategy that involved (1) making the elimination of hunger a central objective of development; (2) creating and maintaining a policy environment supportive of this objective; and (3) adopting an integrated food policy approach to the hunger problem. China and Cuba have both pursued the reduction of hunger as a fundamental element in an overall policy that seeks to ensure greater equity in the distribution of income. Chile, Costa Rica, Jamaica, and Sri Lanka have acted to put in place food and social security safety nets in combination with equity-improving measures, such as agrarian reform. Other policies that have been associated with significant reductions in hunger include according agricultural and food sectors a high priority, pursuing policies geared to the employment of a rapidly growing labor force, and following judicious population policies.

Since the majority of the world's hungry people live in rural areas having limited infrastructure, including inadequate transportation and storage facilities, the only real hope of increased food security lies in increased productivity of local resources, which usually means, as a minimum, improved seed, production practices, fertilizer, markets, and price incentives, together with the trained people and other resources requisite to the maintenance of a productivity-enhancing environment. Most of the effort and investment needed will have to come from the developing countries themselves. However, external aid including food aid can enhance the process and accelerate its development.

Fletcher postulates that food aid can make a useful contribution to food security through good investment projects, targeted supplemental feeding, or food-for-work projects. His specific recommendation to clarify the legislative mandate for food aid and provide a simple management structure for it is pointing in the right direction.

8

Improving American Foreign Financial and Food Assistance Policies to Enhance Food Security

Raymond F. Hopkins

The Domestic Policy Environment for Foreign and Food Assistance

Generally, four kinds of donor assistance may serve to strengthen another country's food security. Such assistance is especially important in countries vulnerable to food shortages, with their attendant high internal prices and increased hunger.

1. Project financial assistance directed to agricultural projects or to inputs, such as fertilizer or research, to improve the agricultural productivity of a country.
2. Food aid can eliminate temporary shortages. Imported food on a free or concessional basis should enhance supply and, if provided in a reliable, compensatory fashion, smooth supply availability and the threat of acute hunger.
3. Nonproject development assistance. This is most often provided in support of policy reform measures or to help a country's structural adjustment programs and can be used to pay for food imports needed to satisfy minimal security requirements.
4. Renegotiation and reduction of debt obligations can improve a country's food security by reducing its general vulnerability

to international and national market fluctuations in the longer run. Debt forgiveness may be a *sine qua non* for economic development.

These four pathways by which external assistance affects food security, whether through official aid flows or debt adjustment, can all be affected by a recipient country's production, import needs, and role in international trade, and that country's domestic policies on food subsidies. The changing context of each recipient is therefore crucial for assessing the "true" effect of aid on food security.

This chapter focuses on the first two of these flows, and particularly the second, food aid. It discusses these in the environment of the American food aid program. Generally, the domestic and international factors that affect food aid from the United States and the international purposes and interests that the United States has sought to serve have changed since the inaugural of the food aid, or PL 480, legislation in 1954; further changes in environmental factors invite further changes in American policy in the 1990s.

Two basic purposes of the U.S. government in continuing to allocate scarce foreign affairs budget resources in order to send foodstuffs overseas are (1) to enhance domestic agricultural interests in the United States and (2) to alleviate constraints on development in other countries rising from food shortages and malnutrition. Given these two purposes it is understandable that USDA and AID are the major executive branch agencies responsible for food aid, and equally logical that the agriculture and foreign affairs committees of Congress are its principal legislative authors.

The political saliency of its purposes has not remained constant, however. As the proportion of food aid in total agricultural exports for the United States has declined from over 30 percent in the 1950s to less than 5 percent in the 1980s, its benefits to American food producers and the U.S. treasury through reduced costs for commodity storage programs have dwindled. Coincident with this dwindling stake in food aid has been a decline in the power of agricultural interests supporting it. With growing urbanization—as the American population has shifted away from farm and agricultural employment—combined with the effects of the Supreme Court decision proscribing unequal electoral constituencies that had favored rural areas—the power of agricultural interests within the U.S. government has eroded. The political context in the 1990s for PL 480, therefore, is far different from what existed in 1953-54 when the initial food aid legislation was drawn up and its share of treasury funds was first negotiated.

The second factor shaping American interests in food aid is that of contributing to the global "collective good" of stabilizing international markets and guaranteeing populations in poor countries access to minimally adequate nutrition. Evidence suggests this has been a steady and growing policy concern. Reasons for this trend include (1) the enhanced capacity to transport and deliver food to remote areas around the world and to respond quickly to anticipated needs (over the last two decades early warning networks have been developed to forecast famines); (2) concern over domestic agricultural policies that may destabilize markets, a problem especially for very poor or very indebted food importers; and (3) a growing normative consensus that hunger is an unacceptable element of the human condition in the last decade of the twentieth century.[1]

Implications of these two changes, declining domestic producer interests and rising global food stabilization and hunger interests, combined with lessons derived from the cumulative experience and research in food aid over the last 35 years lead to a strong case for revising the entire PL 480 program.[2]

This chapter is divided into three sections: it elaborates upon the historical trends already described; it discusses some of the costs and benefits associated with food aid, in particular, for trade and development purposes; and it offers some practical steps appropriate for the future design of American food and financial aid related to food security.

Origins and Changes in PL 480

In 1954, a coalition of cold war, farm commodity, and humanitarian interests supported the creation of a special U.S. government program of noncommercial food sales and donations. Although the United States regularly had provided such aid after World War II, it was not institutionalized (outside the Mutual Security Act) until Public Law 480 of 1954. This law reflected the belief that food aid could simultaneously serve the needs of reducing the costs of our domestic farm programs and, at the same time, serve relief and development interests. America's internationally oriented leaders saw food aid supporting both the humanitarian concerns of Americans to avoid starvation and famine and, more broadly, resistance to the "communist menace." Senator Hubert Humphrey claimed that U.S. surpluses could be "a great asset for checking communist aggression. Communism has no greater ally than hunger; and democracy and freedom no greater ally than an abundance of food" (Ruttan 1989).

Following the enactment of PL 480, President Eisenhower created an interagency committee to oversee this program reflecting the multiple objectives of the legislation. It was chaired by the Department of Agriculture with representatives from the Departments of State and Defense, the agency for foreign aid (after 1961, the Agency for International Development—AID), the Treasury, and the Budget Bureau (now OMB).

Unfortunately, neither the legislation nor the interagency process created a harmonious marriage among interests. The very division of food aid into two disbursement channels, a Title I program, primarily steered by USDA and the State Department, and a Title II program, primarily aimed at supporting humanitarian and development objectives, and in recent years steered by AID (with special ties to voluntary agencies in this country), acknowledges the likelihood that particular food transfers cannot serve all of PL 480's mandated purposes simultaneously.

A 1977-78 review of food aid, carried out by the Carter administration, considered the desirability of allocating fixed proportions of the food aid budget to particular mandates. This idea was rejected in favor of maintaining a diffuse coalition of interests and purposes within the legislation. At least some food aid, it was felt, could simultaneously serve multiple purposes. Much has changed since this review over 10 years ago, however. Conflicts over the shrinking foreign assistance budget and the uncertainty of surpluses have made food aid much closer to a fully funded cost for the United States as it is for other countries (Clay and Singer 1985).

Since its beginning as a surplus disposal, anticommunist effort of the United States, the underlying character of the international food aid "regime" (i.e., the structure and rules for governing the transactions that encompass the entire set of donors and recipients) has changed dramatically. Furthermore, the burden-sharing has shifted. The U.S. contribution, for example, has fallen: from providing more than 95 percent of the world's food aid, the United States now provides between 50 and 60 percent (in dollar terms the U.S. contribution is less than 50 percent). Other bilateral and multilateral donors now have a significant role. Other donors and recipients now set rules and pressure the United States over regime elements (World Food Program 1979).

In 1963, an international organization, the World Food Program (WFP), was created to conduct a special portion of food aid, that is, aid to be used in projects within recipient states that would help people improve their lives, particularly in agriculture. The WFP in 1974 was authorized to expand its authority under a new international committee, the Committee on Food Aid Policies and Programs (CFA), which serves as an overall body to establish principles for food aid and to provide guidance to donors and recipients of food aid. This "governing" task was added to the CFA's regular charge to approve particular food aid projects supported by the multilateral WFP.

By 1990, the regime expanded to the point where more than 25 countries provided food and over 100 received it. Under the Food Aid Convention (FAC), established in 1967 as part of the Kennedy GATT negotiations and most recently renewed in 1986, the United States is obliged to provide a minimum of 4.47 million metric tons (mmt) of food aid while other principal donors to the FAC have pledged another 3 mmt. Ironically, in spite of greater burden sharing among rich states, thus expanding the wealth base for paying for food aid, the physical volume of food aid in tonnage terms has declined. As the burden of providing it became more widely accepted and carried out by other OECD countries, the U.S. effort shrank.

In 1966, a reform of U.S. food aid shifted the emphasis of food aid's purposes toward economic development. It required countries receiving food aid to establish self-help measures to be funded by sales of concessional food. These changes arose in part as a result of concern that food aid could hurt recipient countries through disincentive effects upon local production. Disincentives might be created by weakening a government's interest in providing funding for research for the food and agriculture sector, by lowering market prices for foods and thereby decreasing food producers' income and incentives, and finally by creating tastes for imported foods, such as wheat and rice, that are relatively expensive and/or impossible to produce locally, thus creating an unnecessary dependence.

Food aid allocations also have changed. Over the years, particular interests, sometimes famine alleviation, other times the desire to reinforce foreign policy actions or even support military operations, have played a compelling role in the U.S.'s allocation of food. For example, in the mid-1960s and again in the mid-1980s, famines in India and Africa caused substantial shifts and increases in the size of food aid. Conversely, in the late 1960s and early 1970s, use of food aid as a resource to support the American military effort in Southeast Asia became important. These latter allocative shifts resulted from bureaucratic politics within the United States.

Today further reforms are advocated. Much as the ones advanced in 1966, based on the results of research and evaluations over the last two decades, in 1990 a revamping of food aid was proposed, by Senators Leahy and Lugar, with support from humanitarian groups (Minear 1989) and from domestic farm groups. Food problems in sub-Saharan Africa provide the most pressing examples of why reform has been called for. This region has come to absorb the largest share of food aid over the last 15 years. Per capita food production declined in Africa from 1970 to 1983 by 17 percent. This was a major factor in the general economic malaise of that period. For food aid to help solve food problems that hinder African development, experts have increasingly argued that such aid must be designed to improve national food markets and foster local development actions. Indeed, the U.S. Food for Progress Program was proclaimed with just this link to food in mind.

For food aid to be constructive, especially in the poorer African countries, it is clear that longer term planning, larger resource flows, and formal multiyear commitments are required. How much food aid can African and similar countries absorb? To guard against disincentive effects in its local production, a conservative approach to an estimate would be simply to project "demanded" imports above the average level of commercial imports in the 1980s. For Africa, for example, 4 to 5 million additional tons could be justified. Thanks to the enormous African debt burden, only moderate growth of food imports to Africa is projected, but even these are surely not affordable on a commercial basis (NAS 1989). Imports by the poorer developing countries during the 1980s that required foreign exchange are a reasonable indicator of what economic demand and hence absorptive capacity were available without displacing local production.

For Africa, about half or more of projected import increases cited in a recent National Academy of Sciences workshop may require some aid to finance them. An adequate response to the "need" gap would require grants be tripled to support food imports to Africa. For all food deficit countries where reform measures are moving in directions urged by the United States and the World Bank, an increase in callable food guarantees would be especially deserved, particularly as a compensatory way to balance food needs and prevent shortages. For African countries alone, food aid could increase by $500 million (1989 price) per year, I believe, without violating the spirit of usual marketing requirements set to protect commercial interests.

Successful food aid requires multiyear commitments. Each country's use would work best if the agreement regulating the aid allowed the resource flow to change from year to year in size, type of food commodity, and even between food and cash. For example, if Guinea or Madagascar were to have a banner year in rice production, then donors need the flexibility to switch their plans, perhaps to send them less rice and substitute another food such as wheat and/or cash. This would be appropriate as a reward for their "success." To continue to send food that is not needed or may overwhelm their markets is hardly a reward for successful adjustment or a good crop year.

Major price instabilities strike economies of African states when food production varies much over 10 percent. During the recent 1984-85 drought, cereal production fell as much as 50 percent in some countries and overall staple food production by 15 to 25 percent. Per capita food production in Africa is not only the lowest in the world, but variability in production (1970-86) is high, exceeded only by the Soviet Union. Thus, reducing vulnerability of poor states through a flexible, procyclical food aid program is crucial.

In food insecure states, because of the importance of food in employment and in household expenditures, instabilities in production can wreak havoc in national economic life and in individual lives. Populations in areas hardest hit by shortages migrate, burdening other regions and causing the loss of capital resources as in Chad, Mozambique, and Ethiopia in recent years. Terms of trade are drastically altered; wealthy herders become impoverished. Employment shrinks, demand for nonfood goods falls, and the formal economy is increasingly circumvented by informal exchanges. Even in years when national food production is normal, large numbers of Africans and Asians can be affected by regional variations.

Based on this type of need, quite different from that of Mexico and other food-importing, debt-ridden, but partly industrialized states, and also different from that of 20 years ago, a high priority for food aid should be as a resource for improving weak food markets. Past U.S. rules and practices regarding food aid, however, have made this priority difficult to accomplish. Why? First, the interagency working group has usually had inadequate information about failures in food policy and insufficient leverage or assurance of covering risks in policy change to nurture market improvement. The effort to use food aid in support of a grain market restructuring in Mali is the major exception, and that effort was set back by the 1984-85 dropout. The multiple objectives of PL 480 make market stabilization adjustments at odds (sometimes) with other goals.

In many recipients, unfortunately not only in Africa, policy reforms to improve the food system have been lacking or have been made reluctantly. Food aid should support, not undercut, policy reform. This requires coordination with other donors and fitting U.S. food aid into larger reform financing. A shift toward greater coordination, multilateral aid, and integrating food and cash assistance would fit the changed understanding of food system reforms necessary in the 1990s.

Analyzing Costs and Benefits

The changes in the nature of food aid from the 1950s to the 1980s, sketched out above, raise some basic questions as to its future size and modality (see NAS 1989). Clearly, the benefits it provided to some groups, such as grain producers in exporting countries, have declined. Fortunately, the costs it may have imposed on recipients through distorting their economy are also likely to have declined. This in turn has shifted the extent to which various interests are served or disadvantaged by food aid. The climate within which policy is made, therefore, has similarly changed.

Academic studies have given the most attention to the effects of food aid (for example, the benefits and costs) to recipient countries. Disincentive, distribution, and distortion effects have received wide criticism (Maxwell and Singer 1979). Relatively less attention has been paid to the costs and benefits to donor countries. These, however, are central to understanding the motivation for food aid, and important in formulating recommendations regarding its future size and modalities in an era of shrinking budgets.

What are the benefits of food aid to the United States? Basically, food aid may be construed as an international public good, differing from cash as being tied (doubly tied when the United States insists that its food be used). In this sense, as argued earlier, the public good of stability is a U.S. interest advanced. It should or can advance the U.S. interest as a major stakeholder in a peaceful global order and its interest in international economic development and trade expansion, especially as the economic situation deteriorated in the 1980s.

What is the monetary cost of food aid supplied by the United States, either bilaterally or through international agencies? A simple answer, and one conventionally used for international accounting purposes, is to value the quantity of food at current world prices, the market price. Thus, the value of 10,000 tons of wheat or cooking oil, as recorded by foreign aid bookkeepers, is its cost on the open world market, either f.o.b. or c.i.f., as circumstances of the transfer dictate. Often, however, this price is not a good estimate of the value that donors give up. Thus, other valuations have been used over the years in the bookkeeping of food aid. Each of these plays a role in understanding the true economic costs to supplying countries.

The highest cost that might be used in assigning a value to food aid commodities is their acquisition or treasury cost. During times when domestic farm policy supports higher prices, a government intervenes in the market to acquire surpluses of the commodity. Thus, in the Common Market, for example, domestic-oriented actions of the Common Agricultural Policy (CAP) have generated mountains of butter and powdered milk, while in the United States the Commodity Credit Corporation (CCC) has frequently held large grain stocks. The acquisition costs of such commodities and subsequent costs of storage can result in government outlays substantially higher than the market values of the commodities.

If donor governments use their full budgetary outlays for valuing commodities that are subsequently shipped as food aid, the apparent cost of food aid seems rather high. Indeed, in the United States in the early years of PL 480 aid, the Commodity Credit Corporation's costs were often used to report the value of food aid. In more recent years, especially in reports to those interested in economic development, the value of early food aid has been recalculated to reflect prevailing international commercial prices. Similarly, the European Community reports the international value of its food, not the costs incurred by the various European intervention agencies.

With the decline of large government-held surpluses of grain in the 1970s and again in the late 1980s, this high-priced method of valuing food aid has become less relevant. Still, to appease some domestically oriented policymakers, especially when domestic prices are higher than international prices and when substantial government storage charges may be incurred, there may be advantages to charging the international assistance budget the cost needed to cover some part of government outlays for the food provided as aid. Moreover, congressmen representing farm interests, frequently in the 1950s, were happy to construe the full value and cost of the PL 480 program as part of America's international welfare contribution and not as a cost of domestic farm programs (White 1974). This is no longer true; indeed, global-oriented congressional leaders can now count on support for aid tied to food from "farm" members of Congress regardless of the arrangements.

At the other extreme, considering only alternative uses for the food, zero has sometimes been suggested as the appropriate cost for providing food. When aid is drawn from surplus commodities, as under Section 416 of the Farm Bill (1949), this is the value charged to the foreign assistance account. At the level of the national economy, this valuation rests on the premise that, besides the means of disposing of this food as aid, the only effective option open to government agencies holding large surplus stocks would be to destroy them.

Still another way to assess the economic cost of food aid to the donor is in terms of opportunity costs. In this case, the potential additional costs for farm subsidy programs in the absence of food aid are deducted from the treasury cost to the government for food aid. Leo Mayer calculated in the 1966-68 period that the net cost of PL 480 programs was considerably below apparent government (CCC) costs and below world market prices. The net government cost, according to Mayer's calculations, was reached by reducing CCC costs by the amount the CCC would have had to pay out in set-aside payments to farmers in order to idle the amount of land used to produce the amount of food aid shipped. Thus, he found that the average net cost to the government of wheat food aid in 1966-68 was 49 percent of its gross costs (Mayer 1972). More recently, a USDA study calculated PL 480 costs as less than full value, but higher than set-aside costs to reduce the same amount of "surpluses" (Pinstrup-Andersen 1988).

The alternative chosen for calculating donor costs is important for several reasons. First, it affects the publicly perceived budgetary burden. Second, it can affect repayment obligations if it is a Title I-type arrangement. Finally, it can affect the volume of food aid a particular donor can supply to the extent volume is capped by dollars allocated. Thus, in 1986-88, food authorized under Section 416 for food aid 480 use was a free addition to the foreign aid budget (except for shipping).

All donors, including the United States, budget their food aid in monetary, not volume, terms. Other donors, however, add funds to meet tonnage goals when prices rise. The United States generally has not done so. This is largely because U.S. legal food aid requirements under Title II subminimums and commitments under the FAC are lower than available funds for food aid. Other donors usually just meet fixed tonnage pledges. Great Britain or Australia, for instance, simply adjust their development budget allocations upward (or downward) to meet changing food prices for set tonnage and the adjustment is usually borne by the rest of the development assistance budget.

Aside from the cost of the commodity, another PL 480 cost is the management and personnel expenses required to run a food aid program. Managing food aid requires some additional staff and management expenses that the government would not otherwise have incurred. In the United States, which has a very large bureaucracy at home and abroad working for both the Agency for International Development and the Department of Agriculture, it may be argued that some of the costs of managing food aid are fixed and would otherwise go for staff salaries whether food aid were provided or not. Moreover, the size of the Washington-based food aid bureaucracy compared to the value of the program makes it one of the smaller in government for each dollar spent. Indeed, as one agriculture department official remarked, no other billion-dollar program in the United States government has so few staff members.

Aside from salary costs for personnel, another conceivable cost would be the attention time required of high-level administrators. This is relatively small. Seldom do food aid issues and controversies rise to the level of department secretaries or the White House.

Programming or budgetary issues, even when they have generated complicated and heated intragovernmental bargaining, have seldom diverted the attention of top government leaders. Perhaps the only occasions for this in recent years occurred in 1974, when pledges for the World Food Conference required approval at the highest level, and in 1984-85 when the White House gave attention to responses to African famine conditions.

Food aid benefits the United States in both economic and political ways. In the economic realm, benefits are perceived to come from expanded overseas sales. These are hard to calculate. For example, after World War II, the United States gave substantial food aid to Japan, Germany, and Great Britain. In the 1970s, these countries had become large commercial importers of American farm products. Would food sales to these countries in the 1970s have been any less if there had been no food aid in the 1950s to stimulate subsequent trade? If so, what would be the loss to the United States of such lowered sales? Even if answers to these questions could be estimated somehow, further questions remain as to how much benefit from trade gains is required to offset the food aid costs incurred in the 1950s. What would be the appropriate compound rate for the earlier expenditures? One can at best speculate. In general, officials from U.S. producer and marketing groups offer a generous interpretation of these benefits, while officials in development agencies tend to be skeptical of the value of market development effects. Since historically these effects were considered important by commodity representatives, assuming rationality of producer lobbyists, there must have been some, albeit hard to calculate, economic benefits to a segment of the American populace. Substantial benefits, however, are not really needed to explain or justify food aid, since economic stability, military security, and other foreign policy benefits have also been sought through food aid.

Political benefits have become increasingly important as the justification for food aid, especially for donors other than the United States. Not unrelated is the increase of concessionality in food aid. Even in the United States, concessionality has increased with the relative growth of Title II, and food aid's economic value for market development and domestic supply adjustment has declined. Political benefits are especially difficult to measure in monetary terms; worse, nonmonetary evaluation is subject to great disagreement. The kinds of political benefits from food aid range from rather diffuse claims of an improved "climate" of relations (such as food aid to countries like Tunisia and Kenya) to very specific political payoffs, such as foreign policy support or military base rights in, for example, Egypt and the Philippines.

National prestige, that is, the recognition and favorable attention given to a food aid donor by other countries, can also be a significant benefit. For those whose jobs and/or personal identities are closely associated with their national community, actions that call favorable attention to their own nation and win it respect abroad are naturally prized. Just as philanthropists are rewarded with recognition, flattery, and respect when their donations are given attention or sought, so national communities (or their leaders) can derive satisfaction from the enhanced status and respect that food aid philanthropy provides.

Although philanthropic benefits could be derived from providing commodities other than food, the maintenance of international norms for minimal nutrition and humanitarian goals is more directly advanced by food aid, whatever the argument regarding its efficiency. Moreover, food aid rather than cash may be used by those seeking quid pro quo political benefits because it is more available than cash due to its diffuse "humanitarian" public support. It may also be more available because particular domestic interest groups, notably producers and voluntary organizations, lobby on its behalf. Indeed, its availability, which has allowed it to be used for pursuing foreign policy benefits rather than development or humanitarian relief, has led some to sharply criticize the program (Minear 1989).

The balance of costs/benefits to the United States is clearly that costs have risen while benefits have been hard to assess. This is an important reason for the lack of growth in the tonnage of U.S. food aid since 1975 and for the downturn since the mid-1980s in its real monetary amount. Certainly a need for food aid has grown (NAS 1989). While some skepticism about the value of food aid may have undermined its attractiveness, interest in the potential positive effects among development economists remains substantial (Ruttan 1989). As we saw earlier in the history of American food aid, it is seen as having special noneconomic elements: (1) it assists particular domestic interest groups; (2) it has a more humanitarian and popular appeal for the American public than cash aid; and (3) it emerges as an obligation from international bargaining. Thus, the rise in economic costs and decline in economic benefits in the 1970s may well have been offset by a rise in political benefits. As aid has become a more scarce resource, food aid has become more attractive among the economic tools available to donor country policy elites. In the 1980s, for example, foreign policy elites saw it as an important and valuable tool in Central America and Egypt. AID and the World Bank have also shown interest in it as a resource for its role to help stabilize African economies with special attention to their food security.

Prescriptions: Targeting Food Aid and Financial Assistance to Address Global Food Insecurity

In light of the changed world situation and our increased knowledge of policies to achieve an effective use of food aid, the United States should reform its food aid legislation to coordinate it more reliably with other forms of aid that spur economic and agricultural development and employment.

Having established the initial principles and rules under which food aid became an institutionalized regime in international trade (Hopkins 1984), the United States is now in a position to provide new leadership in the international community regarding food aid. How? By legislation that shifts the U.S. priority to recipient needs, targets resources into areas where the use of food is most appropriate and most efficient in promoting development and that will reduce food insecurity, and sets a more altruistic example in its own behavior through a greater delinking of food aid from agricultural subsidy and protection policies. This would enhance the U.S. position in the Uruguay Round of GATT trade negotiations for agriculture, especially if the United States had a position on bona fide food aid common to other donors (meaning U.S. food aid as grant, not loan, aid). This would also allow aid to be managed in a way that would be more likely to induce policy coordination and increase food provision by other industrial countries, such as Germany and Japan.

To achieve this goal, six steps would be appropriate.

1. Establishing food needs as the principal allocation priority for food aid.
2. Allowing for total monetization of food aid and making this practice normal.
3. Establishing modalities whereby needed tonnages of food aid, particularly for the most stressed populations and locales, currently heavily in Africa, would be protected from price fluctuations.
4. Streamlining food aid to make it fully a grant program and one related to prospects for debt forgiveness.
5. Enhancing policy coordination and cofinancing among donors.
6. Eliminating congressional earmarking, except for projects that attack fundamental problems leading to food insecurity, such as high population growth, soil erosion, forest depletion, or the waste of harvested grain.

Some of these prescriptions have been more precisely put forward as reforms to the existing PL 480 legislation and implementation. The broader aim should be to establish changes not only in U.S. procedures and rules, but in other countries that participate in the new international regime.

The first proposed change—giving priority in allocations of food aid to countries desperately short in domestic production and without adequate economic purchasing power in the world market—has an intuitive sensibility. After all, these are the countries in which the need for food is undeniably large, while the commercial import option to achieve food security is blocked by national poverty and growing debt. These countries need to import food under any circumstances. The important thing is that the food should come in a reliable and responsive way to their needs, which vary from year to year. This requires that other priorities, particularly diplomatic, commercial, and bureaucratic ones, do not force the misappropriation of food for less-efficient uses. Furthermore, inertia, built in to the aid system through the older, multiple-purpose, annual authorization, view of food aid, can prevent quick responses to changes in the level of need—or type of commodity.

Food aid regulations should be formulated in a way that stabilizes poor countries' per capita food supplies, while at the same time meeting one of the newer norms of food aid provision, as stipulated in the Bellmon Amendment of 1979, namely to prevent harm to local markets and producers. Following this scenario, the top 10 countries for U.S. grant or bona fide food aid (not Title I) would not include India, Egypt, or El Salvador, all countries where the United States is the dominant and nearly sole provider. Rather, the allocation of grant funds would be substantially redirected towards countries with high rates of environmental threat, malnutrition, and high population growth, such as Ethiopia, Mozambique, Sudan, Bangladesh, and a number of other smaller African states. The food security allocation criteria of the Leahy-Lugar bill, as introduced in April 1990, would mandate such direction.

The second recommendation is that food normally be sold in the recipient country, regardless of the modality through which it is provided. This forces more attention to the true value of specific commodities, moves food into appropriate markets (such as wheat to cities), reduces transport costs, and then raises the total caloric amount available to targeted populations when local, more appropriate foods are purchased to use in food-for-work, mother/child health centers, or emergency refugee camps by U.S. voluntary organizations or ministries of the recipient country.

Since price fluctuations pose a special problem for food security and may well be substantial in the 1990s, a third recommendation is to provide stability in food resources targeted to needy countries and peoples, especially for extremely vulnerable states in Africa. The creation of a special, earmarked, no-year account for Africa, similar to subminimums already used (in the Title II legislation), could guarantee greater security for the special needs in Africa. An

African tonnage subminimum would guarantee food for Africa and reduce the prospect that people in the world's poorest countries will have to share disproportionately the costs of instability in world food markets in the 1990s. With appropriate links to policy in recipient countries, this subminimum need not have a disincentive effect. Interest in Africa in the United States, however, is not high enough to make this proposed legisltively probable.

The fourth recommendation is to redraft the authorizing legislation so that food aid becomes entirely a grant program. Titles I/III, with their concessional sales—useful for market development and political payment for base rights or other foreign policy goals—could be moved to a separate place in the Farm Bill. Benefits of this change would appeal to farm groups if greater scope of authority for use by USDA, the State, and Treasury Departments were stipulated. The purposes of subsidized food exports from the U.S. government, including market development, surplus disposal, and foreign policy support, would be streamlined. Again, the Leahy-Lugar bill takes a step in this direction. Alternatively, a more autonomous Title I could remain in the development assistance account, although it more appropriately belongs, I believe, in the export promotion account, nested with other export subsidy programs.

This splitting of Title I leaves, roughly, a billion dollars of grant funds per year provided by the development assistance account for U.S. food to be used for development purposes. This is a reasonable target. Under this fourth recommendation, grant aid becomes all of PL 480, while Title I becomes a separately legislated export promotion and foreign policy program. PL 480 reflows, plus other funds sought by USDA, the State Department, or the Treasury Department for ensuring U.S. commercial market shares or addressing debt issues could be authorized for use for these trade and natural security issues.

This separation of programs would provide a double bargaining asset in the Uruguay Round of GATT negotiations. The grant food aid program would send aid to those countries where food can be a valuable resource in attacking the particular problems associated with food insecurity and hunger (and thus conform to concerns expressed in the United States and GATT draft on food security). The export program could be a more direct counter to other countries' agricultural subsidies, and could be a subject for GATT negotiations.

Fifth, in rewriting PL 480, Congress should provide incentives for other countries to coordinate and cooperate with the United States in overseas undertakings using food aid. This would be desirable in order to raise world levels of food aid. Reform of the U.S. program should encourage other donors, such as Japan, to view more positively the leadership and collaboration of it and make it easier for them to utilize U.S. farm commodities in their food aid programs. If the United States adopted the first recommendation (a need approach), it could negotiate with other donors to match or exceed the United States in contributions. Other donors' grants should grow substantially, as they once did from 1968-78. Otherwise, in the Uruguay Round of trade negotiations, the United States will have to defend its call for reduction of barriers against the allegation of inconsistencies in the United States's own program, to wit, Title I programs used for "unfair" market competition as measured by free trade principles.

A sixth reform is to reduce radically the earmarking of both food aid allocation and use of local currency proceeds. Earmarks for use of local currency are cumbersome and inefficient. Their purpose might appropriately be maintained in the legislation much in the manner of the Bellmon Amendment. This requirement, that the secretary of agriculture affirm that any food aid provided will not adversely affect local production or national/international marketing, could be a model for any other congressional constraints. For example, in requiring food aid to be targeted to alleviate food insecurity Congress need not legislate specific modalities, which can change. Another "amendment" could require that priority be given to environmental concerns, such as improved and more efficient agricultural techniques.

Detailed prescriptions in PL 480, however, requiring use of specific kinds, such as private entrepreneurs, should be eliminated. Uses of local currency, however, should continue to give high priority to attacking pressures on arable land and the rapid environmental deterioration in many countries. Irrigation, reforestation, research on production, and other national and international collective benefits—especially to agriculture—should be central to projects supported by food aid.

If food aid allowed recipients to exploit less heavily the marginal soils of Africa and Latin America and to protect the environment more generally, its allocation would be closer to serving the longer term interests of the United States. Furthermore, such uses would be especially attractive for cofinancing with other countries, possibly under the aegis of the World Bank, which already is encouraging such steps. Particular projects, such as food-for-work programs, might be supported by food from the U.S. and food and cash from other donors. Currently, projects developed using food aid are often widely scattered geographically and functionally; they are seldom integrated into national food needs or linked to food production and distribution of the recipient country.

A U.S. priority for integrating projects around a food security objective would be evidence of U.S. leadership. This would be especially resonant among the economically sophisticated members in the aid community, consistent with the current GATT negotiations concern with food security, and could be more successfully monitored by congressional oversight.

Conclusions

The United States remains the world's largest exporter of grains, the largest provider of food assistance, and the most complex policy implementor. Detailed legislative requirements, however, often create undesirable constraints and complex configurations for policy implementation. They can even create disincentives within the bureaucracy and become sources of amusement and scorn among political scientists. Although Congress has often been successful in earmarking specific projects or in initiating higher standards for performance, its efforts have inconsistent effects. Rather than streamlined, efficient management resulting, often the complications that are built into the legislation (as in the case of Title III) yield the net opposite of what was intended.

Furthermore, as the 1990s unfold, the world's most food insecure countries remain extremely vulnerable. Food aid and other efforts to provide backup options to shocks received by poor countries' food systems do not provide adequate guarantees. Furthermore, what food aid is provided is not allocated in relative proportion to levels of insecurity. While many highly food insecure countries suffer from declining agricultural productivity, increasing deforestation, and high population growth rates, a fair number are given relatively low priority in allocating U.S. food aid. In fact, among the top 20 recipients of U.S. food aid in 1987, there was only a modest and nonsignificant correlation between degrees of need and per capita aid. Even in a country like El Salvador, which has rapid deforestation, generous U.S. programs have largely ignored production and environment problems while providing several times the amount of aid need would dictate. This is equally true in Africa where much aid has been dumped under the guise of emergency feeding (that is, free food).

An overwhelming case can be made for changing regime practices. A major start would be to target grant food to food insecure states, tying it to support of appropriate food policy and macroeconomic reforms. Currently, food aid provided to the most needy countries comes disproportionately from other countries than the United States. Thus, the United States has fallen behind in taking leadership to address global food needs and alleviate/prevent emergencies. Potentially explosive situations are developing in the highly concentrated urban populations emerging in the Third World. Cognizance of this danger is required; otherwise urban-based political pressure will accelerate the mining of the earth's soils in the next decade in these poor states.

Recognition of the problems just reviewed has already given rise to some changes in the world's food aid regime and in the attention food and food aid receives among specialized development agencies, notably the World Bank. In 1960, the bank spurned the idea of using food aid. At that point, the principles of food aid were at variance with those of the bank. These initial principles were that food aid was to come from donors' surpluses, to add to total trade, to be provided on an annual ad hoc basis, and to be used to promote commercial trade or to address emergency humanitarian needs.

By 1990 other principles, largely contradictory to the founding ones, have arisen. Now principles of market efficiency and development gains rather than exceptionalism and diplomatic gains have been articulated, most notably by the multilateral food legislature, the Committee on Food Aid Policies and Programs of the World Food Programs. These propose that food aid should (1) be supplied most efficiently, (2) be a substitute for a recipient's food imports, (3) be given under longer term commitments, and (4) provide development investments for recipients. Development economists, international organizations, hunger lobby groups, and voluntary agencies have all espoused these principles.

Each of these newer four principles should be incorporated in future U.S. legislation, replacing the remaining elements of the older ones still embodied in the original legislation. In some cases, as with other established U.S. programs, although new principles have been openly advocated by food aid specialists based on expert consensus, such ideas are not well received by some U.S. budgetary authorities, foreign policy officials, or commodity interests.

The Leahy-Lugar Senate bill for legislation in the 1990 Farm Bill is congruent with these new international principles. The key recommendation is that food aid should go to poor countries most in need of food imports to meet nutrition deficiencies. Such food insecurity should become the principal priority of food aid per se. As such, food aid could better attack the very conditions and causes that justify its existence. Its aims, therefore, would be:

1. The need to improve agricultural production through practices that do not threaten the environment and that take advantage of the most appropriate technology.
2. The support of regional, national, and international markets to smooth out instabilities in domestic food supply and reduce the need for grant food imports in the longer term.
3. The design of flexible, environmentally targeted interventions, perhaps using cash-for-work from food sales proceeds, in which donors, such as the United States and Japan, would provide cofinancing.

With such an emphasis, I believe, the prospect for cofinancing with other donors who could provide both cash and food inputs to longer term efforts seems promising. The World Bank has begun efforts to initiate a framework for such cooperation. Significant aid donors that are not large food exporters, such as Germany and Japan, have exhibited a willingness to associate their financing when such efforts are not competitive with their own domestic industries.

The proposals outlined here call for reform of food aid. The United States, as its principal founder and major contributor (both to its substance and its rules), is the natural leader to press for such reform. It is well placed to assert leadership in attacking food insecurity. The 1990 PL 480 reauthorization affords a chance to reform anachronistic elements in the U.S. law, to contribute to related objectives, such as a liberal trading order, and to simplify food aid to make it more effective, less cumbersome, and more dedicated to the central tasks of economic development and hunger alleviation.

New knowledge about world food needs and effective uses of food aid provide a basis for specific steps for regime reform. Leadership in this realm requires taking advantage of the developed world's rich agricultural productivity and surplus food capability. Along with a concern for efficient world agricultural production, the rationale for food aid calls for rich countries to both donate food and to direct the use of this food more centrally toward the goals of protecting people and reducing vulnerability to acute and chronic hunger (World Bank 1988).

Notes

1. The claim for a normative consensus rests on the growing acceptance of human rights that include material goods, as discussed by political philosophers, such as Amartya Sen in *Poverty and Famines* (1981), and the success of organizations, such as the Hunger Project, Bread for the World, and other lobbying and promotional organizations formed in the 1970s, which focus on the issue of hunger, the establishment of the Select Committee on Hunger in the U.S. House of Representatives, and the results of national public opinion surveys.

2. It should be understood that the U.S. global interest is not essentially altruistic. The United States, as the major food exporter, has an interest in a stable growing demand for food imports. Just as Saudi Arabia in the 1970s recognized the interest it had in stable oil markets and to import capacity for poor countries through its major contribution to the establishment of a special oil facility in the IMF during the 1970s, so the United States has an interest in alleviating poor countries' inability to import goods it exports.

References

Clay, Edward J., and Hans W. Singer. 1985. *Food Aid and Development: Issues and Evidence.* Occasional Papers No. 3. Rome: World Food Programme.

Donaldson, Graham. 1989. "World Development and the Role of the World Bank." Paper presented at the First Marbach Conference on Agriculture and Economic Development, Oehningen, Germany.

Gray, Roger. 1974. *The Price Effects of Grain Reserve.* Washington, D.C.: USDA National Agricultural Conference.

Hopkins, Raymond F. 1984. "The Evolution of Food Aid." *Food Policy* 9 (4): 345-62.

_____. 1988. "The Politics of Adjustment: The African Case." *Food Policy* 13(1): 47-55.

Maxwell, J. and Hans W. Singer. 1979. "Food Aid to Developing Countries: A Survey." *World Development* 7 (April): 225-47.

Mayer, Leo B. 1972. "Estimated Net Costs of PL 480 Food Aid with Three Alternative U.S. Farm Aid Programs." *American Journal of Agricultural Economics* 54(1): 41-50.

Minear, Larry. 1989. "U.S. Food Aid: Give Priority to Human Needs." *Choices* 2: 28-30.

National Academy of Sciences. 1989. *Food Aid Projections for the 1990s: Report of an Ad Hoc Panel Meeting, October 6-7, 1988.* Washington: National Research Council.

Pinstrup-Andersen, Per, ed. 1988. *Food Subsidies in Developing Countries.* Baltimore: Johns Hopkins University Press.

Reutlinger, Shlomo, and Judit Katona-Apte. 1987. "The Nutritional Impact of Food Aid: Criteria for the Selection of Cost-Effective Foods." In *Food Policy: Integrating Supply, Distribution, and Consumption.* J. Price Gittinger and others, ed. Baltimore: Johns Hopkins University Press.

Ruttan, Vernon. 1989. "Food Aid: Surplus Disposal, Strategic Assistance, Development Aid and Basic Needs." Mimeo. University of Minnesota, Department of Agricultural and Applied Economics, St. Paul, Minn. July 10.

Sen, Amartya. 1981. *Poverty and Famines.* New York: Oxford University Press.

Wallerstein, Mitchell. 1980. *Food for War—Food for Peace.* Cambridge: MIT Press.

Wheeler, Joseph C. 1988. *Development Co-operation.* Development Assistance Committee Chairman's Report for 1988. Paris: OECD.

White, John. 1974. *The Politics of Foreign Aid.* New York: St. Martin's Press.

World Bank. 1988. *World Development Report, 1988.* Washington: The World Bank.

World Food Program. 1979. *CFA 5/79.* Rome: World Food Program.

PART IV

Improving U.S. Economic Assistance and Food Aid Programs

Participants in the workshop were organized into two working groups, which met for discussion during each session and were responsible for preparing recommendations related to the workshop objectives. One group focused on poor, low-growth countries located mainly in sub-Saharan Africa and low-income Asia. The other considered emerging middle-income or high-growth countries in Latin America and the Caribbean, East Asia, and North Africa. Each group reported its recommendations in the final workshop session. Following the reports of the working groups, a five-person panel commented on the recommendations. The reports of the working groups and panel comments are summarized in Chapter 9. Chapter 10 restates the major conclusions of the workshop that emerged during the open discussion that closed the final session.

Lehman B. Fletcher

9

Reports of the Working Groups
and Panel Comments

Report of the Low-income
Low-growth Working Group

Raymond F. Hopkins, Chair
Ross Talbot, Rapporteur

The low-income/low-growth working group agreed on the following seven observations and recommendations based on papers and ideas presented at the workshop.

There are sound reasons for optimism in forecasting the economic conditions of the world into the 1990s. However, this observation must be tempered by the realization that severe problems of economic and social maldistribution will prevail. These will especially be a problem within the developing countries, as well as between the industrial and low-income countries. That aggregate numbers tend to disguise this unfortunate element is to be expected.

Serious inequities existing within the developing countries relate to their supplies of food and services. Persons in poverty conditions will be unable to enjoy the benefits of overall expansion in goods and services. In Africa this condition is especially acute and likely to be long-term; in Asia and Latin America it is more cyclical.

Development assistance and food aid should be directed toward the establishment and maintenance of an international scientific research infrastructure linking together and relevant to the problems of the developing nations. The industrial countries have a strong rationale for development assistance based on a global social contract, one that reflects the relations of an increasingly interdependent world. A high priority exists for a transnational exchange (from rich to poor nations) of greater research and development in agriculture. At the same time, the needs of those who are thrown into poverty and experience emergencies must be met. This means that new research or assistance programs should not be initiated and implemented in ways that would put the poor in even greater jeopardy.

In formulating and implementing their development assistance programs, industrial nations should seek to maximize the marginal productivity of their development aid projects and programs. This is facilitated by an explicit and consistent set of objectives. A problem will occur if there is a set of conflicting objectives for which foreign assistance is to be used. Grantors must be aware continually of the lag between their policies and programs, and the effects of these, especially in low-income, low-growth countries. Emergency and refugee aid should continue to have high priority and be fully supported; this aid, however, should be administered efficiently to prevent disincentive effects in the area.

Developing countries should not oppose GATT agricultural reforms; to oppose liberalization among market-economy nations would be contrary to the interests of these low-income nations. No food aid should be provided to low-income, food-importing countries opposing the adoption of GATT policies.[1] Because of the large growth gains that research indicates are possible, there should be food aid incentives for those developing countries who cooperate, especially ones who themselves undertake liberalization.

Industrial and developing countries should promote an understanding and appreciation of large economic gains, especially indirect, that are likely to occur through the removal of net agricultural taxes and internal distortions and through an emphasis on liberal macroeconomic and sectoral policies. In certain cases, subjecting food aid to the conditionality restrictions established in World Bank/International Monetary Fund negotiations is justified. Food security as a food aid program objective should be structured so that economic gains as well as political assistance for sustaining adjustment are paramount. Political goals per se are insufficient.

Those developing nations that give operational support to measures of food sector and macrosector reforms should be given a definite priority in the allocation policies of donor assistance programs. Such developing nations will be especially vulnerable in the medium run, and thus especially in need of help. Donors should make a special effort to assist them in building and supporting institutions that can effectively implement these reform policies. Further, donors should provide more aid to assist agricultural reform policies of developing nations, although emergency/disaster support should continue to have first priority in food aid allocations. Political and commercial interests should not overrule these priorities. Those interests should establish their own programs and modalities for the objectives they seek.

Report of the Middle-income High-growth Working Group

William M. Miner, Chair
James McCormick, Rapporteur

The middle-income/high-growth working group considered that food aid/food security programs are: (1) necessary, (2) inadequate in size compared to anticipated trends in LDC import requirements and food consumption needs, and (3) relevant and appropriate for the goal of overcoming larger poverty problems. It agreed on the following seven recommendations to improve U.S. food assistance policies:

1. Food aid objectives should be separated into three basic categories and food assistance should be provided on one or more of these basic categories:
   - Emergency food assistance would be designed to respond to unforeseen disasters.
   - Economic development assistance would be provided to encourage policy reforms and to support economic growth within developing countries.
   - Market development assistance might be provided through

the food aid program or better as a component of overall trade and marketing programs. Further analysis appears necessary, however, to determine its usefulness and the appropriate administrative arrangements.

It was also recognized that unusual economic, social, and political circumstances, such as political and economic reforms in Poland, might justify special forms of food assistance.

2. U.S. commitments to bilateral and multilateral food aid should be reaffirmed. The commitment to multilateral food aid should be strengthened, in part, to encourage burden sharing among donor countries. Further, a multilateral approach will encourage coordinated actions among donors and recipients.

3. The provision of food aid should be better integrated into the policy formulation process in order to support food security and development objectives more efficiently. This recommendation can best be achieved through delegating more decision making authority to staff in the field.

4. The expertise of the World Food Program and the World Bank should be used in concert with the administration of U.S. food aid to encourage policy reforms within developing countries, particularly if aid and policy reforms are directed toward achieving food security.

5. The authorization of food assistance programs should be available on a multiyear basis.

6. Food assistance legislation should incorporate a mechanism to allow the forgiveness of Title I debt obligations in response to appropriate economic policy reforms in recipient countries.

7. A new framework is needed to foster greater technical cooperation in agricultural development among donors and recipients, and new methods are required to measure the need for food aid and its effectiveness.

Panel Comments

Leo Mayer

Having spent a career in Washington arguing that we should not consider issues single-dimensionally, I suggest we should consider food aid in relation to other things that are part of the broader picture. In 1970, I wrote a journal article on the trade-offs between land retirement and food aid. It seems that not too much has changed in the interim, in terms of questions relating to food aid. It is still a question of how we use our resources. Should the United States retire land or produce surpluses that become food aid? That is a very basic question that is continuously faced in the Department of Agriculture.

At present there are some new players in the decision making on this question. There is a big interest group, and an important one, that would argue that nonuse of resources is just as important as the use of resources for food aid. Who are they? They are the environmentalists who pushed a conservation reserve program of 40 million acres and who are still pushing to increase it substantially, despite the fact that we had a drought in 1988, that we have drawn down stocks to bare minimum levels, and we had a partial drought again in 1989. There is still a major effort going on in Washington, D.C., to expand the conservation program well beyond the minimum 40 million acres that are now in the law.

What is that going to do to prospects for food aid programs? It is very clearly going to place limits on the amount of food that is going to be available. This broader perspective is important because we can discuss at great length how to use food aid but not recognize that the first step is producing it. That is the critical step in this whole process.

Next on the use of food aid, there is the question of development versus emergency aid. Development implies a multiyear commitment of food aid. Emergency aid implies a one year or even less commitment. In fact, the U.S. program has too many informal multiyear commitments. The food aid program is almost impossible to change. The distribution between countries is pretty much locked in.

I was in Korea in 1981. I was astonished to find out we still had a food aid program going there. We still had an AID mission there. It should have been phased out.

I was in Indonesia in 1988. To my great surprise, I found that the United States has a food aid program there, too. Yet Indonesia is one of the fastest growing countries in the Pacific Rim area and has recently become self-sufficient in rice production.

Why do these programs persist? I call it institutional lethargy. If we cannot bring ourselves to phase out countries where we have been successful, then we cannot, under the limited resources available in the budget, phase into countries where aid is needed.

As a developmental resource, if we want food aid to do something really useful and we want to get public support behind it again, we have got to come up with something imaginative to generate support for it. In my judgment, we should focus food aid programs on the 30 poorest countries in the world and develop a five-year strategy of shifting it to them. Only an approach like this is going to give us the national priority that is necessary to get the food aid program rejuvenated.

What is it we want to achieve with food aid? I don't think we know. Perhaps that is why the United States has lost the momentum for food aid that existed following World War II. In one sense, putting land into trees and grass is a very selfish kind of measure. It is "save it for ourselves," as opposed to "produce food aid and give it to others." It is indicative of where we are in history that food aid is losing this fight. If we really want to rejuvenate food aid, or even maintain it, it is essential to figure out what it is we are really trying to achieve with it. If we cannot find a valid justification for food aid, there is no chance of expanding it in the present budget environment; even maintaining it is going to be very difficult.

Charles Hanrahan

My comments are directed to the broad outline of the legislative proposal for reform in food aid that has emerged in this workshop and fairly explicitly reflected in the recommendations of the middle-income/high-growth working group, and more generally and broadly included in the recommendations of the low-income/low-growth working group.

The political and economic context in which these proposals will be taken up and considered could be characterized as a "political economy" approach. In discussing developing country agricultural policy reforms, the question was asked: Why do governments undertake policy interventions that appear to be inefficient or inappropriate? Is it by design or is it by mistake? The answer given was that behind the policies and programs in developing countries are people who have vested interests, or something to gain or lose. Interest groups are important, which is a starting point for my assessment of food aid reform.

Proposals presented to the workshop would separate food aid into new titles defined by function, not by funding mechanism. Market development would go to the Department of Agriculture. Economic development, with a strong emphasis on food security assistance and refugee aid, would go primarily to AID. Foreign policy food aid would be combined with Economic Support Fund (ESF) assistance under the State Department. Given the current allocation, this would work out to a $1 billion allocation for development food aid to AID and $400 million for market development and/or foreign policy food aid.

The $1 billion would fund both program and project food aid. Monetization of food aid would take place as needed. Food aid would be provided on a multiyear basis.

These proposals have some obvious merits. First, from a legislative point of view, the changes would result in a clean bill. Second, from an administrative management point of view, the program would become much simpler to administer. The proposals respond to the perceived interests of many, although not all of the interest groups involved with food aid, and are a direct response to problems of hunger and food security in developing countries, particularly African countries.

Now, that being said, let me make four sets of comments by way of discussing the context. My first remark is that the forces that have historically made for changes in the food aid program do not seem to be at work in the current domestic and international economy or food system. Historically, the main factors driving change in food aid programs, as in most aspects of domestic and foreign agricultural policy, has been the existence of commodity surpluses.

When you look back at Section 416 in 1949, 480 in 1955, a number of changes in the 1985 Farm Bill, and the expansion of Section 416 and then Food for Progress, they are all driven mainly by the desire to reduce burdensome stocks. All were accompanied by perceptions of immediate needs overseas, such as famines in India in the mid-1960s and drought and famine in Africa in 1984 and 1985. Existence of surpluses, together with emergencies overseas, provided an environment in which fairly major changes could be made in food aid legislation.

There are important forces at work now that might make for change in the food aid program. Congressional staff, powerful members of Congress, committees, a number of interest groups, USAID, and commodity organizations are all arguing for changes in the program. That is an important combination of forces and factors. However, the environment for change would be facilitated if surpluses existed and if there were immediately perceived foreign food emergencies. Long-run projections of deficits, however credible, are not as persuasive as immediately perceived problems.

My second set of comments has to do with the conclusion that the views of interest groups matter. I am including as interest groups those in government as well as those outside of government. Some have suggested that the old coalition in support of food programs has weakened and a new coalition in support of food programs is needed.

At least four sets of interests with respect to the food aid program can be identified. First are the commodity organizations. Major commodity organizations are on record as strongly supporting a market development orientation for the existing Title I program. Testimony before the House Agriculture Committee in July 1990, for example, indicated that most of the commodity groups also favor reform in the interagency decision making process. But perhaps we need to be less sanguine about the political arithmetic. At least it is my interpretation that when commodity organizations say that Title I ought to be more oriented toward market development, they are thinking about the $900 million that is currently allocated to Title I rather than to the $400 million that would be allocated to market development in the proposal presented to the workshop. Budget reallocation between those titles would be hard to effect given the current configuration of interests and budget pressures.

The second important set of interests is the private voluntary organizations. One has to distinguish between the mainline organizations like CARE as well as smaller social justice or religiously oriented private voluntary organizations. The mainline groups have expressed fairly strong views before congressional committees that they see no major legislative reforms needed in the current program. That is coming from a group known as the Food Aid Coalition.

They do, however, call very strongly for reform of the inter-agency decision making process. The smaller, social justice oriented PVOs have echoed sentiments like those reflected in the proposal to put greater emphasis on development of food security, food aid for emergency purposes, and for refugees.

Third are the governmental bureaucratic interests: USAID, USDA, Treasury Department, and State Department, to name a few. It is fair to say that these groups do not yet speak with one voice with respect to food aid policy reform. USAID appears to be leading the effort, both intellectually and politically, within the bureaucratic interests, to orient food aid more toward economic development. USDA seems to be taking a wait and see attitude. State seems to be opposed but how adamantly is unknown. The Office of Management and Budget (OMB) has not yet demonstrated that it feels threatened by proposals for change, although it is taking at least a mild interest.

The fourth group includes the agribusiness and maritime interests. They, themselves, have not said very much about their intentions. So perhaps we have yet to hear from them in a formal, public sense. But there is some indication that they like the program pretty much the way it is. Their views, of course, would have to be taken into consideration. All of these interests, of course, will be interacting with the various congressional committees that have jurisdiction over authorization, appropriation, and oversight of these programs: for example, the House and Senate Agricultural Committees, House and Senate Appropriation Committees, and the House Select Hunger Committee.

Some reforms seem more likely than others at this point. But perhaps it is too early to make predictions, although as all of us are aware and particularly those on the Hill, the legislative clock is ticking away. The time for consideration is growing short. This configuration of interests suggests to me that the growing coalition for the reform of food aid has not yet fully emerged. We may not need the old line to ensure support. But surely we need a new one to get major changes. I think this is the major challenge: the requirement for getting food aid policy reform through the legislative process.

My third set of remarks has to do with administrative reform of the program at two levels: one at the interagency level and one within USAID. It seems to me that this may be a relatively propitious time. Certainly there is widespread dissatisfaction both in and out of government with the way the program is administered. That may be the one agreed upon aspect of the program throughout most, if not all, of the interest groups, Congress, and the affected bureaucratic agencies.

It is not inconceivable that the administration, with strong congressional urging, could review the food aid charter of the DCC, the Food Development Coordination Committee, eliminating or at least mitigating OMB and State Department micromanagement of the program and replacing it with something like an annual budget and foreign policy review and leaving day-to-day management decisions to USAID and USDA.

Finally, it seems to me that one other area deserves a fair amount of consideration. It has been mentioned as a rationale for both expansion of food aid and refocusing on food security. That is the situation in Africa. It seems to me that there is a huge reservoir of support in the Congress for food aid and development assistance for Africa. That might provide a basis around which a number of interests might effectively coalesce for getting future reforms in the program.

Richard E. Bissell

There are a couple of basic issues that we in USAID are trying to face. It is difficult at this point in the consideration of the 1990 Farm Bill to be particularly definitive. As Charles Hanrahan noted, at some point USAID will come up with a position on how to reform food aid programs. Sequentially, the administration will then come up with an integrated view.

Right now, I can only express a personal view that comes from AID experience, which I think has been properly characterized as frustrating in recent years, as to how food aid programs are designed and implemented. I think there are a couple of major issues that need to be worked out.

Let me address the kinds of dilemmas that come up, from my point of view, in trying to recategorize food aid. Categorizing it always raises problems in terms of having to create what people may want to describe as mutually exclusive categories, as opposed to being overlapping. It was illustrated for me, setting aside the market development issue, by my USDA colleagues trying to design an emergency food aid category on the one hand and, on the other hand, creating an economic development/humanitarian category. Being a "nose to the grindstone" kind of person, I immediately began thinking of contrary examples of what I would do with specific food aid programs. It is fairly easy to take a classic civil war catastrophe in Mozambique and put it into an emergency category. But moving away from that, into a food aid program say in Ethiopia, which is clearly affected by civil war but has been perhaps more greatly affected by the disastrous economic policies of the government, the categories start to merge in terms of how we design a program to address such problems. We in the aid community have to think through the design of programs to elevate them to the level we want.

We clearly have emergency food aid as a first response, hoping we can turn it later into a development program. Whether or not that is humanitarian, and it depends on how you interpret the word *humanitarian,* it seems to me not to clarify the issue at all.

I have two categories to suggest. First is what I call compensatory food aid. This can be compensatory in a number of different situations. It can compensate for national disasters, civil wars, or emergencies. But it is clearly provided by drawing upon the historic charity of the American people. It is frequently implemented as simply as possible through private voluntary organizations (PVOs) and others. Therefore, it reaches people as directly as possible.

On the other hand, my second category is developmental programs. Developmental programs are not compensatory in the sense of trying to simply address an actual food shortage. They have to be integrated into the overall economic development plans of the recipient country. This is not a simple thing, and there are several reasons. One is the historical roots of the American food aid program. A second is that there is an enormous amount of thinking, analysis, planning, and both macroeconomic and microeconomic work that has to go into a development program. But at USAID we are trying to run a $100 program on two cents of overhead: we do not have the people. We do not have the people in Washington, and we do not have the people in the field to carry out the ambitions that people have for food aid as a development tool. We can do compensatory programs and we have cooperating institutions that implement programs for us in the compensatory area.

But, as a development tool, we really do not have the staff and we have not found, generally speaking, in working with Congress, the money to cover personnel needs. The ambitions for food aid go well beyond our current design and implementation capacities.

With regard to forgiving Title I debts in certain countries, which came up in the recommendations, we have had experience with regard to the issue of forgiving debts and foreign assistance over the last year in the development assistance economic support fund area for the least developed countries in Africa. Last year's Appropriations Bill provided for this in Section 572. We have gone through an interagency process that resulted in initiating debt forgiveness for African countries beginning in October 1989.

The issue of forgiving Title I raises a different problem. I want to touch on this because it is something that I have been personally involved in to a great extent. In the 150 account, food aid debts—Title I debts—are treated differently from other outstanding loans. They, in fact, are offset specifically against the food aid programs on the budget line. Other loan payments that come from developing countries go into a miscellaneous account and are simply attributed against the account overall, as we say, below the bottom line. Food aid loans, in fact, are an offset and, thus, they have a direct budget impact. We have done some numbers and depending on how widely one defines Title I loans, Title I loan forgiveness can be considerable.

Charles Hanrahan noted the special place that Africa plays in congressional thinking. Title I loans in Africa are far less than they are in Asia and in Latin America. It may be if one follows this route of looking at forgiveness of Title I loans, it would make a lot more sense to begin with Africa just because of the enormous impact. However, the budget impact would be great if any kind of an across-the-board forgiveness of Title I debts is undertaken.

This brings me to what is an important issue for many concerned with food aid to think about. What is the state of the food aid budget overall and the role that dollars play in it? Currently, we are told that we have to give special attention to Poland and Eastern Europe. We are constantly giving priority to one area or another. The present program in Europe is inadequate according to many in the Congress. But, the fact is that the budget is extremely constrained. When the administration asked agencies to come up with commodities for Eastern Europe, we came up with animal feed because that was available in Section 416.

If you move away from surplus commodities, you are talking dollars, not just commodities. So, as a result, we have moved into a phase where we have to think about food aid as a dollar issue. It is not really a commodity issue anymore. It is not just a Gramm-Rudman fact of life. It is a fact of life of the priority programs that come along, like Poland, at the end of the fiscal year. These are all playing together to put pressure on people like me as chief budget officer in USAID to realize that PL 480 is a dollar issue as much as development assistance, economic support funds, or any other part of the 150 account. I hope that everybody keeps that in mind.

James Phippard

Although I participated rather actively in one of the working groups and contributed to formulating its proposals, I now have the happy opportunity to comment on those same proposals. Having had some experience in the field in the design and operation of food programs, I hope that I can perhaps bring a slightly different perspective to this discussion.

Regarding the purposes of food aid, there has been much discussion and perhaps some uncertainty as to purposes. But, at the same time, there is a coalescing view as to what the purposes of food aid should be.

Perhaps they should not necessarily be what they are now. But there is uncertainty as to how to translate food aid into the real live programs it must become. That is probably particularly true for what we call the developmental aspect of food aid.

We have talked about the importance of policy changes. I do not think that we have talked enough about project food aid and how or whether you should use local currencies for project food aid and some of the implications of that for actual operations in the field.

I would like to underline one of the recommendations. If we are going to agree in food aid legislation that economic development is a bona fide goal of at least a portion of the program, and we also agree that whatever portion it is, we should focus on that and not have the current conflict of goals, which tends frequently to obscure the various goals involved, then it seems we really need to provide for implementation. We need the analytical capability in the field to integrate these programs into the overall developmental assistance package. Merely declaring economic development a goal is not going to make it happen. I think there are a variety of things that people are going to have to look at to really make it happen.

With respect to policy changes, there is a lot of uncertainty about the use of food aid or, indeed, use of economic resources. Some people talk about leverage. Others talk about encouraging policy changes. My own view is that talk about leverage is overblown. I do not think you are able to force changes that people do not see as being in their own self-interest. You may be able to ease the way. Here is a proposal based on Phippard's Rule on this: the amount of U.S. influence on policy changes is in inverse proportion to the amount of assistance provided. That rule may be heavily colored by my own experience in Egypt: we have poured in a vast amount of food aid and have had very little influence on Egyptian policy. And in Tunisia, with very little food aid, we managed to talk with the Tunisians and help them implement the agricultural policy change they wanted.

I think we have to be very careful about setting overly high expectations as to what the United States can accomplish with policy change. The danger is that if you set very high expectations and you fail, then you conclude that you cannot achieve anything.

There has been talk about multiyear commitments. I think from a field perspective it is extremely difficult to accomplish anything, whether it is projects funded through the food aid process or a continuing policy dialogue, if you only know from year to year what level food aid is going to be.

A reference has been made to bureaucratic inertia. I think that is quite right. There is a feeling that we deliver the wrong political signal if we reduce country programs. So we continue to give countries much the same as they received year after year. Whether it is politically possible to change that, I do not know. But until it is, I think the economic development results of food aid will be rather limited.

Janet Breslin

I would like to address my comments to two different areas. One is to give a sense of what it feels like politically to work on the food aid issue, and what I think is going to happen; and then talk a little bit about some of the policy issues that have been raised.

From a political point of view, I look at food aid as a piece of legislation that has to be passed. It is part of the Farm Bill. Last year the biggest domestic increase in nutrition funding in the last decade, the Hunger Prevention Act, passed. I look at this issue as similar to that one—which was a big spending bill. It was the end of the Reagan administration. Nobody thought the nutrition bill was going to happen. Certainly, President Reagan had not come out for big increases in food stamp spending, but factors came together in the right way and made it possible.

I see the same prospects for PL 480 reform coming into the new

Farm Bill. Events are coming together in a certain way that are providing some openings; certain changes happening right now make some types of reform possible.

Let me make a couple of comments about the Senate Agriculture Committee. Nine of the 16 members on the committee are up for reelection in 1990. That is a substantial proportion of the committee up for reelection. They are equally divided between both parties. However, neither Chairman Leahy nor Senator Lugar is up for reelection.

The new bill must be passed in a timely way. Most people, including Senator Lugar to some degree, are saying that we cannot do it as quickly as we are trying to do. But from the committee's view, we have no choice. Hearings on PL 480 began before the end of 1989. The Farm Bill will be about 1000 pages long. Doing this bill is an incredibly complex, time-consuming operation.

Now, let me make some comments about the policy issues that have been raised. In February 1989, Alan Woods, the AID administrator, convened a day-and-a-half conference of congressional staff talking about foreign aid. At the summary meeting there was an attempt made to summarize the goals of foreign aid. The idea was that if anybody disagreed, the goal would not be accepted. There had to be consensus. This could also be said about food aid. The reality was that none of us could agree. The only things we could agree on were weak and useless, because everybody in Congress and the American people reflected in Congress, have different views, different goals, and different desires for what foreign assistance and food aid are supposed to be used, and what USAID is supposed to do. USAID has a problem in trying to come to grips with this. That is why the State Department appears to be more focused. It has a clearer design of what it is about. I am very sympathetic to the problems of identifying the goals of food aid as distinct from foreign aid.

Let me mention some of the things members of Congress and staff have concluded about food aid. They reflect a lot of the comments made here. The program has always been known as a very effective balance of interests; a balance of five agencies, of commodity groups, and foreign policy interests. It has been very effective over the years. Some things are changing. The challenge ahead in the Congress is in dealing with a different balance or a new grouping of interests.

Some of these changes are in the policy area. A good example is the impact of the environmental groups. Their approach is supportive of the budget process, because we can spend on agriculture by taking land out of production. This is a different way of supporting prices with less direct federal budgetary costs. There is an interaction here between environmentalists and agricultural interests.

One perspective developing across the country is that it may be of value to do food aid with less food, that the error has been dumping. This is definitely one school of thought. Given a high production level in this country, then it is used overseas, one hopes effectively. I think that this approach is not possible any more because of environmental and budget constraints. Also, I think there is a sense in some areas with strong foreign policy orientations that we can be effective, possibly even more effective, with less.

It has been my observation that in those parts of the world where the USAID missions are not the largest donor, we are more sensitive to the political reality of the country and are more politically adept than in those places where we supposedly have the most influence.

So, I suggest the Senate Agriculture Committee is comfortable with the idea of making the best use possible we can of the limited amount of both money and food, because we are in an environment of budget constraint and because such an approach reflects changing production patterns. That is not bad and it might be a useful approach. We are obviously balancing trade against humanitarian interests. Also, we as a people respond to international crises. That orientation is something we cannot lose track of.

The other orientation from an agricultural point of view is that the commodity groups are very interested in having an intelligent international economic policy. It is not just trade. I think that the commodity groups are changing their orientations toward foreign aid. I do not think that the relationship is as hostile as it used to be. They are potentially a very effective resource to have in the foreign aid and foreign policy community to push for effective international economic policy or other types of assistance. That needs to be pursued more. We need to be sensitive to both hardheaded economic policy and humanitarian orientation. Whatever we come up with in PL 480 and Section 416 will reflect, we hope, both of these concerns.

From a political point of view, for a bill to succeed we have to get a majority vote. All of the members of the committee represent different states. We have Republicans who have an ear toward the administration. The only way you succeed politically is if everybody gets something, especially if they have to give up something. What we are trying to get a feel for in working with the administration and all of the groups is whether there is a better way of putting this legislation together in a way that everybody gives something up and everybody gets something. That is why when market development and export subsidies go to USDA, USAID or the development community should get other things.

My last comment is on the issue of debt. This is obviously important not just for food aid but for foreign aid. How repayments flow back into the PL 480 account is very important. PL 480 is funded through agriculture appropriations. OMB also makes assumptions about the reflow level. That determines our program level and the recommendations for spending. We have had a fight about this because OMB is assuming higher reflows. Congress is pretty good about maintaining appropriations levels. As I understand it, that does not happen in reflows of development assistance loans. We cannot just simply wave a wand and say, okay, we are going to forgive all the debts. It will show up as less money. We would then have to appropriate more to maintain funding. Politically, I think that is possible. My own feeling is that is possible to do in the long run. PL 480 is so much an institution that adjustments can be made and a basic level of support will stay. But whatever reform efforts are made, either to food aid or foreign aid, I am hoping that progress can be made on this very, very difficult problem of what to do about official and commercial debt of the developing countries.

Notes

1. Later discussion clarified that the intent of this recommendation applied only to development food aid and not humanitarian food aid for emergencies and refugees.

10

Conclusions and Recommendations

Lehman B. Fletcher

The U.S. foreign assistance appropriation was not much different in 1990 from other recent years. A small increase raised the total to $14.3 billion, benefiting both bilateral and multilateral development assistance. Congressional earmarks continued; of $3.25 billion appropriated for the Economic Support Fund, all but $58 million was designated for particular countries or programs.

The 1991 budget made no significant changes in the direction, level, and execution of U.S. economic assistance. That possibility remains for the near future. A task force of the House Committee on Foreign Affairs carried out a yearlong review of foreign aid and reported to the committee in 1989. Congress is now deciding whether or not to reorient and reorganize U.S. policies and programs for foreign development assistance. When and if this happens, it will be the first reorientation of the congressional foreign aid mandate since the 1973 "New Directions" legislation.

The workshop affirmed continuing justification for a strong development assistance program by the United States and other industrial countries based on a global social contract reflecting increasing world economic interdependence. It pointed to the expansion and maintenance of an international scientific infrastructure for agricultural research, oriented to the needs of poorer nations, regions, and producer groups, as priorities for that assistance.

The workshop recognized that massive poverty and hunger persist and grow in the low-income and debt-burdened Third World

countries, and that these countries are not expected to participate
fully in the global economic expansion of the 1990s. It emphasized
that worsening hunger and malnutrition are evident in sub-Saharan
Africa. While famine and starving refugees are the most visible signs
of this food crisis, the steady decline in African food production
per capita is the most telling indicator of the scope and scale of
Africa's problems. The workshop fully accepted the urgency of
humanitarian and emergency food aid for alleviating hunger but
called for greater efforts to enhance the developmental role of food
aid.

The relationship between food security and food aid was
debated. Some felt that food aid, by its very nature, is an especially
relevant resource for promoting a country's food security. Others
argued that the current understanding of food security as access to
adequate food by all people at all times has more to do with
employment, income generation, and productivity growth of the
poor than with food aid. While food aid can be useful in targeted
feeding programs for those adversely affected by policy reforms or
left out of the growth process, only its effective use as a development
resource offers promise of permanent alleviation of poverty and
hunger.

A strong consensus developed around the need to reform U.S.
food aid legislation and implementation policies. A clean separation
of export market promotion, including credit sales, from
humanitarian/developmental grant food aid was strongly supported.
Allocation of food aid to countries whose policies favor its productive
use, multiyear commitments, and integration with financial aid were
all recommended. The need for adequate USAID personnel to
design and implement integrated food/financial development
assistance was recognized, as was the need to draw more heavily
on WFP and other multilateral experience and capabilities.

The workshop viewed the total level of food aid in the 1990s
and beyond as problematical. Generous food aid in the past has
been associated with large crop surpluses in the United States and
Europe. It seems unlikely that such surpluses will emerge in the
1990s, especially if environmental concerns further restrain the use
of erodible land and polluting chemicals. As a result, food aid will

become closer to full-cost assistance and more completely fungible with financial aid; hence the greater urgency to use it productively as a development resource.

This perspective on the diminishing availability and demanding nature of development food aid contrasts sharply with the view of it, also expressed at the workshop, as a panacea for a panoply of adjustment, environmental, and social problems. The softening, greening, and fragmenting of food aid the latter view entails invariably exceed the financial and managerial capacities of both recipient countries and granting agencies, and weaken the growing resolve of donors to use it only when it meets the test of parity with financial assistance.

Statistical Appendix

Tables on world food production, trade, and food aid were prepared as background materials for the workshop participants. Selected tables have been revised and are included here for use by the readers of this book.

Table SA.1. Cereal production, imports, exports, total supplies per person and food aid in developing countries

Countries	Unit	1981/82	1982/83	1983/84	1984/85	1985/86	1986/87
ALL DEVELOPING COUNTRIES							
Production (a)	mil. tn.	682.47	698.81	750.55	772.57	776.31	795.43
Per capita production (a)	kg	203.91	204.65	215.45	217.36	214.06	215.15
Imports (b)	mil. tn.	97.04	105.30	112.23	110.49	97.74	110.04
Exports (b)	mil. tn.	32.12	36.42	34.90	38.06	36.91	34.61
Food aid (c)	mil. tn.	8.57	8.91	9.77	12.34	10.74	12.03
Food aid as percentage of imports	percent	8.83	8.46	8.71	11.17	10.99	10.94
Total supplies per capita (d)	kg	223.30	224.83	237.64	237.74	230.84	235.55
LOW-INCOME FOOD-DEFICIT COUNTRIES							
Production (a)	mil. tn.	479.57	497.24	552.36	569.10	557.94	576.44
Per capita production (a)	kg	186.94	190.24	207.41	209.72	201.77	204.69
Imports (b)	mil. tn.	48.60	50.19	50.79	47.95	40.87	45.43
Exports (b)	mil. tn.	1.83	1.87	2.52	7.43	9.12	8.15
Food aid	mil. tn.	7.26	7.64	8.62	0.78	9.37	10.03
Food aid as percentage of imports	percent	14.95	15.22	16.98	22.48	22.93	22.07
Total supplies per capita (d)	kg	205.17	208.73	225.53	224.65	213.25	217.92

Table SA.1. (cont.)

LEAST-DEVELOPED COUNTRIES

Production (a)	mil. tn.	46.85	46.88	46.17	43.11	49.61	52.08
Per capita production (a)	kg	155.72	151.75	145.60	132.42	148.43	151.38
Imports (b)	mil. tn.	6.13	6.01	7.93	10.09	7.29	7.81
Exports (b)	mil. tn.	0.32	0.46	0.45	0.18	0.46	0.65
Food aid	mil. tn.	2.79	3.06	3.06	5.16	4.46	4.11
Food aid as percentage of imports	percent	45.53	50.84	38.58	51.09	61.20	52.72
Total supplies per capita (d)	kg	175.03	169.73	169.20	162.87	168.86	172.17

SUB-SARAHAN AFRICA

Production (a)	mil. tn.	43.41	43.25	41.13	38.27	49.17	52.39
Per capita production (a)	kg	116.99	113.07	104.33	94.16	117.34	121.13
Imports (b)	mil. tn.	9.81	9.45	10.29	0.30	9.68	9.24
Exports (b)	mil. tn.	0.56	1.02	0.77	0.13	0.80	1.59
Food aid	mil. tn.	2.40	2.54	2.75	4.98	3.78	3.08
Food aid as percentage of imports	percent	24.48	26.92	26.74	37.41	39.01	33.33
Total supplies per capita (d)	kg	141.92	135.11	128.48	126.56	138.53	138.81

SOURCE: FAO.

(a) Data refers to the calendar year of the first year shown. Rice is in terms of milled rice.
(b) For total grain, season beginning 1 July of first year shown: for rice, calendar year of second year
(c) Excludes Israel, Malta, Poland, and Portugal.
(d) All supplies per person are based on production and net imports, taking no account of stock changes.

Table SA.2. Annual growth rates of food production, total
and per capita, 1962-87 (percent per year)

| | Total production | | |
	1962-70	1970-80	1980-87
World	2.90	2.30	2.10
Developed market economies	2.10	2.00	0.90
United States	2.00	2.30	0.30
Canada	2.90	1.90	2.70
Western Europe	1.80	1.80	1.10
Japan	3.10	1.60	1.40
Oceania	3.80	1.50	1.30
South Africa	2.70	2.90	0.10
USSR and Eastern Europe	3.40	1.40	1.90
USSR	3.90	0.90	2.00
Eastern Europe	2.40	2.10	1.80
Developing Countries	2.80	2.70	2.40
North Africa	2.90	1.80	3.40
Egypt	3.10	1.80	2.80
Sub-Saharan Africa (a)	2.90	1.30	2.40
Latin America	2.80	3.10	1.90
Mexico	4.10	4.00	1.60
Brazil	3.10	3.70	3.10
Argentina	1.50	2.20	0.80
Near East	3.00	3.40	2.60
South Asia	2.30	2.20	2.40
India	2.10	2.20	2.20
Southeast Asia	3.00	4.00	3.30
Indonesia	3.00	4.10	3.80
Other East Asia (b)	4.10	4.30	2.60
China (c)	5.70	3.60	4.80

(continues)

Table SA.2. (cont.)

| | Per capita production | | |
	1962-70	1970-80	1980-87
World	0.80	0.40	0.40
Developed market economies	1.10	1.20	0.20
United States	0.80	1.30	-0.60
Canada	1.20	0.60	1.70
Western Europe	1.00	1.40	0.90
Japan	2.00	0.50	0.80
Oceania	1.60	-0.10	-0.20
South Africa	0.00	0.30	-2.30
USSR and Eastern Europe	2.30	0.50	1.20
USSR	2.70	0.00	1.10
Eastern Europe	1.70	1.40	1.30
Developing Countries	0.30	0.30	0.00
North Africa	0.40	-0.80	0.50
Egypt	0.90	-0.60	-0.20
Sub-Saharan Africa (a)	0.30	-1.40	0.50
Latin America	0.10	0.60	-0.30
Mexico	0.90	1.10	-0.70
Brazil	0.20	1.10	0.50
Argentina	0.00	0.50	-0.60
Near East	0.20	0.30	-0.60
South Asia	0.00	0.00	0.10
India	-0.20	0.10	0.10
Southeast Asia	0.60	1.70	1.00
Indonesia	1.10	1.70	1.50
Other East Asia (b)	1.50	2.20	0.80
China (c)	2.70	1.70	3.50

SOURCE: USDA/ERS (1989), "World Agriculture: Situation
and Outlook Report," WAS-55, p 8.

(a) Excluding South Africa
(b) Excluding Japan and China
(c) Excluding Taiwan

Table SA.3. Percentage of production of all cereals by trade (percent)

	1961-70	1971-75	1976-80	1981-85	1985	1986	1987
WORLD:							
Exports	9.60	11.00	12.60	13.50	12.40	11.20	12.50
Imports	9.40	10.80	12.40	13.30	12.20	11.10	12.30
INDUSTRIAL COUNTRIES							
Exports	24.00	31.20	36.50	37.00	32.80	30.00	35.80
Imports	16.30	17.50	16.90	13.80	12.80	12.30	12.70
DEVELOPING COUNTRIES							
Exports	3.40	2.80	3.30	3.70	3.50	2.90	2.40
Imports	7.60	8.30	10.20	11.90	10.90	10.60	12.20
DEVELOPING COUNTRIES							
Excluding China							
Exports	5.30	4.50	5.40	6.30	5.90	4.90	4.10
Imports	9.50	11.20	13.80	16.60	16.10	15.40	16.80

SOURCE: USDA/ERS (1989), "World Agriculture: Situation and Outlook Report." WAS-55, p. 62.

Note: Exports do not match imports largely because of differences in timing and reporting. An export
      may be counted as occurring in one country in one year and by the importing country in the next year.
      Exports reported by crop year are assigned to a calendar year based on the year in which the harvest
      occurs.

Table SA.4. Developing countries ranked by per capita food deficits, 1989/90

Rank	Status quo deficit	$ US	Nutrition deficit	$ US
1	Cape Verde	$90.03	Rwanda	$109.84
2	Jamaica	$86.82	Sierra Loone	$81.64
3	Tunisia	$78.17	Jamaica	$67.53
4	Costa Rica	$62.64	Cape Verde	$60.02
5	Liberia	$40.44	Mozambique	$50.33
6	Swaziland	$39.32	Lesotho	$49.58
7	Lesotho	$35.86	Bolivia	$47.85
8	Egypt	$33.58	Tunisia	$45.71
9	Malawi	$33.06	Malawi	$45.49
10	Afghanistan	$29.13	Haiti	$44.70
11	Mauritania	$28.75	Costa Rica	$44.55
12	Sri Lanka	$27.37	Honduras	$43.56
13	Honduras	$26.45	Guinea	$39.48
14	Bolivia	$24.93	Liberia	$38.07
15	Haiti	$24.74	Somalia	$36.91
16	Nicaragua	$23.70	Niger	$33.37
17	Peru	$23.66	Ethiopia	$30.91
18	Sierra Loone	$22.88	Chad	$30.62
19	Somalia	$21.31	Peru	$28.23
20	Mozambique	$18.58	El Salvador	$26.72
21	Angola	$18.32	Kenya	$24.71
22	El Salvador	$18.23	Togo	$24.59
23	Domican Republic	$16.81	Sri Lanka	$24.37
24	Rwanda	$9.78	Mauritania	$21.56
25	Madagascar	$9.74	Dominican Republic	$20.17
26	Guatemala	$9.65	Guatemala	$19.29
27	Togo	$9.62	Nepal	$17.76
28	Guinea	$9.53	Angola	$17.50
29	Sengal	$8.99	Egypt	$16.75
30	Central Afr. Rep.	$7.37	Benin	$15.97
31	Gambia	$5.96	Afghanistan	$15.85
32	Bangladesh	$5.88	Bangladesh	$14.20
33	Chad	$5.48	Ghana	$14.02
34	Ethiopia	$5.09	Zambia	$13.59
35	Guinea-Bissau	$4.95	Madagascar	$12.92
36	Zaire	$4.77	Senegal	$12.48
37	Benin	$4.62	Sudan	$12.11
38	Pakistan	$3.88	Nicaragua	$11.06
39	Ghana	$3.80	Central Afr. Rep.	$7.37
40	Kenya	$3.19	Zaire	$6.02
41	Niger	$2.71	Mali	$4.36
42	Tanzania	$1.66	Pakistan	$3.48
43	Nepal	$0.73	Philippines	$3.32
44	Indonesia	$0.02	India	$3.00
45	Uganda	$0.00	Burkina Faso	$0.91

SOURCE: Economic Research Service (1990). Agricultural Outlook.
Washington, D.C.: U.S. Department of Agriculture.

Table SA.5. Cereal food aid shipments by developing country regions and groups
(in thousand tons, grain equivalent)

	1977/78	1978/79	1979/80	1980/81	1981/82
World total	9211.30	9499.70	8886.90	8942.20	9140.20
Total developing countries	8785.80	9116.30	8588.10	8672.60	8714.10
Africa	3390.70	3535.30	3662.20	4511.90	4937.60
Asia	4914.20	4884.20	4066.80	3550.00	2916.60
Latin America	368.00	605.00	720.90	583.30	711.90
Other developing countries	11.00	12.00	13.50	7.30	2.80
Unspecified	101.90	79.80	124.70	20.10	145.20
Low-income, food-deficit countries	7070.80	7294.10	7373.40	7002.80	7264.50
Sub-Saharan Africa	1248.10	1136.10	1545.50	2319.60	2338.80
Least developed countries	2283.90	2458.00	2651.60	2511.00	2789.40

	1982/83	1983/84	1984/85	1985/86	1986/87
World total	9238.00	9848.70	12494.20	10804.90	12204.90
Total developing countries	9154.80	9806.70	12418.30	10791.30	12204.90
Africa	4658.30	5133.20	7640.20	5801.70	6083.90
Asia	2984.30	3341.20	3348.50	3335.30	4242.40
Latin America	1264.50	1295.80	1353.80	1600.30	1786.40
Other developing countries	0.10	2.20	-	0.70	3.10
Unspecified	247.60	34.30	75.80	53.30	107.10
Low-income, food-deficit countries	7636.80	8625.10	10799.00	9369.90	10090.20
Sub-Saharan Africa	2495.90	2613.30	4778.60	3702.80	3085.40
Least developed countries	3057.80	3060.80	5157.00	4462.60	4055.40

SOURCE: Compiled by FAO from data provided by donors, the International
Wheat Council, the World Food Program and other international organizations.
Taken from WFP/CFA 25/P/5.

Table SA.6. Shipment of noncereal food aid by commodity (in thousand tons)

Commodities	1978	1979	1980	1981	1982
Vegetable oil	284.90	189.70	261.70	308.80	346.40
Butter oil	53.10	47.30	29.80	59.20	40.50
Edible fat (a)	4.10	4.60	5.40	5.70	6.60
Skimmed milk powder	236.20	256.10	228.20	332.50	268.40
Other dairy products (b)	30.10	30.40	38.20	36.00	25.10
Meat and meat products (a)	6.70	7.30	6.50	6.10	5.80
Fish and fish products	12.70	13.40	12.90	8.80	10.50
Pulses	(d)	(d)	(d)	(d)	(d)
Sugar	(d)	(d)	(d)	(d)	(d)
Dried fruit	(d)	(d)	(d)	(d)	(d)
Other foodstuffs	(d)	(d)	(d)	(d)	(d)
Total non-cereals	627.80	548.80	582.90	757.10	703.30
Share of multilateral % (c)	46.60	58.30	52.90	50.40	48.90

Commodities	1983	1984	1985	1986	1987
Vegetable oil	344.20	342.60	383.70	525.00	550.00
Butter oil	21.80	56.10	49.50	47.00	40.00
Edible fat (a)	5.60	6.30	6.30	4.00	(d)
Skimmed milk powder	255.00	366.50	320.60	343.00	290.00
Other dairy products (b)	49.70	41.20	61.60	52.00	44.00
Meat and meat products (a)	8.50	10.10	11.60	7.00	3.00
Fish and fish products	10.70	16.30	23.90	9.00	13.00
Pulses	29.90	87.50	96.00	63.00	47.00
Sugar	12.30	37.30	38.40	13.00	13.00
Dried fruit	14.90	14.60	20.90	5.00	2.00
Other foodstuffs	2.70	1.00	9.40	4.00	5.00
Total non-cereals	755.30	6.60	1021.80	1072.00	1007.00
Share of multilateral % (c)	59.40	59.60	69.70	57.00	60.00

SOURCE: Compiled by FAO from data provided by donors, the World Food Program and other international organizations. Taken from WFP/CFA 25/P/5.

(a) Up to 1982, figures refer to shipments made by the World Food Program only.
(b) Includes also the dairy component of blended foods.
(c) Estimates.
(d) Data not available.

Table SA.7. Cereal food aid receipts by main category, 1975-1986 (in million tons, grain equivalent)

	Average 1975/80	1980/81	1981/82	1982/83	1983/84	1984/85	1985/86	1986/87 (a)
Program aid	6.00	4.90	4.40	6.00	5.70	6.70	5.10	6.30
Project aid	2.00	2.10	2.30	2.50	2.80	2.70	2.70	3.30
Emergencies	1.00	1.10	1.80	1.20	1.50	3.20	3.30	1.90
Total	9.00	8.10	8.50	9.70	10.00	12.60	11.10	11.50

SOURCE: Data provided by WFP country offices; data from donors for countries in which there are no WFP country offices. Taken from WFP/CFA 25/P/5, p. 44.

Note: To express cereal food aid in grain equivalent, wheat, rice and coarse grains are counted on a one-to-one basis, while wheat flour and blended food have been converted as follows: 0.73 ton of wheat flour to 1 ton on grain equivalent; 0.58 ton of blended food to 1 ton of grain equivalent.

(a) Provisional

Table SA.8. Bilateral and multilateral food aid by members of the Development Assistance Committee (DAC) of OECD

	1977	1978	1979	1980	1981	1982	1983	1984	1985	1986
At current prices (millions of dollars, net disbursements) :										
Total food aid (a)	1913.00	2048.00	2292.00	2629.00	2934.00	2473.00	2527.00	2975.00	3113.00	2912.00
Multilateral (b)	369.00	424.00	482.00	650.00	629.00	611.00	615.00	687.00	685.00	680.00
Bilateral (c)	1543.00	1624.00	1810.00	1979.00	2305.00	1862.00	1912.00	2288.00	2428.00	2232.00
Grants	843.00	972.00	975.00	1083.00	1307.00	1164.00	1206.00	1597.00	1556.00	1534.00
Loans	700.00	652.00	835.00	896.00	998.00	698.00	706.00	691.00	872.00	698.00
As a percentage:										
Multilateral as % of total food aid	19.30	20.70	21.00	24.70	21.40	24.70	24.30	23.10	22.00	23.30
Grants as % of total bilateral food aid	54.60	59.90	53.90	54.70	56.70	62.50	63.10	69.80	64.10	68.70
Multilateral plus bilateral grants as % of total food aid	63.40	68.20	63.60	65.90	66.00	71.80	72.10	76.80	72.00	76.00

SOURCE: Compiled by FAO from data provided by OECD. Taken from WFP/CFA 25/P/5, p. 33.

(a) Includes contributions by DAC members to multilateral agencies, but not actual amounts disbursed by these agencies.
(b) Includes contributions by the EEC channelled through multilateral agencies but excludes contribution channelled by member countries through EEC to recipient countries.
(c) Includes bilateral grants by the EEC.

Table SA.9. U.S. food aid share of total grain exports

Year	Grain exports	Food aid	Food aid share of shipments
	(mil. tn.)		(percent)
1955	10.50	4.70	45.10
1956	13.00	8.90	68.60
1957	20.90	13.40	64.10
1958	16.60	8.50	51.40
1959	18.50	9.90	53.20
1960	20.60	12.50	60.60
1961	26.00	14.70	56.70
1962	31.00	16.40	53.00
1963	28.70	15.20	53.00
1964	36.80	15.80	43.00
1965	35.30	17.20	48.70
1966	41.70	17.00	40.70
1967	34.20	12.20	35.70
1968	38.10	14.50	38.00
1969	29.90	9.70	32.50
1970	33.80	10.70	31.70
1971	34.60	10.80	31.30
1972	38.80	10.70	27.50
1973	65.80	7.40	11.20
1974	60.50	2.50	4.20
1975	61.50	4.00	6.50
1976	75.50	4.10	5.40
1977	69.50	8.10	11.70
1978	84.00	6.80	8.10
1979	88.90	6.60	7.50
1980	101.60	5.30	5.30
1981	107.90	5.10	4.70
1982	99.60	5.00	5.00
1983	87.70	5.70	6.50
1984	93.80	6.50	6.90
1985	78.90	6.90	8.80
1986	61.40	5.90	9.70

SOURCE: Shapouri, S., and M. Missiaen (1990), "Food Aid:
Motivation and Allocation Criteria," USDA/ERS, FAER No. 240.

Table SA.10. Food aid share of EC grain exports

Year	Grain exports	Food aid	Food aid share of shipments
	(000 tn.)		(percent)
1970/71	8581.00	857.00	10.00
1971/72	11224.00	986.00	8.80
1972/73	12253.00	1017.00	8.30
1973/74	9578.00	1238.00	12.90
1974/75	11190.00	1469.00	13.10
1975/76	12854.00	1023.00	8.00
1976/77	6784.00	1202.00	17.70
1977/78	10993.00	1423.00	0.90
1978/79	14862.00	1182.00	8.00
1979/80	17509.00	1270.00	7.30
1980/81	22717.00	1299.00	5.70
1981/82	23145.00	1778.00	7.70
1982/83	22805.00	1735.00	7.60
1983/84	22688.00	1957.00	8.60
1984/85	29251.00	2251.00	8.60
1985/86	27250.00	1569.00	5.80
1986/87	26000.00	1769.00	6.80

SOURCE: Shapouri, S., and M. Missiaen (1990), "Food Aid: Motivation and Allocation Criteria," USDA/ERS, FAER No. 240.

Table SA.11. Food aid share of Canadian grain exports

Year	Canadian grain exports	Canadian food aid	Food aid share of shipments
	(000 tons)		(percent)
1970/71	16122.00	1304.00	8.10
1971/72	9052.00	1093.00	5.70
1972/73	19432.00	808.00	4.20
1973/74	14130.00	664.00	4.70
1974/75	13722.00	612.00	4.50
1975/76	17221.00	1038.00	6.00
1976/77	17885.00	1201.00	6.70
1977/78	20029.00	902.00	4.50
1978/79	16974.00	758.00	4.50
1979/80	20557.00	740.00	3.60
1980/81	21046.00	600.00	2.90
1981/82	25901.00	600.00	2.30
1982/83	27924.00	843.00	3.00
1983/84	28480.00	817.00	2.90
1984/85	21329.00	943.00	4.40
1985/86	22247.00	1229.00	5.50
1986/87	27905.00	1240.00	4.40

SOURCE: Shapouri, S., and M. Missiaen (1990), "Food
Aid: Motivation and Allocation Criteria," USDA/ERS,
FAER No 240. Table 8.

Table SA.12. Major recipients of U.S. food aid, per capita ranking

1975 Aid recipient	Per capita (kg)	1985 Aid recipient	Per capita (kg)
Egypt	15.70	Jamaica	56.40
Cape Verde	15.70	Cape Verde	41.90
Bangladesh	15.20	Egypt	40.80
Sri Lanka	11.00	El Salvador	33.40
Honduras	10.60	Lesotho	20.70
Pakistan	10.20	Sudan	19.90
Guinea	6.90	Honduras	19.70
Lesotho	6.40	Morocco	18.80
Haiti	6.20	Haiti	18.00
Tunisia	4.30	Bolivia	17.20
Mauritius	3.20	Mauritania	17.00
Togo	3.20	Mali	13.50
Somalia	2.60	Dominican Republic	13.10

SOURCE: Shapouri, S., and M. Missiaen (1990), "Food Aid: Motivation and Allocation Criteria," USDA/ERS, FAER No 240.

Table SA.13. Major recipients of EC food aid, per capita ranking

1975 Aid recipient	Per capita (kg)	1985 Aid recipient	Per capita (kg)
Egypt	21.10	Cape Verde	74.00
Mauritius	15.30	Mauritania	36.50
Mauritania	13.40	Mozambique	7.30
Tunisia	8.70	Ethiopia	7.10
Niger	5.10	Nicaragua	6.30
Yemen Arab Republic	3.60	Lebanon	5.20
Egypt	2.70	The Gambia	5.20
Sri Lanka	2.60	Chad	4.80
Benin	2.20	Lesotho	4.60
Mali	2.10	Sierra Leone	3.90
The Gambia	2.10	Haiti	3.80
Bangladesh	1.90	Senegal	3.60
Somalia	1.60	Zambia	3.40

SOURCE: Shapouri, S., and M. Missiaen (1990), "Food Aid: Motivation and Allocation Criteria," USDA/ERS, FAER No 240.

Table SA.14. Major recipients of Canadian food aid, per capita ranking

1975 Aid recipient	Per capita (kg)	1985 Aid recipient	Per capita (kg)
Niger	4.40	Sri Lanka	6.60
Mali	3.70	Lebanon	6.10
Sri Lanka	3.40	Mauritania	6.00
Pakistan	2.90	Bangladesh	5.00
Bangladesh	2.40	Nicaragua	3.00
Ghana	2.30	Ethiopia	2.00
Lebanon	2.20	Honduras	1.50
Cape Verde	2.10	Zambia	1.50
Somalia	1.70	Sudan	1.50
Tanzania	1.30	Ghana	1.40
Ethiopia	1.10	Senegal	1.20
India	0.60	Rwanda	0.90
Haiti	0.60	Yemen Arab Republic	0.90

SOURCE: Shapouri, S., and M. Missiaen (1990), "Food Aid: Motivation and Allocation Criteria," USDA/ERS, FAER No 240.

Table SA.15. U.S. concessional cereal exports to the world ($ US millions)

Year	Title I/III Program	Title II Program	Barter shipments	Section 416	Commodity import program	Credit & Guarantee program	EEP	Total Concessional Exports
1955	73.00	187.00	125.00	0.00	451.00	69.00	0.00	905.00
1956	439.00	248.00	298.00	0.00	354.00	62.00	0.00	1401.00
1957	908.00	217.00	400.00	0.00	394.00	73.00	0.00	1992.00
1958	657.00	224.00	100.00	0.00	227.00	203.00	0.00	1411.00
1959	724.00	161.00	132.00	0.00	210.00	93.00	0.00	1320.00
1960	824.00	143.00	149.00	0.00	167.00	35.00	0.00	1318.00
1961	951.00	221.00	144.00	0.00	186.00	61.00	0.00	1563.00
1962	1048.00	249.00	198.00	0.00	74.00	104.00	0.00	1673.00
1963	1145.00	263.00	47.00	0.00	13.00	162.00	0.00	1630.00
1964	1105.00	270.00	43.00	0.00	23.00	197.00	0.00	1638.00
1965	1300.00	239.00	32.00	0.00	26.00	167.00	0.00	1764.00
1966	1047.00	267.00	32.00	0.00	43.00	278.00	0.00	1667.00
1967	981.00	267.00	6.00	0.00	37.00	438.00	0.00	1729.00
1968	1023.00	250.00	1.00	0.00	17.00	216.00	0.00	1507.00
1969	772.00	265.00	0.00	0.00	11.00	167.00	0.00	1215.00

Table SA.15. (cont.)

Year	Title I/III Program	Title II Program	Barter shipments	Section 416	Commodity import program	Credit & Guarantee program	EEP	Total Concessional Exports
1970	815.00	241.00	0.00	0.00	12.00	279.00	0.00	1347.00
1971	743.00	280.00	0.00	0.00	56.00	488.00	0.00	1567.00
1972	677.00	380.00	0.00	0.00	67.00	457.00	0.00	1581.00
1973	658.00	288.00	0.00	0.00	84.00	1095.00	0.00	2125.00
1974	575.00	290.00	0.00	0.00	76.00	298.00	0.00	1239.00
1975	672.00	337.00	0.00	0.00	123.00	249.00	0.00	1381.00
1976	649.00	255.00	0.00	0.00	216.00	957.00	0.00	2077.00
1977	762.00	341.00	0.00	0.00	419.00	755.00	0.00	2277.00
1978	737.00	335.00	0.00	0.00	477.00	1583.00	0.00	3132.00
1979	793.00	394.00	0.00	0.00	304.00	1591.00	0.00	3082.00
1980	865.00	476.00	0.00	0.00	183.00	1417.00	0.00	2941.00
1981	790.00	543.00	0.00	0.00	159.00	1871.00	0.00	3363.00
1982	722.00	385.00	0.00	0.00	82.00	1390.00	0.00	2579.00
1983	810.00	385.00	0.00	0.00	130.00	4060.00	0.00	5385.00
1984	775.00	602.00	0.00	129.00	104.00	3830.00	0.00	5440.00
1985	928.00	698.00	0.00	279.00	90.00	2807.00	94.00	4896.00
1986	766.00	420.00	0.00	147.00	129.00	2413.00	709.00	4584.00
1987	696.00	248.00	0.00	133.00	60.00	2744.00	1693.00	5574.00
1988	766.00	684.00	0.00	412.00	NA	3706.00	3301.00	8869.00 (a)

SOURCE: Compiled from Schouten, D. (1989), "Background Data for workshop on Food, Trade, Food Security and Aid in the 1990s," CARD, Iowa State University/USAID. September 20-22, Washington, D.C.; and K. Z. Ackerman, and E. S. Mark (1990), "Agricultural Export Programs: Background for 1990 Farm Legislation." USDA/ERS.

Note: Does not include CCC direct sales. (Market value of commodities sold by CCC was not available prior to 1978.)

(a) Does not include exports under CIP.

Workshop Participants and Contributors to the Volume

Steven Abrams
Associate Administrator
OICD/USDA
2121 K. Street, 317 A
Washington, D.C. 20250

James Anderson
Director
Office of International Training
Room 207 SA-16
Agency for International Development
Washington, D.C. 20523-4200

Bruna Angel*
Graduate Assistant
Center for Agricultural and Rural Development
Iowa State University
Ames, Iowa 50011

Alan Batchelder
Economist
Office of Economic Affairs
Bureau for Program and Policy Coordination
USAID
2201 C. Street
Washington, D.C. 20535-0001

* *Contributor to this volume.*

Rodney Bent
Chief, Economics Affairs Branch
International Affairs Division
Office of Management and Budget
8235 New Executive Office Building
17th and Pennsylvania Avenue
Washington, D.C. 20503

Richard E. Bissell
Assistant Administrator
Bureau for Program and Policy Coordination
USAID
Room 3938, NS
2201 C. Street, NW
Washington, D.C. 20523

Fred Blott
Program Analyst
OBPA, Room 117A, Administration Bldg.
U.S. Dept. of Agriculture
14th & Independence Avenue, SW
Washington, D.C. 20520

Janet Breslin
Deputy Staff Director
Committee on Agriculture, Nutrition and Forestry
U.S. Senate, SR-328A
Washington, D.C. 20510

Anita Brown
Legislative Assistant
1301 Longworth HOB
Committee on Agriculture
U.S. House of Representatives
Washington, D.C. 20515

Mary Chambliss
Director of Program Analysis
Export Credit
Room 40795
Washington, D.C. 20250

Eugene R. Chiavaroli
AID Affairs Officer
SAA/S&T
Room 4942 NS
Agency for International Development
Washington, D.C. 20523

Richard Cobb
Supervisor, General Development Officer
AFR/TR
Room 351 SA-8A
Agency for International Development
Washington, D.C. 20523

Owen Cylke
Deputy Assistant to the Administrator
Bureau for Food for Peace and Voluntary Assistance
Room 206, SA-8
USAID
Washington, D.C. 20523

R. C. Duncan*
Chief, World Bank
1818 H. Street, N.W.
Room S7053
Washington, D.C. 20433

* *Contributor to this volume.*

Donald S. Ferguson
Agricultural Economist
OICD/USDA
2121 K. Street, N.W.
Washington, D.C. 20250

Lehman B. Fletcher*
Professor of Economics
377 Heady Hall
Iowa State University
Ames, Iowa 50011

Bill Furtick
Director for Office of Food and Agriculture
S&T/FA
Room 513, SA-18
Agency for International Development
Washington, D.C. 20523

Bruce Gardner
Professor of Agriculture and Resource Economics
University of Maryland
College Park, MD 20742

Margaret Goodman
Staff Consultant
House Committee on Foreign Affairs
2170 Rayburn HOB
US House of Representatives
Washington, D.C. 20515-6128

Walter E. Grazer
Policy Advisor for Food, Agriculture, and Rural Development
U.S. Catholic Conference
3211 4th Street, N.E.
Washington, D.C. 20017-1194

* Contributor to this volume.

Charles Hanrahan
Senior Specialist in Food and Agriculture
Congressional Research Service
Library of Congress
101 Independence Avenue, S.E.
Washington, D.C. 20540

Dale Hathaway
Vice President
Consultants International Group
1616 H. Street, N.W.
Washington, D.C. 20006

Rev. Thomas Hayden
Executive Director
Africa Faith and Justice Network
Box 29378
Washington, D.C. 20017

Stephen Hellinger
Co-Director, Development Group for Alternative Policies
1400 I. Street, N.W.
Suite 520
Washington, D.C. 20005

John Helmuth
Associate Professor of Economics and Assistant Director
Center for Agricultural and Rural Development
578 Heady Hall
Iowa State University
Ames, Iowa 50011

Raymond F. Hopkins*
Chair, Polititcal Science Department
Swarthmore College
Swarthmore, Pennsylvania 19081

* Contributor to this volume.

Geoge M. Ingram
Senior Staff Consultant
Committee on Foreign Affairs
2170 Rayburn HOB
U.S. House of Representatives
Washington, D.C. 20515

S. R. Johnson*
Charles F. Curtiss Distinguished Professor of Agriculture
Director, Center for Agricultural and Rural Development
578 Heady Hall
Iowa State University
Ames, Iowa 50011

Mary Kilgour
Deputy Assistant Administrator
Coordinator of Food for Peace
Room 402, SA-8
Agency for International Development
Washington, D.C. 20523

Lawrence R. Klein*
Benjamin Franklin Professor of Economics and Finance
Department of Economics
University of Pennsylvania
3718 Locust Walk
Philadelphia, Pennsylvania 19104

Anne O. Krueger*
Arts and Science Professor of Economics
Duke University
Durham, North Carolina 27706

* *Contributor to this volume.*

Senator Patrick Leahy
Chairman
Committee on Agriculture, Nutrition and Forestry
SR-328A
U.S. Senate
Washington, D.C. 20510

Alex F. McCalla*
Professor of Agricultural Economics
University of California-Davis
Davis, California 95616

James McCormick
Professor of Political Science
519 Ross Hall
Iowa State University
Ames, Iowa 50011

John Mellor
Director, International Food Policy Research Institute
1776 Massachusetts Avenue, N.W.
Washington, D.C. 20036

William M. Miner*
Senior Research Associate
Institute for Research on Public Policy
275 Slater Street
Ottawa, Ontario, Canada KIP 5H9

Jon O'Rourke
Food for Peace Officer
FVA/PPM
SA-8, Room 21
Agency for International Development
1400 Wilson Blvd.
Roslyn, Virginia 22209

* *Contributor to this volume.*

Robert L. Paarlberg*
Professor and Chair
Department of Political Science
Wellesley College,
Wellesley, Massachusetts 02181

Stephanie Patrick
Public Affairs Officer
Cargill, Inc.
1101 15th Street, N.W.
Suite 205
Washington, D.C. 20005

James Phippard*
Committee on Agriculture, Nutrition, and Forestry
U.S. Senate
Room 328A, Russell Building
Washington, D.C. 20510

Lorette Picciano-Hanson
Director of Program Priority Campaign
Interfaith Action for Economic Justice
110 Maryland Avenue, N.E.
Washington, D.C. 20002

Donald Puchala
Director, Institute of International Studies
University of South Carolina
Columbia, South Carolina 29208

Gordon Rausser
Economist, USAID
320 21st Street, N.W.
Room 5879NC
Washington, D.C. 20523

* *Contributor to this volume.*

Khalid Riaz*
Graduate Assistant
Center for Agricultural and Rural Development
Iowa State University
Ames, Iowa 50011

Terry L. Roe*
Professor of Agricultural and Applied Economics
337 COB
1994 Buford Avenue
University of Minnesota
St. Paul, Minnesota 55108

Jim Ross
Director of the Trade Assistance and Planning Office
FAS/USDA
14th and Independence Avenue
5057 S. Bldg.
Washington, D.C. 20250

George Rossmiller
Director, National Center for Food and Agricultural Policy
Resources for the Future
1616 P. Street, N.W.
Washington, D.C. 20036

Vernon W. Ruttan*
Regents Professor
Department of Agriculture and Applied Economics
University of Minnesota
332 Classroom Office Bldg.
1994 Buford Avenue
St. Paul, Minnesota 55108

* *Contributor to this volume.*

Lyle Schertz
Editor, *CHOICES*
12709 Oak Farms Road
Herndon, Virginia 22071

Maurice Schiff*
Economist
World Bank
Washington, D.C. 20250

David Seckler
Director, Agricultural Policy and Resource Development
Winrock International
Route 3, Petit Jean Mountain
Morrilton, Arkansas 72110

Emmy Simmons
Supervisor, Program Officer
APR/DP
Room 3909-D NS
Agency for International Development
Washington, D.C. 20523

Mark Smith
Agriculture Economist
Commodity Economics Division
Commodity Trade and Analysis Branch
USDA/ERS, Room 734
1301 New York Avenue
Washington, D.C. 20005-4788

---

* *Contributor to this volume.*

Daniel Speckhard
Policy Analyst/Food Aid Budget Examiner
Economics Affairs Branch
Office of Management and Budget
8235 New Executive Office Building
17th and Pennsylvania Avenu
Washington, D.C. 20503

Scott Steele
Deputy Director, Program Analysis
International Affairs and Commodity Programs
U.S. Department of Agriculture
14th and Independence Avenue, S.W.
Washington, D.C. 20520

Ross Talbot*
Professor Emeritus
Department of Political Science
529 Ross Hall
Iowa State University
Ames, Iowa 50011

Philip Thomas
Assistant Director for Agricultural Trade
National Security and International Affairs Division
U.S. General Accounting Office
Room 5492
441 G. Street, N.W.
Washington, D.C. 20548

Gerald Trant*
Executive Director
United National World Food Council
Viale delle Terme di caracalla
00100 Rome ITALY

---

* *Contributor to this volume.*

Charles Uphaus
Supervisor, Agricultural Development Officer
ANE/TR
Room 4440 NS
Agency for International Development
Washington, D.C. 20523

Alberto Valdés*
Economist, Agriculture Division, Technical Department
IFPRI
1776 Massachusetts Avenue, N.W.
Washington, D.C. 20036

Ann Veneman
Deputy Under Secretary for International Affairs, USDA
Room 212-A
14th and Independence Avenue, S.W.
Washington, D.C. 20250

James Vertress
Policy Analyst for Trade Economics Staff
Office of the Assistant Secretary for Economics
U.S. Department of Agriculture
Room 438-A
Washington, D.C. 20250

T. Kelley White
Director, Agriculture and Trade Analysis Division
USDA/ERS, Room 732

* Contributor to this volume.

Acronyms

BLS	Basic Linked System
CAP	Common Agricultural Policy
CARD	Center for Agricultural and Rural Development
CCC	Commodity Credit Corporation
CFA	Committee on Food Aid Policies and Programs
CGIAR	Consultative Group on International Agricultural Resource
CIP	Commodity Import Program
CMEA	Council for Mutual Economic Assistance
DAC	Development Assistance Committee
DCC	Food Development Coordination Committee
EC	European Community
EEC	European Economic Community
EEP	Export Enhancement Program
ERP	Effective Rate of Protection
ERS	Economic Research Service
ESF	Economic Support Fund
FAC	Food Aid Convention
FANA	Food Aid Needs and Availabilities
FAO	Food and Agriculture Organization of the United Nations
FAPRI	Food and Agricultural Policy Research Institute
GATT	General Agreement on Tariffs and Trade
GNP	Gross National Product
GDP	Gross Domestic Product
IDCA	International Development Cooperation Administration
IFPRI	International Food Policy Research Institute
IIASA	International Institute for Applied Systems Analysis
IME	Industrial Market Economies
IMF	International Monetary Fund
LDC	Less-Developed Country

MERM	Multilateral Exchange Rate Model
NIC	Newly Industrialized Countries
OECD	Organization for Economic Cooperation and Development
OMB	Office of Management and Budget
PVO	Private Voluntary Organization
ROW	Rest of World
UMR	Usual Marketing Requirement
UNCTAD	United National commission on Trade and Development
USAID	U.S. Agency for International Development
USDA	U.S. Department of Agriculture
WEFA	Wharton Economics Forecasting Group (from The WEFA Group)
WFP	World Food Program
WHO	World Health Organization